D0842118

BLACKWOLF

Ernest Thompson Seton

ARTIST—LECTURER—AUTHOR

BlackWolf

THE LIFE OF ERNEST THOMPSON SETON

BETTY KELLER

Douglas & McIntyre
Vancouver/Toronto

Douglas & McIntyre Ltd., 1615 Venables Street, Vancouver, British Columbia V5L 2H1

Canadian Cataloguing in Publication Data

Keller, Betty.
   Black Wolf

Includes index.
Bibliography: p.
ISBN 0–88894–439–X

1. Seton, Ernest Thompson, 1860–1946. 2. Artists –
Canada – Biography. 3. Authors, Canadian (English)
– 19th century – Biography.* 4. Naturalists –
Canada – Biography. I. Title.
QH31.S48K44 1984   574'.0924   C84–091230–7

Cover photographs courtesy Seton Village, New Mexico
Design by Barbara Hodgson
Printed and bound in Canada by D. W. Friesen & Sons

Contents

Preface

Several hundred thousand copies of Ernest Thompson Seton's *Wild Animals I Have Known* were sold between the release of the first edition on 20 October 1898 and the author's death nearly fifty years later, yet comparatively few of those copies exist today. Most large university libraries hold one or two first or second editions — usually in their science divisions — and there are quite a number of autographed copies tucked away in private collections, but it is only the eleventh or fourteenth edition copies with battered covers and missing pages that occasionally turn up in secondhand bookstores, because Seton's books simply did not survive all the love bestowed upon them. Three generations of boys and girls, caught up in the drama of their animal heroes' lives, thumbed these books until their pages were dog-eared and their bindings had disintegrated.

Many who first read about Lobo and Raggylug and Vixen fifty or sixty years ago can retell their stories in detail even now, often repeating the exact phrasing used by Seton. They can tell you how to track deer as Yan did in *The Trail of the Sandhill Stag* and how to light a fire without matches exactly as they learned the technique from Seton's woodcraft manuals.

For these readers, Seton remains the greatest of all animal story writers. Few of them realize that he considered these stories only a means to an end. In 1901, at the height of his writing career, he acknowledged that he only wrote in order to make his "everlasting fortune" so that he could "grub in the field of science and live happily ever after." More than anything else in his life, Seton wanted to gain renown as a naturalist; his second goal was to be acclaimed as an artist.

This biography tells the story of Seton, the artist-naturalist who became the most widely read animal story writer of all time. It covers his attempts to have his work hung in the Paris Salon, his natural history achievements, his storytelling success and his part in establishing the Boy Scouts of America. It does not explore in any depth his place in the scientific world; that has been done most efficiently in such works as John Wadland's *Ernest Thompson Seton: Man in Nature and the Progressive Era: 1880–1915* (Arno, 1978) and in the Manitoba Naturalists Society's *Ernest Thompson Seton in Manitoba 1882–1892,* published in 1980. And it does not analyze his animal stories in detail except as they relate to the events in his life; his stories have already been thoroughly examined in books such as Margaret Atwood's *Survival* (Anansi, 1972). *Black Wolf* is instead an intimate look at the private life of a creative genius.

I was given invaluable assistance in my research for this book by the descendents of Joseph Logan Thompson: Beverly McKie of Langdale, British Columbia; Jean Thompson of Toronto; John Carl Thompson of Waterloo, Ontario; Andrew Rutherford Thompson of Vancouver; David Arthur Thompson of Guelph, Ontario; Edgar Seton (Bill) Thorne of White Rock, B.C., G. Scott McIntyre of Vancouver and especially Dee Seton-Barber of Santa Fe, New Mexico, who gave so freely of her hospitality and of access to her father's papers.

I am grateful also to the descendents of the artist Charlotte Schreiber for their kind assistance: Lorna Schreiber of White Rock, B.C.; Beatrice M. Geary of Ottawa, and E. Jane Turman of Willowdale, Ontario, and to the grandsons of Prof. James Mavor: James Mavor Moore, and Francis Mavor Moore of Toronto.

I wish to express my appreciation for the services rendered to me by the following: Helen and Wayne Heine of Edmonton; Edith Simmons of Gibsons, B.C.; Sylvia Crooks of Vancouver; Anne Yandle and the Special Collections Division of the University of British Columbia Library; Maureen Wilson of the Map Division of the University of British Columbia Library; Bert Billesberger, Provincial Archives, Manitoba; Rachel Grover of the Thomas Fisher Rare Book Library, University of Toronto; D. P. Snidal, MD, Associate Dean, Faculty of Medicine, University of Manitoba; Sidney G. Hutchison, Archivist, Royal Academy of Arts, London, England; T. Graham, Central Library, South Shields, England; Dr. Hartwell Bowsfield, Archivist, York University; Charles C. Hill, Curator of Canadian Art, National Gallery, Ottawa; Betty Jones, Librarian, Philmont Scout Ranch, Boy Scouts of America, Cimarron, New Mexico, and William C. McKee, Chief Archivist, Glenbow-Alberta Institute, Calgary, Alberta.

My gratitude is also extended to the staff members of the Public Archives of Canada, Ottawa; California State Library, California Section, Sacramento, California; Rice University Library, Interlibrary Lending, Houston, Texas; City of Toronto Archives; the Archives of Ontario, Toronto; Interlibrary Loans, London Public Library, London, Ontario, and Harlan Hatcher Graduate Library, University of Michigan.

To my sons, Perry Neil Keller, who helped with research in eastern Canada, and Christopher Philip Keller, who assisted in Vancouver and New Mexico, I am deeply indebted. Finally, I would like Dr. Yvonne Duncan to know how much I appreciated her help.

Care has been taken to trace ownership of copyright material contained in this book. The author will gladly receive information that will enable her to rectify any reference or credit in subsequent editions.

This book was completed with the aid of a Canada Council Explorations grant.

1

"The Most Selfish Person in History"

Throughout his long life, Ernest Thompson Seton regarded the majority of his fellow men with love and respect, he looked on some others with humour, and on a few with anger and contempt. But for three individuals he nursed a passionate, implacable hatred: his father, St. Paul the Apostle and Gen. George Custer. Although it is certainly not surprising that a man who lived for eighty-six years should have found reason to hate three of his fellow human beings in that span of time, it is rather remarkable that his feelings for all three should have been established by the time he was twenty-five and that these feelings should have remained unaltered and undiminished to his final years. His second wife, Julie, in attempting to explain this aspect of his personality, wrote that it was Seton's "blessing or curse" to have the kind of memory that not only brought back to him the minute details of past events but "all the emotions he had felt at the time. . . . His later feelings were not a remembrance of the hatred he felt in his childhood, but the same hatred itself fanned to even greater heat."[1]

It seems far more likely, however, that the vehemence of these three hatreds had more to do with the power of his imagination than with the vividness of his memory. Two of the men he hated had never caused him direct injury. St. Paul earned Seton's wrath because of the part he had played in establishing the doctrine that Woman was created by God to serve Man, a doctrine that condemned Seton's devout mother to submit without protest to the despotic rule of her husband. Custer, who died at the Battle of the Little Bighorn in 1876 — six years before Seton left his family's home in Toronto — earned Seton's hatred for his crimes against the Cheyenne and the Sioux. But the power of Seton's vigorous imagination allowed him to identify completely with both his mother and the Indians — in fact, with all underdogs — so that he felt the injustices and the abuse inflicted on them exactly as if he had been the recipient, and he smouldered with rage at those he considered responsible.

This type of identification is not unusual in highly creative and sensitive people, but that part of Seton's imagination that fueled his hatred for his father was distinctly aberrant. Seton's memoirs and papers tell how, as a child, he was beaten unmercifully by his father, the same man who also required him at age twenty-one to repay all the monies ever spent on him — even the doctor's fee for his birth. The father in these memoirs was, in fact, so reprehensible that Seton described him as "a worthless loafer, a petty swindler, a wife-beater, and a child-murderer,"[2] and he was so egotistical that he denied his wife and children the basic necessities of life in order to indulge himself; he was, wrote Seton, "the most selfish person I ever heard of in history or in fiction."[3]

Although Seton discussed these grievances with his friends and acquaintances until all of them were thoroughly familiar with the persecution he had suffered as a child, as long as his father was alive, Seton never complained to members of his immediate family. And only once — on the occasion of his mother's funeral — did he ever confront his father on the subject. But when Seton was forty-two his father died, and less than a year later he unburdened himself at last to his elder brother William, pouring out the whole dreadful story of the brutality he had suffered at his father's hands. William reacted with horror, but not for his brother's sufferings. He wrote in his memoirs:

I really believe that the poor boy actually believed that father had so treated him, for he shed real tears in the recollection! But no one believes that there is anything but a very small foundation for his ideas, for everyone of the family knows that father thought more highly of Ernest than he did of any other of his family of ten boys, and really sacrificed more to advance his education. Poor Ernest got the idea into his head and nursed it and coddled it and exaggerated any little imaginary slights until he actually came to believe what was nothing more than a distortion of the truth, a figment of his own imagination.[4]

William was the second in that family of ten boys, thirteen years older than Seton, who was the eighth in line. They had lived together under their father's roof from the time Seton was born in 1860 until he was fourteen, but William never witnessed the cruelties of which Seton complained. His brother Harry, who was the fifth son, never saw them either.

The "very small foundation" to which William refers may be attributed partially to the fact that parents do not treat all their children the same. Some of this difference can be the result of the parents growing older; their aspirations and standards for their children change with time and circumstances, becoming more indulgent or less patient with the younger children, more generous or more miserly, and less or more dependent on them. But part of the difference is surely the result of parents' reactions to their children's personalities. And Seton, from all reports, was not the easygoing kind of child that most of his brothers were.

There is little doubt that William's version of the family's life and his description of his father's personality are the correct ones; they are corroborated by the available family correspondence and the incomplete diaries and memoirs of the other brothers. Although this means that most of the grievances on which Seton based his feelings for his father were a sham, the feelings themselves were not. He was absolutely convinced that his father had monstrously abused him, and as a consequence, the hatred he felt in response to that abuse — even though imagined — was so real that it became the most vital influence in his formative years.

He grew up with the image of himself as an innocent victim of persecution, like some wild animal made sport of by cruel humans. And what made his plight even more bitter was the fact that he was the only one of the family to be singled out for this persecution, though he was convinced that he was more talented and more intelligent than any of his brothers. His resentment at this unfairness affected his relationship with all his brothers, but especially with those nearest him in age, and it drove him unceasingly to prove to the father who had undervalued him that he was the really worthwhile member of the family.

The imagination that nurtured his persecution complex and his hatred for his father also encouraged him to believe that his father had denied him his rightful heritage. At seventeen he decided that he must assume the family's "true name." In the process of assuming it over the next twenty-five years, he was known variously as Ernest Evan Thompson, Ernest Evan Thompson Seton, Ernest Thompson-Seton, Ernest Seton-Thompson, Wolf Thompson, Wolf Seton and Chief Black Wolf, much to the confusion of his publishers, readers and friends. To resolve the problem, he took the legal name of Ernest Thompson Seton in 1901, but as books published before that date still bear his earlier names, confusion lingers. In this book, he is simply called Seton, since that is the name that he was so stubbornly determined to have as his own.

Not all the consequences of Seton's imagination were destructive, controversial or trivial. The animal stories by which he is known in North America, Europe and Japan were unique in their time and, because of that, had an enormous influence for good. He was the first to produce stories in which the animals were not given human traits to make them more interesting, the first to write "true" stories about individual specimens in their wilderness habitats, and the first to promote conservation and ecological concepts within a popular framework.

Seton's ability to live so totally within his imagination does not mean that he was incapable of objective observation. He was what his second wife called "a strange combination of exact scientist and imaginative romancer."[5] The natural history journals that he kept for more than sixty years attest to his meticulous recording of events in the field, and his scientific papers and books earned him the respect of naturalists throughout the world. His two-volume *Life Histories of Northern Animals* (1909) was described by J. A. Allen of the New York Museum of Natural History as "the best work of its kind ever written,"[6] and his four-volume *Lives of Game Animals* (1925–28) won the John Burroughs Bronze Medal for the best production of nature literature published during 1927.

Most of Seton's problems throughout his life, however, were caused by this "strange combination," for it was extremely difficult for his contemporaries to decide which facet of his personality to credit for his stories, illustrations, natural history documents and youth training concepts. Where did fact leave off and fantasy begin?

2

A Little Colony in Itself

Seton began life as Ernest Evan Thompson, the eighth son of Joseph Logan Thompson of South Shields, a town at the mouth of the River Tyne in Durham County, England; eight miles upriver in the heart of northern England's coalfields lies the city of Newcastle. In 1820, when Joseph Logan Thompson was born in South Shields, it had already existed for six centuries, "a smokey old town"[1] blackened by the soot from the coal-fired furnaces of the chemical works in the valley to the west. In Joseph's youth there had been a pithead right in the centre of town. The mine had angled downward, then snaked out under the North Sea. Although some of the men of South Shields worked in this mine and others worked in the chemical factories up the valley, most of them were employed building ships or sailing them. The ships were mostly colliers, wooden-hulled sailing vessels, manned by crews of a dozen or fifteen men. They were seldom more than five hundred tons and many were as small as two hundred tons, yet they carried the coal and chemicals of the Tyne to North America, Africa and China, and brought back cargoes that made their owners comfortably wealthy.

Seton's forefathers had lived in South Shields for several generations, building and sailing ships. His maternal grandfather,

William Snowdon, had been a prosperous shipowner and master; when he was lost at sea around the year 1840, he left his widow with a respectable income and each of his children with a nest egg of £1,000. Grandfather Enoch Donkerly Thompson was also a shipowner and master, though he was semi-retired by the time Seton became acquainted with him. Seton's brother William remembered their grandfather as a portly gentleman, the picture of dignity in a swallow-tailed coat, a flowered silk or satin vest and a shiny high hat, but his many years of having his own way as a ship's master, coupled with a naturally ferocious temper, landed him in the local police court on at least one occasion on charges of assault and battery. He was extremely crafty and tight-fisted with his money, but woefully lacking in business sense except when it came to finding profitable cargoes for his ships. He suffered enormous financial losses when a bank in which he had bought shares went bankrupt.

Seton's father, Joseph Logan Thompson, inherited his love of ships and persuaded his father to let him go to sea as a cabin boy. However, the master of the ship had been in cahoots with Enoch Thompson, and agreed to make the young fellow's life so miserable that he would return to dry land and stay there. Joseph did just that, setting himself up as a ship's broker and insurance agent, branching out into sail-making and ship provisioning and eventually acquiring his own small fleet of merchant ships.

A civic minded individual, Joseph served for several years on the town council and on the River Tyne Commission, which was charged with the responsibility of maintaining the river for deep-sea ship traffic. He acted as a committeeman for the ship insurance associations and served as a life governor of the Winterbottom Marine School. He was chosen for the latter position by the man who had bequeathed the funds to build the school, a doctor who for many years represented the borough as a Conservative. The appointment came as a surprise to Joseph since he was a staunch Liberal and had always voted against the old man.

In business Joseph Logan Thompson was considered the soul of integrity, and when jurors were chosen from among the prominent businessmen for the twice yearly debtors' court, he was generally asked to serve. There was only token compensation for the jurors' service. Each suitor merely paid a one-shilling fee to be allowed to plead his case and enlist the court's aid in collecting monies owed to him. These fees were then divided amongst the jurors in lieu of salary; Joseph gave his share to his children for pocket money.

Both Seton and his brother William considered their father to be a man of strict moral principles. Although he had enjoyed a glass of wine and a good cigar in the early years of his marriage, after his fifth child was born he decided that it must never be said that his sons learned bad habits in their father's home. From that time on, he abstained from tobacco altogether and confined his liquor intake to special occasions. Being a practical man, however, he did not throw the wines and cognacs in his cellar away; he simply did not replenish the stock as it was used up.

Joseph Thompson's manners were those of a gentleman and his language was almost scholarly, though his schooling had not been extensive. He was, however, an omnivorous reader, and his library contained the latest scientific works, especially those on astronomy, chemistry and mechanics. He was also keenly interested in nature study; on long Sunday afternoon walks with his sons, he delighted in identifying all the wildflowers and mushrooms that they found. Alan, the youngest, declared later that he had received a liberal education just by being in his father's company and listening to him talk.

Joseph was not a witty man. Seton and William agreed that his anecdotes were so convoluted and laborious that his listeners could predict the punch lines long before he got to them. William could remember only one occasion on which his father attempted a joke: after his eldest son, John Enoch, joined him in business and promptly secured several new agencies through well-timed advertising, Joseph remarked that the firm's name should be changed to "John Enoch Thompson and Father."

The pace of his humour was in keeping with his whole temperament, for he was lethargic by nature, and though extremely thorough and careful in everything he did, he was painfully slow. He disliked the bustle of business, preferring to do his company's bookkeeping and office work himself while sending his clerk out to drum up business.

Seton, however, remembered some far less attractive traits in his father. "There were times when we seemed in absolute accord," he told his wife in later years, "two really harmonious companions with common interests abounding. Then, suddenly,

some trifle would happen. . . . a little nothing that was wrongly
construed. And a storm was started that swept all good things out
of life for days."[2] According to Seton, the trifles usually stemmed
from Joseph's craving for "proper respect" from his family.
Seton's Aunt Tate (his mother's sister) had told him how Joseph
once beat Seton's eldest brother with the flat of his hand because
the child had refused to sit up properly at the table. In spite of his
wife's pleading, he stopped slapping John Enoch only when the
child fell to the floor unconscious. Aunt Tate, who claimed to
have witnessed the beating, said the boy was one year old at the
time.

According to Seton, his father also boasted that he had taught
his second son, William, to understand obedience by using the
same method, and at different times had ordered three of his sons
to leave home because they failed to show him due respect. One
of these banishments came when he discovered that the grapes he
had been cultivating for himself had disappeared, another when
he found one of his sons in the outdoor privy at a time when he
was accustomed to use that convenience himself.

In his memoirs William makes no mention of being beaten; it is
possible that he was too young to remember, though he does
recall another event that happened when he was two. Aunt Tate's
story of child-beating is not corroborated by any other source
and may originally have been a story about Enoch Donkerly
Thompson, who certainly did have a reputation for physical violence. William recalled his striking a South Shields businessman
with an umbrella because the man had disagreed with him.
Joseph, on the other hand, was known in South Shields as a sober,
serious man, devoted to his family and "a credit and a respect and
comfort to his parents."[3]

"We were taught to treat him like the Pope or a Roman
Emperor," Seton complained, "to stand aside and at attention
whenever he approached or passed. If he entered the room where
we were sitting, we were trained all to rise and stand meekly
behind our chairs with downcast eyes until he was seated. If one
of us looked at him with more than a brief glance, he would say:
'At whom are you staring, sir? A more modest demeanor would
comport more suitably with your station.'"

One of his sons was expected to anticipate his desire to leave or
enter a room and to stand ready to open the door for him. Seton

recalled his mother waiting patiently by the front door for hours, ready to open it on her husband's return home each evening. If by chance he was forced to open a door for himself, he would demand indignantly: "Am I no one that you treat me as if I were merely one of yourselves?"[4]

William's only reference to his father's dignity appears in a story about "a stuck-up young bank clerk from Dale Miller's Bank" who came to Joseph's office with bank drafts to be signed. He refused to take off his hat when addressing Joseph and "even when asked to do so, continued to disregard the modern code of correct behaviour, so father complained to the bank and he was never sent again."[5]

Although Seton's tone makes Joseph sound like an ogre, the description itself is probably fairly accurate. Children of mid-nineteenth century middle-class English homes *were* expected to stand aside for their elders, wait for their elders to be seated first and open doors for anyone senior to themselves. Staring *was* considered the height of ill manners, just as it was not "correct behaviour" to keep the head covered when addressing an older person. Joseph, in insisting on these standards, was certainly in step with his times, but Seton's account distorts the facts as recounted by his brothers.

Other than the beatings of which he accused his father, Seton's most serious charge against Joseph was his greed and selfishness. He recalled that all monies coming into the household were used to satisfy Joseph's desires first, and the "most vital interests of his family were always cheerfully sacrificed to his most trifling passing convenience."[6] When his wife inherited £4,000 from her mother, Joseph confiscated the money, bought himself an acre of garden opposite the family home, had greenhouses constructed and hired gardeners to operate them. He bought fancy sporting rifles, microscopes and the best telescope in South Shields. When his wife pleaded that he spend a little of the money on a pony chaise for her to get about in, since she was so frequently pregnant, he told her to call a hack when she needed to ride. But he refused her money to pay the fare.[7]

William recalled that "father, afraid of us learning bad habits and failing to recognize the true value of money was by no means liberal with pocket money. At boarding school he only allowed us one penny per week and I have no recollection of him ever giving us money, all I ever got was given by mother. But father was very far from being a mean man, this was simply English carefulness, so different from our Western prodigality."[8] In another section of his memoirs he describes his father returning from his frequent business trips to London "laden with toys or books or some other presents," and writes of the donkey he bought for his children and the swing he built for them.[9]

Seton's story of the squandering of his mother's inheritance does not fit with William's memoirs. Grandmother Snowdon died in 1859, one year before Seton was born, but William, who was six years old when the family home was built in 1853, recalls the greenhouses being built at the same time as the house. The acre garden was in reality only a quarter acre of rented land which their father fenced so that he could grow vegetables for his family. This bit of land was known to the family as The Far Garden to distinguish it from the tiny garden in front of the house; the family gardener helped with the work but always under Joseph's supervision, for he loved to work with growing things.

Cultivating a garden was so important to Joseph that in 1851 he rented a house at Harton, a village in the rolling countryside two miles beyond South Shields. He was by this time married and had a family of four sons and another on the way. From Harton he walked to his office in South Shields each day, cheerfully accepting this inconvenience in exchange for the pleasure of a house in the country and a quarter acre of garden.

After a year, however, the inconvenience outweighed the pleasure, and he brought his family back to town where he was building a new home for them on Wellington Terrace, on "the very outskirts of the town, the most modern, newly built part."[10] Across from the house was a large wheat field, and beyond that the farmlands of eastern Durham County stretched to the sea. The lot on which the house was built was a standard twenty-seven feet in width, but the house was three stories high with a full basement to accommodate the two kitchens, and behind it stood the three conservatories, or greenhouses. The dining room at the front on the first floor and the drawing room directly above it were the pride of the elder Thompsons because of the mahogany and horsehair furniture, the plate glass bay windows and the ornamental ceilings with their "gasoliers" hanging down on brass chains. The walls were decorated with scarlet and mauve flocked hangings interspersed with oil paintings of the Thompson ships framed in ornate gilt. Each room had a fireplace with a marble mantelpiece.

But it was the bathroom that the young Thompsons would later remember most vividly. In an age when many of the best houses in England still had no indoor plumbing of any kind, the new house on Wellington Terrace had a flush toilet and a shower, both supplied with water from a tank in the room above. The bath was unique. It had been constructed of five grey marble slabs, and was so large that five young Thompsons could be bathed in it at once. Its supply of hot water was piped up from a tank that was heated by the fireplace in the basement kitchen.

At the back of the house on the first floor was the nursery where, in their earliest years before being sent off to the local school, the boys were educated by governesses. When his eldest son was ten, Joseph Thompson became concerned that his sons would grow up speaking with the "unpleasant vernacular of the locality,"[11] and he enrolled him and his next two sons at a boarding school: Skerne Lodge Academy at Darlington, about thirty-five miles from South Shields. The three boys — John Enoch, commonly known by his second name (born in 1846), William (1847) and Joseph Jr. (1849) — spent about six years at this school. The next three sons — Charles (born in 1851), Harry (1852) and George (1854) — spent less time there as their school years overlapped a decline in the Thompson family fortunes. By the time that Arthur (born in 1859) was ready for school, there was not enough money for either governesses or boarding schools.

All of the Thompson boys appear to have had a strong bond with their mother, Alice Snowdon Thompson, but Seton was convinced that his bond was the most special because of the story his mother told him of how she prepared for his birth. In the winter of 1859–60, when she discovered that she was pregnant again, she asked the family doctor what she could do to make sure that her next child was more gifted than the others. The doctor told her that she should keep calm, fix her mind on the highest plane of thought and keep healthy. Determined to follow his orders precisely, she avoided all excitement and read the Bible every day. Then, to start her unborn child in the right direction, she read the newly published novel *Ernest Maltravers*, the story of a fine Christian country gentleman, hunter and sportsman. To keep healthy, she walked down to the ocean every day with the family nurse, "Old" Ellen Robertson, and took a dip to improve her circulation. But one day in late July, she insisted on carrying out this ritual even though it meant wading into a storm-tossed sea. She was knocked down by the waves and would have drowned if Old Ellen had not caught her by the hair and dragged her ashore.

As a result of the shock, she gave birth to the baby several weeks ahead of schedule, on 14 August 1860. Of all her children, only this one feared water and for the first two years of his life screamed whenever he was put in the bathtub. The baby was given the name Ernest in honour of the uplifting novel his mother had been reading, and Evan for one of his ancestors, Evan Cameron, the fabled wolf hunter of Scotland.

As a little girl, Alice Snowdon's ambition was to grow up to be "a widow with two daughters."[12] Instead, at twenty-one she married Joseph Logan Thompson and became the mother of eleven children. Mary Ann, the only girl among them, was born in 1856 with "a dislocated spine"[13] (probably spina bifida) and was unable to walk, feed herself or speak. She died at age six and her mother promptly declared this to be God's will, especially as among so many boys she would surely have been spoiled.

Alice Thompson's entire life was bound up in her family and her God. Even though she always had the help of Old Ellen — who acted as nursemaid and major-domo of the household — a cook and a maid, and always hired an extra maid when her older sons were home from school, the task of raising ten sons occupied most of her time and energy. What was left she devoted to her God by doing charitable works and praying. Her sons were all highly impressed with their mother's capacity for prayer. Down on her knees, she would pour out her soul to God, and when she arose, her face would be shining with the conviction that she had been heard and the answer to her prayers would very shortly be forthcoming.

Seton regarded his mother as a saint and a martyr, though basically weak in character. Thus, whenever she slipped from the pedestal on which he had installed her, he could blame her lapse on her inability to sustain her saintly nature in the face of his father's far stronger wicked one. He blamed his father also for inflicting on her a life of servitude by forcing her to have so many children. But as time went by and he grew disenchanted with Christianity, he began to spread the blame for his mother's lowly estate equally between his father and the church, since he perceived that it was the church to which his mother was devoted that decreed she should bow to the dominion of her husband and sons. Finally he settled on St. Paul as the real perpetrator of this iniquitous doctrine because he had set up an all-male hierarchy when he established his church. Seton concluded that Paul must have been a woman-hater and accepted as fact the theory that he had been syphilitic. In this way St. Paul joined Seton's private pantheon of those who deserved his unending hatred.

But Alice Thompson was really far from downtrodden. She expected and received obedience and respect from her sons, though she indulged them in many ways, such as preparing picnics for them and baking cakes for them to take to boarding school. She was blunt and plain-spoken, and on occasion seems to have been somewhat insensitive. Her child-rearing methods combined the standard Victorian father-knows-best approach with guile and manipulation, but whenever these did not work, she would invite her erring child to kneel with her while she consulted God. This technique generally had the desired effect.

Her devotion to God, however, did not prevent her from appreciating Shakespeare and many of the poets of her own day. Alice had an exceptional talent for memorization, and could recite an appropriate quotation for any of life's events. Her son William was quite sure that he knew more Shakespeare from listening to his mother than he had ever learned in school.

Alice had strong views on her sons' education and their future careers. Because she had lost her father and two brothers at sea, she was adamant that none of her sons was to become a seaman. It helped, of course, that Joseph's seagoing experiences had been so unpleasant. It also helped that her first two sons showed an aptitude for "figures" while at school and a willingness to enter business. At sixteen Enoch was welcomed into the ship brokerage firm of his Uncle Snowdon in Newcastle. William was taken into his father's office in January 1863.

Unfortunately, by this time, Joseph Thompson's business was in decline. Seton would later blame this decline on his father's lethargy, and while this might have been part of the cause, most of the trouble was the result of changing technology and Joseph's unwillingness to adapt to it. Like his father, who had believed that railways were a passing fad, Joseph clung to the old ways while he waited for the new ways to pass.

The Thompsons' shipping businesses depended on the fact that for centuries the town of South Shields and its twin across the river, North Shields, had served as the port for the city of Newcastle because the course of the Tyne had been interrupted by a series of sandbanks and islands upriver. At low tide at Newcastle the channel was little more than six feet deep. Control of the river had always been claimed by Newcastle, but the port towns, knowing they would lose the majority of the coal shipping business if they allowed the river to be improved, managed to block work on it for nearly a century.

In 1850 the matter was taken out of local hands by the passage of the Tyne Improvement Act which empowered a commission from all the Tyne's cities and towns to straighten and dredge the river, and build dikes and piers at its mouth. The result was a waterway capable of floating a battleship, and the beginning of a vast change in the traditional life of South Shields. It was intended that improvement of the river would benefit all the towns along its banks, but while the new dikes and piers did eliminate the treacherous entrance to the harbour of the two Shields, competition increased almost immediately with the construction of massive new docking facilities upriver.

The businessmen of South Shields might have recovered from this setback by vigorously promoting other aspects of their traditional business if the river's improvement had not coincided with a more revolutionary change. In 1852 the Palmer Shipyards at Jarrow, just upriver from South Shields, built the first screw-propelled, iron-hulled collier in the world. The sailing ship owners of the Tyne had already lost much of their exclusive domestic coal markets when the coalfields of South Wales and Yorkshire had begun to expand in the first half of the century, but they had been making up their losses by searching out foreign markets. Now they were faced with competition in these markets which would effectively wipe out sail-powered colliers within twenty years.

In his younger days Joseph Thompson had been a very progressive man, "a strong upholder of free trade." He had introduced cricket to South Shields, "was the first to have a Christmas tree for his boys, the first to wear a moustache and was called a Frenchman for doing so,"[14] and the first in his town to accept homeopathic medicine. Prior to this, whenever one of the young Thompsons complained of an ache or came home with a cut finger, Alice Thompson had been in the habit of calling the family doctor. After a while, Joseph noticed that the doctor's approach to the curing of these ailments had altered; he investigated, found the doctor had been converted to homeopathy, and decided he approved. He then bought books on the subject and a chest of the medicines used by the doctor and, with Alice's help, proceeded to treat his family without calling the doctor except in the case of major illnesses.

But all these things had happened in Joseph's younger days. After he built his fine brick home on Wellington Terrace and became prosperous in a business which relied on the continuation of sailing ships, he was content with life as it was. In his civic-mindedness, he worked diligently as one of the commissioners for the improvement of the Tyne which would eventually make his sailing ships obsolete, yet he seemed to feel that progress was for others. He watched as his competitors switched to steam-powered, iron-hulled vessels, while he continued to send out the sail-powered *E. D. T.* (named for his father's initials), the *Alice Thompson* and the *Marathon*.

The *E. D. T.* was a 359-ton vessel built to order by the Sunderland shipyards. In 1864 she set sail from Shields with a cargo of "heavy goods" destined for Spain. After discharging her cargo in Barcelona, she sailed for the Levant with cattle, then into the Black Sea to load up wheat and head for home. Somewhere on the return journey she foundered and all hands were lost.

The *E. D. T.* was not the first of Joseph Thompson's ships to go down, but its loss came close on the heels of another kind of disaster. In the late 1850s, the insurance company in which Joseph was a partner had been the managing owner of a large ship called the *New Zealand*. Nearly seven hundred tons register, she was the largest sailing ship up to that time to load at the North Eastern Railway Company's newly opened Jarrow Docks, under construction just upriver from South Shields. Unfortunately, as she left the dock after loading, she swung into shallow water and went aground. When the tide went out, the weight of the thousand tons of coal she was carrying broke her back and she was left a total wreck.

Instead of turning to the underwriters of the vessel's insurance for compensation, the managing owners elected to sue the North Eastern Railway for allowing such a large vessel to enter their docks before they were complete. But the North Eastern was an immensely wealthy company and could afford to prolong the litigation for years. Whenever the owners of the vessel secured a verdict in their favour, the railway would appeal and the whole process would begin again. The suit was finally settled in February 1862, but by this time Joseph and his partners had spent such enormous sums on legal fees and court costs that the victory was an empty one.

In the midst of these years of litigation, Joseph had begun to realize that his business would soon no longer decently support his family, and it was at this time that he first brought up the subject of emigrating to Canada. In the beginning the talk was confined to Sunday afternoons when he and his sons, accompanied by his brother-in-law Thomas Tate and Tate's son Tom, would walk along the sand dunes bordering the North Sea then out along the "rock tops," the pier that had been built to improve the harbour. At its farthest end, almost a mile out into the North Sea, the Thompsons and the Tates would watch the ships heading to sea and talk of the opportunities to be found in Canada. Joseph had been to Quebec on his voyage as a cabin boy and liked the little he had seen of the country. The Tates joined in the conversation wistfully, for Aunt Tate ruled the Tate household and she made it a rule never to entertain an idea put forth by Joseph.

In the winter of 1864–65 Joseph announced his intention of emigrating. He told his family that Canada would provide better opportunities for his sons and a better climate for his wife, who suffered each winter with chest trouble. For himself, he envisioned a vast estate of virgin land where he could grow acres of garden and go hunting in his own forest. He set the embarkation date as June 1866.

To prepare for their new life, the Thompson boys were now to learn trades which their father believed would be useful in the new environment. William had spent two years in his father's office as assistant bookkeeper, but he had also learned sail-making and proved to be very adept with his hands, so his father found him a job with a cabinet maker. Joseph Jr. went to a contractor to learn carpentry. Charlie, the fourth son, was apprenticed to Rennoldsons who specialized in marine steam engineering.

Enoch, who had been employed in his Uncle Snowdon's office in Newcastle, took over William's duties in Joseph's office. All the family acknowledged that Enoch showed definite talent as a ship's broker so it was accepted that if he decided to accompany the family to Canada, he would carry on in this line of business in some Canadian port.

Joseph began making inquiries to the Canadian government about this time, and his letters finally found their way into the hands of the immigration officer for the county of Durham, Ontario, a certain Mr. Roche. He assured Joseph that the land he wanted was to be found in Durham County, and that he would be at the Thompsons' service when they arrived to claim it. With this assurance, Joseph sold his business, his remaining ships, his house and most of its furnishings.

The logistics of transporting a family of ten sons (two more had arrived after Seton's birth) and a mountain of baggage across an ocean were somewhat formidable given the cost of the journey and Joseph's limited resources. Part of the problem was resolved by arranging to ship the family's goods aboard the *Marathon,* which had been sold to Enoch Donkerly Thompson. It was scheduled to sail for Quebec City with a cargo of coal, firebricks and rope about the time the Thompsons were due to depart. When it was decided that the two family dogs would also sail aboard the *Marathon,* three of the boys — William, Joseph Jr. and Charlie — asked to make the voyage on her, too. This was granted, but only after Alice had been persuaded that the saving in passage money outweighed the dangers from the stormy seas.

In the midst of the preparations for departure, Joseph was feted at a number of testimonial dinners. The congregation of the Presbyterian Church where he had served as session clerk presented him with a set of leather-bound books. The Third Durham Artillery Volunteers in which he had been a lieutenant asked God to look kindly on his future endeavours, and the mayor and council gave him "a beautifully illuminated parchment scroll on which was engrossed a highly laudatory letter addressed to himself." Then the mayor added that once the Thompsons were settled in Canada, he expected that "in the course of a few years there might be ten times ten, a little colony in itself."[15] There is no record of Joseph's response.

"I was not quite six when we left England," Seton wrote three-quarters of a century later. "I can clearly see yet the bustle of preparation in that summer of 1866 . . . the piles and piles of boxes all lashed with strong, tarry rope that told of ship tradition."[16] Most of these boxes were trundled off to Jarrow Docks where the *Marathon,* under Captain Hyeres, was being readied for departure. The remainder was forwarded to Glasgow where the rest of the family would embark.

On 19 June the elder Thompsons and seven of their sons boarded the steamship *St. Patrick.* With them was eighteen-year-old Mary Ann ("Polly") Burfield, the second daughter of Alice's sister. Polly had been adopted into the family in 1862 to help with the younger children and had become indispensable to the household. Old Ellen Robertson had wanted to emigrate, too, but her mother was dying and she stayed behind, promising to follow later.

The *St. Patrick* was the smallest of the Ocean Steamship Company's Glasgow line and considered primarily an emigrant ship. Although she had first-class cabins on board, Seton's later comment that all the rats on the ship seemed to have selected the family's stateroom as "the meeting place where they came for their social pleasures"[17] implies that they travelled as "intermediate" passengers who were provided with bed, bedding and meals but little else. Even this would have cost them $40 Canadian each. It was ironic, of course, that they should embark for their new life in an iron ship, the very thing that had destroyed the family fortunes.

3

Immigrants' Idyll

The *St. Patrick,* with 309 passengers and general cargo, docked in Quebec City on 8 July 1866. Seton's only memories of the occasion were of hotel windows which stared out at an expanse of solid rock, and the sour bread which was served to the Thompsons at their first breakfast in Canada. After eighteen days at sea, his normal curiosity had been dulled.

A day later the Thompsons boarded the Grand Trunk Railway for Lindsay, nearly five hundred miles to the west. Most of the journey took them through "interminable swamps of spruce and tamarack," but Seton cherished one beautiful memory of the trip. After nightfall Joseph Thompson called his sons to look out the window: there, drifting among the trees and streaking past the train, were hundreds of tiny, brilliant "shooting stars." Joseph explained that they were fireflies, and the young Seton stored this experience for the rest of his life as "one of those delicious rare moments when your dream fairy comes to you, and you know it really is true."[1]

At Port Hope on Lake Ontario they changed to the Port Hope, Lindsay and Beaverton Railway line for the final forty-two miles to Lindsay in Ops Township. The town of Lindsay was not at all what the Thompsons had expected to find in the wilds of Canada. The streets were wide and the buildings were brick — they learned later that the whole town had burned a few years earlier and had just been rebuilt. They saw "fashionably dressed young couples parading the streets, well-filled stores and a great many of the comforts of civilization" they thought they had left behind.[2] And over it all hung the fragrance of the cedar that was being sawn into boards at the nearby mill.

The townspeople of Lindsay found the Thompsons interesting, too, and there were quite a few smiles on the faces of those who saw them step down one after another from the train. Joseph Thompson had come prepared for the life of an English squire and had dressed for the role. He had brought all his sporting guns with him; his scientific instruments and his library were following on the *Marathon*. Seton later wrote that he thought his father had done most of his preparation for pioneering by reading *Robinson Crusoe, The Swiss Family Robinson* and the stories of Mayne Reid.

Alice Thompson stepped onto the platform after her husband with Polly Burfield close behind her. They were followed by Enoch, looking exactly like a youthful edition of his father and utterly out of place in farm country. By contrast, fourteen-year-old Harry and twelve-year-old George appeared strong and healthy, though rather citified in their English clothes.

There was little to distinguish between the four youngest Thompsons — Arthur Septimus, Ernest Evan (Seton), Walter and Alan Cameron — except their size, for they were seven, six, four and two years old. All wore the standard English juvenile costume of the day: cloth caps, white collars, knee pants, white stockings and patent leather shoes. As if to guarantee that they would continue to stand out among their Canadian neighbours, Joseph Thompson had even brought along more clothes and shoes in graduated sizes to replace the present ones when they were outgrown. It was his firm belief — a conviction that Seton would share in later years — that British was best, Canadian-made a poor second.

Although dressed the same as his brothers, the third from the youngest was somewhat different from them in appearance. He was not quite as solid and robust as they were, tending instead to be slender and wiry, and a little short for his age as well. He had the same dark brown, almost black, wavy hair that was typical of the Thompsons, but it framed a face that was more finely boned, a little more tense, or perhaps wary. But the feature that set Seton apart was his eyes. Dark brown and penetrating, they were the eyes of an extremely observant, questioning child. Only one thing marred them: whenever Seton was excited, nervous or frightened, his eyes crossed.

At four years of age, he had been playing "horsy" on the arm of the tall horsehair sofa in the family parlour, when he slipped off and landed on his head. Alice Thompson had not been unduly alarmed; she picked him up, placed him on the sofa and comforted him. His screaming soon subsided, and then he announced that he could see two mamas, and two clocks — in fact, two of everything. As this problem was not covered by their homeopathy books, Joseph and Alice called in the family doctor who, though unable to do anything for the child, was of the opinion that his eye condition would correct itself as he grew older. He had not outgrown it by the time he arrived in Lindsay, and it would be many more years before he did.

Mr. Roche, the government immigration agent, was on hand to greet the family at the railway station. Joseph had thoughtfully mailed him a photograph of himself so that Roche would have no difficulty identifying him, but a family with that many sons would have been difficult to miss anyhow. Roche installed the Thompsons in a rented house before he set off with Joseph and Enoch to look at land. "Father's idea at first," wrote William, "was to have bought up about a thousand acres of wild land and with the help of his ten sons clear it and thus become what is an Englishman's ideal of felicity, a landed proprietor,"[3] but Roche soon dissuaded him, and instead he bought a hundred acres of semi-improved land at a sheriff's sale.

On 20 August the *Marathon* docked in Quebec City, and the Thompsons received a wire announcing that the three boys and their dogs had arrived safely. A week later the family was reunited and they promptly set off in a horse and buggy to look at their new home five miles southeast of town on Omemee Road. The first thing they learned was that there was no house on the property. The former owner was a bachelor who had made do with the mandatory "claim shanty" and a few log out-buildings when he had homesteaded there. Before he abandoned the land many years earlier, he had cleared about sixty acres of it; as soon as he left, the neighbours tore down much of the fencing in order to pasture their cattle and sheep on it. Any of the land that had been cultivated was now covered in a thick crop of thistles, but the Thompsons were assured that this meant the land was fertile. Forty acres of the farm were still in bush.

Beside the gateway that led into the clearing stood two enormous elm trees which the bachelor had left as guardians over his property. Joseph Thompson christened them Gog and Magog after the giant figures at the palace gates in London, and he named the farm The Elms. Gog, the larger of the two elms, met a sad fate a year or so later. As it was actually on the road allowance, the "road master" gave permission to a local farmer to cut it down for firewood, and the Thompsons arrived home from a trip to Lindsay to find their much-prized tree being split and hauled away.

Although the family's first view of the farm was disappointing — they had expected something more substantial — they were not disappointed in the forest around it or the stream which flowed through it. That first afternoon the older boys built a campfire — the first Seton had ever seen — and the Thompsons spread out a picnic lunch beside the stream. On the way back to town, one of the livery team balked, and no amount of beating would make it move. The family at last climbed out of the wagon and began walking. (Neighbours came to their rescue with a fresh horse to take the balky one's place.)

The shanty, though in need of major repairs, was solidly built. It was a two-storey log building with sleeping accommodation upstairs, so it was decided that the older boys would move out to the farm immediately to renovate the shanty and begin constructing barns and henhouses. In the meantime, Joseph let a contract to a local builder for a substantial brick house to be ready for the family in the spring. The younger sons and their parents remained in the rented house in town, and it was here that Seton first demonstrated his creative genius. To amuse himself, he constructed hens and roosters out of some corks and chicken feathers which he had picked up in the neighbourhood. What delighted his father most about them, wrote William, was the lifelike qualities the child had been able to get from these crude materials.

By October the shanty had been repaired, and the family moved in, cramming themselves and their possessions into the two rooms. According to Seton, the cabin was infested with rats and the wind whistled between the logs, but this seems unlikely considering the Thompson boys' training in carpentry and their parents' fastidiousness. The older boys had boxed off one corner of the main room for their parents' bedroom and another corner for Polly. The youngest children slept in hammocks in the main room; the rest bunked upstairs.

While the first six sons worked the farm and built furniture for the new house, Arthur and Seton attended school. They set off soon after eight each morning for the mile walk to Salem schoolhouse, a one-room log building heated by a wood stove. They carried a lunch of "a meat sandwich, a jam sandwich, and a hard-boiled egg."[4] Each recess the older boys cut and split the day's supply of wood which was fed into the stove during school hours by a boy selected by the teacher for the honour. The first time that the honour fell to Seton, he bungled it. As a city child, he had no understanding of the fine art involved in feeding a fire, and had to be shown the correct way by one of the local boys.

The teacher was sixteen-year-old Agnes O'Leary, a member of one of the numerous Irish families in the district. To Seton she was the fount of all knowledge; she in turn apparently recognized that he was a very bright child, though there was little she could do to encourage him.

At three each day the boys walked home, threading their way through the sheep and cattle that had wandered onto the road, ducking through the rails of the snake fences to avoid the rams and bulls. At home each boy was assigned a share of the chores: Seton had charge of Jenny, a brindle cow with a crumpled horn. A calm and sedate animal, she produced her annual calf with no difficulty. His other charge, however, was a rather scruffy-looking sheep named Nanny whose deliveries were fraught with drama and tragedy. By the simple process of observing these and other barnyard events before he was seven years old, Seton had acquired all the basic sex education he would need for many years to come.

At Roche's suggestion, Joseph Thompson hired a man named William Ramsay, "an all-round Canadian farmer and bushwhacker," to teach him and his sons how to farm.[5] Under Ramsay's supervision, Joseph bought a team of workhorses, a double wagon, ploughs, harrows and all the other tools necessary for a productive farm. Ramsay then taught his new charges how to chop cordwood, split and pile it, fell trees so that they would drop just where they were wanted, burn and clear land. He taught them to take care of the cattle and horses, "how to plough, harrow and sow broadcast . . . mow hay, stack it, cradle wheat, bind sheaves and all the ins and outs of farming."[6] Ramsay stayed with them a year so they could complete a full round of instruction.

The Thompsons were unprepared for the winter of 1866–67. In South Shields, proximity to the sea had protected them from extremes of temperature, and though they were familiar with snow, they had never experienced any quantity of it. In Ops township the temperature dropped to minus thirty degrees Fahrenheit and the snow fell and drifted until it covered the fences, sealing the world in white until the spring.

At first the snow was a delightful diversion for Seton and Arthur on their daily trips to school, but as the winter deepened and the numbing cold set in, their pleasure in it disappeared. One afternoon Seton decided it was too cold to walk the rest of the way home and he lay down in the snow. Arthur got him home by threatening him with violence, and after that he was allowed to remain at home until spring. Shortly afterwards the new house was ready for occupancy. It measured thirty-four by forty feet, was two stories high, had twelve rooms and a cellar. For Seton the only room that held any interest was the big workshop because it was here his older brothers taught the smaller ones the skills of carpentry and handicrafts. Seton spent the remainder of that first Canadian winter creating his own toys and his own entertainment. The training with basic tools that he received from his brothers was all the instruction he would ever get in these skills, but from it he developed the exceptional craftsmanship that he would reveal in his carvings and later in the construction of his own homes.

Seton learned all about domestic animals while he was a farm boy, but he learned even more about wildlife. Some of his informal lessons in this subject came from Charles Peel, one of the Irish neighbours. Peel enjoyed sitting by the Thompson fireside telling tall tales of the bears that had once roamed the township — enormous, ferocious beasts of infinite cunning and resourcefulness. Seton would sit listening as long as he dared, then, when ordered to bed, would dawdle on the stairs to catch another sentence or two of these marvellous epics. Cuddled under the blankets, he would watch the eerie patterns made by the flickering light from the box stove, terrified of the wild animals who waited in the night, but equally fearful that the days of such beasts might be gone forever.

The remainder of the wildlife knowledge he accumulated during these years came to him on independent expeditions into the forest and surrounding countryside, sometimes alone, but most often with brothers Arthur and Walter. It was an ideal time in their lives since they were not yet big enough to do the backbreaking work assigned to their older brothers, and their parents were too busy with the management of the farm to fuss over them.

In spring the three boys looted the woods of mosses, lichens and fungus to decorate the shadow boxes which they had constructed in the workshop during the winter, and Seton marvelled at the intricacy and infinite variety of the tiny plant forms. Later they went hunting for the nests of small animals and birds, toppling the dead stubs of trees in a burned-over area to get at the squirrels and mice that had nested there, but the animals inevitably died when they plummeted to earth. One of Charlie Peel's daughters gave Seton a baby crow and he fed it every hour as he had been instructed, but left it to fend for itself when it was time for school. When he got home, the crow was dead of starvation, and he vowed — for the first of many times — never again to pin his affections on a wild creature.

Seton's greatest joy was the birds, and he would lie by the hour in the straw that capped the barn roof, staring up into the sky. One day he heard a croaking trumpet and saw the long-necked forms of a pair of white cranes. Other days he spotted woodpeckers and flickers and hummingbirds; unfortunately, many of the birds he saw he could not identify. The only reference work available to him was his father's two-volume *Knight's Pictorial Museum of Animated Nature*. Seton had delighted in these books long before he could read, and they already showed signs of wear and soiling from his hands when they were brought from England, but most of the birds illustrated in them were not native to Canada.

Then one day, probably in the summer of 1867, he was told of a collection of stuffed birds owned by the town's hardware merchant, Charlie Foley. After much pleading, the boy was taken by an older brother to see them. Although Foley was in conversation

ABOVE: Joseph Logan Thompson, 1866. This is the photograph sent to the immigration agent at Lindsay (John Carl Thompson).

TOP LEFT: Seton's grandfather, Enoch Donkerly Thompson, 1863 (John Carl Thompson).

BOTTOM LEFT: Alice and Joseph Logan Thompson with Ernest Evan Thompson (Seton), 1854 (John Carl Thompson).

CLOCKWISE FROM TOP LEFT: Aunt
Tate, c. 1865 (John Carl
Thompson); Old Ellen Robertson
and her mother, 1866 (John Carl
Thompson); Seton's second
brother, William Snowdon
Thompson, 1863 (John Carl
Thompson); Ernest Evan
Thompson (Seton) aged 17
(Courtesy Seton Village); Seton's
Oldest brother, John Enoch
Thompson, 1863 (John Carl
Thompson).

"THE ELMS", FARM HOUSE NEAR LINDSAY, ONT.
FAMILY RESIDENCE 1867-1870.

ABOVE: The Elms farmhouse near Lindsay, Ontario, 1867–70 (John Carl Thompson).

RIGHT: No. 4 Wellington Terrace, South Shields, England, 1853–66 (John Carl Thompson).

with another man when they arrived, he took time to point out and name some of the forty or so birds standing on the shelves among his hardware supplies. Seton was awestruck, and from this time on, his goal in life was to acquire a collection of stuffed birds of his own.

Determined to be part of the world of winged things, he constructed birds' nests out of mud and grass and twigs, carefully duplicating the ones he found in the woods; but the birds scorned them. Then, in spite of being stung many times, he built nests of mud for wasps and hornets, too, but these were also ignored. He was more successful with the wooden nesting boxes he made, which proved acceptable to the swallows and wrens.

One summer day, while he was tagging along behind his brother George and a neighbour friend as they went to bring the cows home for milking, two crows flew high overhead. As Seton stopped to watch them, out of a low tree darted a grey bird with a bright red crest, and not much larger than a sparrow. Uttering a shrill cry, it attacked the crows, which dodged and fled as fast as possible into the woods. When the boy asked the name of the grey bird, his brother told him that it was a kingbird.

"An' he kin lick anything that flies," added the neighbour.[7]

To Seton this was almost unbelievable: somehow, one of Knight's exotic birds had flown right into his life in Ontario! "I had dreamed of it. I thought it a rare bird of far countries. Now I had seen it in our own land, with my own eyes, it had all become real. It lived and fought right here among *our* crows."[8] Seton was no longer in a backwoods of unnamed, uninteresting species of birds. Always looking for heroes, he now idolized the kingbird, both because it belonged among the exclusive birds which were written about in books and because it had made such a spirited attack on the much larger crows. As he learned more about the bird, his worship increased, and in 1876 he wrote a poem to honour it. He revised "The Kingbird" several times in the next couple of years, but though he considered it complete in 1879, it was apparently never published until it appeared in his autobiography in 1941. It is of interest mainly as the first of his nature writings.

When his brother Joseph shot a deer, he watched while his brothers gutted it, revealing its unborn young. He saw his first woodchuck, or groundhog, after it had been killed by the family terrier, Snap; seventy years later he would write of the "mixed sense of attraction and disgust" that he felt as the creature was paraded for all to see.[9]

Life on the farm became more civilized after the Thompsons moved into their new home and furnished it. Joseph bought a fine little mare, a buggy and a cutter, and the older boys put them to good use in their social lives. Their father allowed them to join the Lindsay Cricket Club to make up in some measure for the drudgery on the farm.

Farm life also became easier for Alice Thompson in the spring of 1867 with the arrival of Old Ellen Robertson, whose mother had died during the winter. According to Seton, Ellen arrived to find his mother on her knees scrubbing floors, and promptly reordered the allotment of farm and household tasks so that Alice was relieved of all the heavier work. Ellen herself took over the feeding of the poultry. The old woman's greatest value to Alice, however, was not the relief she provided from the drudgery of farm life but the companionship she gave, for Alice did not find the neighbouring farm wives a congenial lot. Ellen understood the world from which Alice had come.

On Sundays the Thompson boys would hitch up the farm team to the double wagon and, with Harry as teamster, the whole family would drive to the Presbyterian church in Lindsay to hear the Reverend Mr. Muir preach. After Muir left the district, the family often went instead to the Methodist church a mile from the farm to avoid having to sit on a bare plank over five miles of rutted road. Joseph, though devout, was not overly concerned with sectarian differences. He had been brought up in the Established Church (Church of England), but became a Presbyterian when he married Alice because she was one and because he had found the simplicity of the Presbyterian services to his liking.

The Reverend Burns of the Methodist Church served three parishes, so on two out of three Sundays lay preachers took his place in the pulpit. For Seton, wedged between older brothers on a bench, all of their sermons and hymns were uniformly dull. His memories of Sunday afternoons were of prayers, Bible readings and making up verses about Biblical characters; his older brothers remembered buggy rides and visiting lady friends.

Joseph Thompson sold the farm in Ops Township in 1870. In their four years at The Elms, the Thompsons had been remarkably unsuccessful as farmers, for even though William Ramsay's farming lessons had been thorough, he had not been able to prepare them for all exigencies. Cows died at calving time, sheep died of unexplained causes, crops failed because they were harvested too soon or too late. Added to these problems was a lack of manpower. By Christmas 1869, only five of the Thompson boys remained on the farm. Enoch had gone to Toronto in the first spring after their arrival on the farm; a friend of the Reverend Mr. Muir had invited the young man to the city, provided him with a home and found him a position as a clerk for an insurance agency. In the fall of 1868, when an offer came from another friend of jobs for two more of the boys, Joseph, acknowledging that the farm could not support the entire family, gave his approval for William and Joseph Jr. to accept. William, who had spent two years in his father's office, became a bookkeeper in a branch of a huge lumber concern near Portage-du-fort on the Ottawa River; the same company hired his brother as a "shanty clerk."

When Joseph saw that his fourth son was not suited to farm life, he wrote to a business firm in Glasgow and Charlie was accepted in 1869 as a warehouse clerk. And Harry, the fifth son, was offered a position in the dry goods company of his parsimonious Uncle Farrar in Leeds. He sailed for England in March 1870. One more family member also left them — Old Ellen. She died in October 1869 and was buried in the Lindsay cemetery.

Joseph's capital was almost all gone by 1870; he could not afford to hire farmhands and he could not do all the necessary work with only the young children to help. The farm was sold to William Blackwell, the son of a local pioneer. The Thompsons left Lindsay for Toronto on 12 April 1870, and though all of them had regrets, none mourned the loss of The Elms more than Seton. At ten years of age he had developed the intense interest in the natural environment that would become the foundation of his life's work.

4

The Berserker Streak

Toronto in 1870 was a boom town. Along the water-front and north to King Street stood foundries, breweries, distilleries and factories for making biscuits and heavy machinery and clothing, products that would find an easy market south of the border in an economy still recovering from the destruction of the Civil War. Thousands of workers from western Europe and Britain, attracted by the city's prosperity, came looking for better lives, swelling its population to nearly seventy-five thousand, far beyond its housing capacity. Some of the newcomers were absorbed into the tenement areas that were sandwiched between the factories; the remainder crowded into the run-down boarding houses just north of Queen Street in the centre of the city, a slum area that would become notorious as The Ward a decade later.

In 1870 Joseph Thompson found a home for his family at 184 Elizabeth Street on the northern edge of this slum. His choice of a home was dictated partly by the difficulty of finding any house big enough for his family in a town with a housing shortage, and partly by his comparative poverty. The Elms had swallowed all his capital and brought little when it was sold.

No. 184 stood on the west side of the street almost opposite Walton Street. It was serviced by a well in the backyard and a privy behind the house, for though piped water, sewers, gaslights and indoor plumbing were available in the better part of the city, it would be another twenty-five years before they came to Elizabeth Street. The house itself was quite comfortable, and was large enough for the parents, Polly Burfield, the five youngest sons and William and Joseph Jr., who had taken this opportunity to leave the woods and find jobs as carpenters in the city. Enoch remained with his patrons for another year; Harry and Charlie were in Britain.

The four youngest Thompsons enrolled in the Elizabeth Street School right next door to the Thompson house. There were approximately three hundred children attending this school and nearly sixty of them to each class. In his memoirs, Seton remembered his classmates as

newsboys, Negroes, and the toughest youngsters I had ever met, including some jailbirds. Their common talk was of successful robberies that they had taken part in, or fights in which they had used a knife with effect.

Rarely did I hear a sentence of their speech that was fit for publication. . . . Fights were of daily occurrence, and more than one boy I saw stabbed in these affairs. Here, indeed, it was that I first learned the value of the knife and the method of handling it.

The attitude of this wild mob toward strangers was fundamentally hostile. They bullied and pelted us poor newcomers with brutal delight — at least for a time, until we were initiated. Those early days in that school were a nightmare of horror and misery.[1]

As he was somewhat undersized for a ten-year-old, Seton was fair game for the neighbourhood toughs, and his eye problems made him an even more frequent target. During the years on the farm, his eye condition had gradually improved, just as the doctor had predicted, but unfortunately his eyes still crossed every time he was under stress, and on the Elizabeth Street schoolgrounds there was little but stress. As soon as his schoolmates realized that he was afflicted in this way, they began tormenting him with: "Come on, Squinty, cross your eyes!"[2] Enraged, Seton would wade into battle against his tormentors, most of them bigger and all of them more competent in a fight than he was. His own fighting strength came from what he called "the berserker streak of my wild ancestor, Fighting Geordie [Cameron]."[3] These battles were an almost daily affair — Seton later estimated that they "numbered in the scores, if not hundreds"[4] — and eventually resulted in damaged nose cartilage and innumerable facial and body scars, but he was enormously proud of having fought them.

If battling in the schoolyard five and a half days a week left scars on Seton's body, Sundays left scars on his soul. As long as the Thompsons had lived in South Shields, they attended the old Presbyterian Meeting House where Joseph was session clerk; in Lindsay, circumstances had forced them to worship at the most convenient church. In Toronto, however, there was an abundance of Presbyterian churches to choose from, and the family joined the congregation of the Second United Presbyterian Church at the corner of Gould and Victoria streets. This congregation had originally been part of the Bay Street Presbyterian Church, but in a dispute over a minor point of doctrine, they had set up a church of their own where they practised a very fundamental evangelical form of their faith.

Seton's recollections of his experience with Presbyterianism in this period of his life are all unhappy ones. He recalled going to Sabbath morning school at Cooke's Church on Elizabeth Street, then being marched off to the Second United Presbyterian Church to hear the Reverend John M. King, "a grim, hard doctrinaire of irreproachable personal life, in his eye a strange gleam which his followers called inspiration."[5] For nearly two hours, King would "dilate on the hot horrors of the world we most of us were bound to land in"[6] after which the Thompsons returned home for their midday dinner. At three o'clock the younger children attended more Sunday School classes, this time in the basement of Second United. At seven, after a brief respite for supper, they were back at church for the Reverend King's evening sermon in which they were forcefully reminded "that all human beings were born foredoomed to hell unless redeemed and saved in some miraculous manner."[7] Then, according to Seton, at home after the sermon, the family assembled for prayers and Bible readings, after which they went to their rooms for individual prayers before bed.

When allowances are made for Seton's bitterness and for the distortions of time on human memory, his recollections of the Thompson family's Sunday activities agree with William's memories and with general Presbyterian practices of that day. Although it was probably not Cooke's Church he attended for

Sabbath morning classes, since that was fourteen blocks away on Queen and catered entirely to the city's Irish, there were other nearby churches that held morning classes. And since the Reverend King was only the morning pastor at Second United, the evening's hell-fire sermons must be blamed on someone else. But the regimen he described in his memoirs was probably not overly exaggerated; the Victorian middle-class of Ontario took its religious life very seriously.

The Thompson boys' reactions to their religious upbringing varied, mostly according to their places in the family lineup. The older ones, products of the discipline of boarding schools, seem to have accepted the strictures of their church's teachings without rebellion. William, and probably Enoch as well, taught Sunday School, and in their adult years remained Presbyterians, attending church regularly and reserving Sundays for religious purposes. The middle sons, Charlie and Harry, both away from home at age eighteen, took a more moderate route, attending church but not being remarkably devout. The two youngest were more interested in worldly things, but Alan became a staunch Presbyterian in his later years.

By the time he was twelve, Seton, who was far more imaginative and impressionable than any of his brothers, had become convinced by the Presbyterian regimen that he was "a hopeless reprobate."[8] He had ample proof of this in the fact that his senses still delighted in so many earthly joys even after the Reverend King had made it clear that his mind should never stray from the fate of his eternal soul. He was racked with guilt over his inability to be saintly like his mother, while at the same time he took a perverse kind of pleasure in the terror of walking along the rim of Hell, waiting to see whether God would really strike him down.

But while he blamed the Reverend King and the Presbyterian church for his fear of damnation, it was his father he held responsible for subjecting him to this joyless faith. He readily acknowledged that his mother was really much more pious than his father, that she was, in fact, the type of woman who had "filled the convents of Dark Ages Europe, or the Flagellant ranks of the Middle Ages."[9] It was his mother who said, after one of her sons burned his finger, "Now that is what Hell is like, only it is all over your body and it lasts forever and ever."[10] And she was the one who marshalled the family for Bible readings and prayers.

Seton preferred, however, to blame his father for punishing him with this "strange school of theology" because he wanted to believe that it was only the weakness of his mother's saintly character which allowed her to follow Joseph's leadership in choice of faith — this in spite of the fact that Presbyterianism had been Alice Thompson's religion first. But Seton was subconsciously searching for things to blame on his father so he could justify his growing hatred for him. In reality there was only one reason for the hatred he felt: his father was a failure.

At the time Seton was born, Joseph Thompson was a wealthy man, his family lived in a fine house and his elder sons were being educated by governesses and boarding school masters. Seton was a happy child during these years, and his contentment is reflected in the anecdotes he later told about this period of his life.

There is only one incident in his first six years that involved punishment. This concerned some chickens owned by his cousin Harry Lee which had strayed into the yard of his Snowdon cousins next door. Seton and his cousin Willie Snowdon had armed themselves with the long pointed irons which were used by their elder brothers to set lines in the harbour for overnight fishing, and with these they attacked the chickens. Seton wrote later: "It was gloriously exhilarating; and when the squawking hens, losing breath and courage, tried to hide in the dark, lurksome corners, we closed in joyously, shouted, and speared them to their death." Afterwards, Seton received a "terrible spanking with [his] father's slipper," but he apparently felt that it had been deserved.[11] The next day Harry forgave him, then, a half hour later, Harry fell to his death from a scaffold in the shipyard.

The most curious aspect of this story is the unlikelihood that Seton actually killed any of the chickens himself. Harry Lee died in November 1863 when Seton was little more than three years old and hardly capable of wielding, let alone aiming, a heavy weapon. Just being in attendance at the scene of the crime seems to have caused his feelings of guilt, and to have somehow associated the events in his mind with his later displays of the "berserker streak" in the Elizabeth Street schoolyard.

The only sign of discontent in these first years comes in an anecdote about a neighbour lady who had doled out cherries to Seton and his friends according to their ages. Six cherries for a six-year-old, five for a five-year-old. When Seton's turn came, though he told her that he was four, she only gave him three cherries. In old age, he still remembered: "All my gratitude for the gift was swallowed up in indignation at the injustice of it. I have never forgotten or forgiven her for the highhanded dishonesty — she robbed me of one of my cherries."[12] Seton would never again in his entire life forget an injustice, real or imaginary, but he would cherish most those he believed his father had inflicted upon him.

The year 1866 brought an end to the Thompsons' good life in England, but though Lindsay had been a terrible comedown for the family as a whole, as far as Seton was concerned the country life style had compensated for the lack of riches. The Elms, of course, could not compare with Wellington Terrace in luxury, but measured by Lindsay's standards, Joseph Thompson still had status, and as long as other people considered him important, Seton was satisfied.

The anecdotes Seton told about this period mainly concerned his discoveries of wildlife and woodworking, and the hard lessons the family had learned about farming. In retrospect, he condemned his father for buying the farm and for his inability to make it pay, yet there are no specific examples from this period of clashes between the two. It appears, however, that Seton's anger surfaced in the final years in Lindsay — Seton's eighth to tenth years — for during this time he quarrelled more and more frequently with his brother Walter. When Joseph forbade this quarrelling, Seton began to turn his anger on his father.

The family's poverty had been hidden from the community in Lindsay, but the reality of it and Joseph's inability to rectify it were inescapable in Toronto. The Thompsons lived in a slum reserved for immigrants, and Seton and his younger brothers were compelled to get their education in an overcrowded school filled with "thieves" and "latent murderers." Seton's resentment at finding himself a slum kid was enormous. He condemned his father bitterly for denying him the privileges that his older brothers had enjoyed, and he accused him of laziness and of waiting for his sons to support him in his former style. The facts, however, do not bear out the charge of laziness. In Toronto Joseph took the only job for which he was suited — bookkeeper — and he worked stoically in an insurance office from eight to six each weekday, half-day on Saturday. He was certainly neither an aggressive nor a competitive man; instead, he was a plodder who did everything with meticulous care and thoroughness. Even Seton had to admit that his own "dogged persistence" had been inherited from his father.[13] By the world's standards, it was probably quite true that Joseph Logan Thompson was a failure, but it was the failure not of a lazy man but of one raised in a slower world that allowed for plodders.

In his own manhood, Seton would become a prodigious and efficient worker, routinely putting in sixteen-hour days at his desk and easel, and he was scornful of those who did less. His brother William, after spending a few months with him in the bush in 1886, was struck by his indefatigable energy and his ability to concentrate on his work despite distractions, but he was convinced that the underlying reason for Seton's success in the world was the fact that he had always known what he wanted. From a small child, he had driven himself to gain financial success and worldly acclaim; he had only contempt for those who settled for less.

Seton's behaviour changed radically after the family moved to Toronto. Propelled into a schoolyard battleground, he discovered after a short time that he actually enjoyed the fighting, even though he did not often win. As his battle tactics improved he became more sure of himself and more belligerent, and this significantly altered his relationship with his parents and brothers.

Combined with his new aggressiveness, there was a growing self-esteem. In Lindsay, though he had been acknowledged as the "brightest pupil,"[14] there was only a handful of children in the school. In Toronto he was declared the smartest boy in a school of three hundred students. And at twelve years, already in the highest form, his teachers' praise convinced him that he was very special. His ego grew accordingly.

At home his scholastic achievements and creative abilities were the pride of his parents, yet they did not reward him for his accomplishments with the extra attention or privileges he felt he deserved. To Seton it seemed unreasonable that his "taciturn and moody" brother Arthur,[15] who, though a year and a half older, was in a lower form at school, should receive equal attention from their parents. Seton was not the kind of child — or later the kind of man — who willingly gave up the limelight or the applause that goes with it.

Although he could do little to punish Arthur at this stage of their lives, he did so thirty years later in his semi-autobiographical novel, *Two Little Savages.* In this book Arthur becomes the insensitive brother "Rad" who hasn't "a human fiber or a drop of red blood in his make-up."[16] Rad finds himself "increasingly detested as he grows up," a fate Seton seems to have wished unsuccessfully upon Arthur.

The pride Seton felt in his own successes, both as a fighter and as a student, made him contemptuous of his brothers, and even more contemptuous of his father since he considered him such an obvious failure. Joseph Thompson must have been aware of his son's contempt and been annoyed by it, though he probably considered it just another facet of the boy's hair-trigger, awe-inspiring temper. And displays of temper were not allowed in the Thompson household, possibly because Joseph's memories of his own father's rages were too fresh, but also because emotional displays were not considered correct behaviour for persons in the Thompsons' social class.

Seton, however, was proud of his temper. He referred to it as his "berserker streak" or his "ancestral red rage,"[17] a tangible link to his primitive but noble Scottish forefathers. His first wife, who did not appreciate being the focus of Seton's tantrums, felt that his temper came from the "devil" in him.[18] And all the evidence points to him as the young Thompson whose temper provoked Old Ellen to announce, "You're yer ard granfither ower agyen. He'll niver be deed as lang as yeer alive."[19]

By Seton's own accounts, his rages were certainly spectacular. In describing the beating he gave to a curly-haired boy named Long who made the mistake of calling him "Squinty," he wrote: ". . . how I clutched my fingers into those golden curls and held him, as I banged his nose with my fist till he was spouting blood and yelling for mercy. He was completely cowed."[20]

When pursued by a gang who were chasing his brother Walter, Seton found himself backed into a corner of the schoolyard fence.

Then I surely did see red. What my friends called my "awful look" came over me. I whipped out my long-bladed knife and yelled: "Come on, I'll kill you all!"

Campbell too jerked out his knife and madly retorted "I'll get you first!" . . .

As the cold steel touched his flesh, he gave a yell; the rest sprang back. I rushed among them, mad and reckless, slashing right and left. . . .[21]

In his constant quarrels with Walter, the younger boy could bring their father running whenever he complained that Seton was in "one of his rages," that his "awful look" had come into his face.[22] Seton repaid Walter by beating him in secret, then threatening to kill him if he reported it to their father. Walter, who realized by his brother's face that he meant business, never told. Seton finished his punishment of Walter and his youngest brother Alan in *Two Little Savages,* in which the two become the character Alner, a selfish, money-grubbing little brute.

In keeping with the Victorian belief that spanking was the best method of teaching obedience and self-control, Joseph Thompson disciplined all his sons by spanking them — usually with a leather slipper — when he felt that they required correction. When he dealt with his eighth son's "red rages" in this way, there was no improvement in the boy's behaviour. In the first place, Seton believed that his rages were perfectly justified since they were provoked by other people picking on him. If his embattled Scottish ancestors had come down on their enemies in fury, so could he. In the second place, Seton considered the "beatings" he received from his father to be simply the base attacks of a cowardly failure venting his frustrations on someone weaker than himself. By his own estimation, he was a brave little martyr faced with an ogre. Julia recorded his telling of one beating by his father: "White with rage, he would hiss at me: 'I'll beat it out of you! I'll flog you within an inch of your life!' "[23] And on another occasion: "Times without number he beat me black and blue with the hard leather and sharp-cornered ironbound heel of his slipper for some trivial transgression often beyond my understanding, which was construed into disrespect, or disobedience, or loss of temper."[24]

Seton told his wife that after one of these beatings he fled to his room weeping over the wrongs he had suffered. There, lying on his bed, he imagined how sorry they would be when he died, presumably from the wounds inflicted by his father. As his sorrowing, conscience-stricken family crowded around his deathbed asking what they could do to atone for slighting and mistreating him, he told them to carve upon his gravestone one word only — Misunderstood.

The incident is certainly not unusual. Almost every imaginative child who feels that his family does not appreciate him has indulged in similar fantasies, but Seton's enthusiasm for martyrdom was almost entirely destructive. It ruined his relationships with his family, and in time became his standard reaction whenever he was thwarted in his drive for recognition and fortune.

Even in old age Seton was convinced that he had not deserved any more than two or three of the "floggings" he received from his father, and he deeply resented the injustice of all the others. While it is true without doubt that Seton was spanked with a leather slipper by his father, the ferocity and the frequency with which such punishments were administered is questionable. In 1903 William Thompson absolutely denied that Seton had received such terrible treatment and he included this denial in his 1923 memoirs. When Seton began his own memoirs in the mid-1930s, he sent the early chapters to three of his surviving brothers for comment, then, because of their objections, deleted much of the material he had written about his father. Julia Seton, in her own book in 1967, included the passages he had decided "against his better judgement" to leave out, but she was not risking, as Seton had been, being called a liar by any of the Thompson brothers, because they were all dead by then.

The Thompson family fortunes revived somewhat in 1872. With the remaining proceeds from the sale of the farm combined with the salaries of Joseph Thompson and his three eldest sons, they were able to leave Elizabeth Street. Enoch was now an accountant; William and Joseph Jr. were in business for themselves as builders; George was apprenticed to a printer. The new house was at 137 Mutual Street, only seven blocks east of the old house, but in a thoroughly respectable residential area.

The two youngest boys, now eight and ten, were deemed too small to walk the distance to their old school and were transferred to the Victoria Street School three blocks from home. Seton and Arthur, twelve and fourteen, were left in their old school for the remainder of the term. By now they were no longer accorded more than their fair share of abuse in the Elizabeth Street schoolyard, but the journey to and from Mutual Street provided fresh perils, since they had to travel against the schoolboy traffic headed for the Victoria Street School. Each morning they set off side by side as ordered by their parents, Seton eager for the battles to come, Arthur "sometimes full of fighting courage and sometimes inexplicably declining a perfectly proper fight."[25] At the end of the term, they transferred to the Victoria Street school. Arthur left school in 1872 to begin an apprenticeship in his older brothers' contracting firm.

The new school was certainly not refined, though it was well disciplined and the children came from solid middle-class homes. Seton was placed in the top form and by the following spring was head boy. He was caned only once in this school — for drawing an insulting cartoon of the headmaster William Spotton on the blackboard.

In the winter of 1873–74 Enoch Donkerly Thompson and his wife died of pneumonia within a few days of one another. Although he had been worth nearly £30,000 at one time, Enoch had lost much of his fortune by bad management and spent most of the remainder establishing his daughters' husbands in business, yet there was still a tidy sum left in his estate. A portion of this came to Joseph Thompson in the spring of 1874, allowing him to move his family once more, this time to fashionable South Pembroke Street. By this time Enoch had been married two years and William was about to marry, so the house was less crowded.

That same spring the Jarvis Street Collegiate Institute, following its annual custom, offered twelve two-year scholarships to the top students of the public schools of Toronto. As the Collegiate's fees were far beyond the reach of the average family, these scholarships represented the only opportunity most students would have for higher education. Not all of them were allowed to compete, however; only the six top-ranking students in each of the city's ten public schools were chosen as candidates and they were subjected to a three-day examination ordeal.

In 1874 Seton was allowed to sit for the Collegiate scholarship examinations, and of the twelve students finally selected, he was the youngest, being not yet fourteen. He had at last achieved public recognition of his brilliance, even though he remained convinced that he was unappreciated at home. He registered for classes full of "pride and exultation. 'It's mine, I won it; it's mine' was the thought and the thrill."[26] And he predicted that he would be a success at the Collegiate, win another scholarship and go on to Toronto University.

Everything about the Collegiate was right. The students were clean and wore "white collars." Foul language was never used. And nobody wanted to fight. Not that Seton made no attempts to start fights, but the boys he challenged were not interested in battling him. Seton thought the Collegiate's principal was perfect, too, but he only held this opinion for the first two months of school. In the second week of November the first snow of the winter fell, and the boys began a snowball fight in the schoolyard. According to his memoirs, Seton was the only one caught and sent to wait on the high wooden bench outside the principal's office. Archibald MacMurchy had risen from Mathematics master at the Toronto Grammar School to principal when the school became the Collegiate in 1872. The son of Highland Scottish immigrants and a stern Presbyterian, he seldom spoke when action would suffice. When he finally turned his attention to Seton, the boy was sufficiently terrified that, without further punishment, he would no doubt have behaved perfectly for the rest of his days at the Collegiate, but MacMurchy caned him nonetheless. Seton immediately placed MacMurchy in the same category with his father. "I despised him in my heart," he wrote, "and I did so to the end of my acquaintance."[27]

5

One Little Indian

All of the Thompsons had loved The Elms in spite of the drudgery and their inability to make the farm profitable, but Seton probably felt more like an exile in the city than any of the others because he was cut off from the wild things that had been the focus of his life. For the first few weeks the Elizabeth Street neighbourhood seemed completely sterile; then he discovered that even in a slum there is a certain amount of wildlife — rodents and birds — to be found. He still had difficulty identifying the creatures that he saw, but the displays in Passmore's Taxidermy Shop on Yonge Street near Shuter provided him with the names of some of the birds, and in 1873 a naturalist shop opened a block away from Passmore's, offering Seton another source of free information. On Saturday afternoons he made repeated close inspections of the stuffed bear outside a nearby furrier's shop, and once made a pilgrimage to the home of one of his older brothers' friends to see a stuffed, mounted woodpecker. The highlight of these forays came the day a friend gave him a mounted wood duck that he no longer wanted; Seton carried it home reverently, and "learned to know its every tint and its every feather."[1]

But not all the creatures he found in the city were stuffed and mounted. He and his younger brothers made wooden birdhouses and attached them to the house gable where they attracted white-breasted swallows, bluebirds, purple martins, house sparrows and English sparrows. After they nested Seton spent hours watching them and noting their habits. When William and Joseph Jr. rescued a fox that was being harried by dogs, Seton rushed off after school to take it food, planning to make a pet of it; to his sorrow, it was claimed almost immediately by its owners.

He began assembling a zoo by buying a pair of rabbits. He constructed hutches for them and fed them on dandelions and other greens from neighbouring yards, keeping them alive through the winter on kitchen scraps and on hay which he carried in bundles from a farm in Rosedale two miles away. Two years later he was able to sell some of the progeny of the original pair to raise part of the cost of a "wonderful" new book, Ross's *Birds of Canada,* which he subsequently found to be full of errors.

For additional exhibits in his zoo, Seton decided to capture some kittens that had "gone wild." But knowledge of the cats on the farm had not prepared him for these city cats: they refused to cower and submit peacefully when caught and he was forced to release them. Thwarted, he decided to paint stripes on the family's orange tomcat so that he could exhibit it as a wildcat, but the tom refused to co-operate and thereafter really did become wild, staying just close enough to home that Seton could observe all its exploits, but never again entering the house. Although the zoo did not materialize, these encounters were not wasted. His observations of rabbit and feline behaviour became the basis for "The True Story of a Little Grey Rabbit" and "The Slum Cat."

In his first summer in the city, Seton discovered Queen's Park just a half dozen blocks northwest of his home. It was still untouched woodland at this time, and the boy returned again and again to explore it. The following spring, he discovered the Toronto Marsh. From this vantage point he could see Toronto Island but had no way of getting there. Finally there came a summer day in 1871 when he was able to afford the ten-cent fare on the *Bouquet,* the little steam ferry that travelled back and forth to the island. This day marked the real beginning of his life as a naturalist because he was at last able to investigate first-hand the myriad variety of birds that inhabited the area, and to meet men whose way of life had given them intimate knowledge of those birds.

On their first trips to the island, Seton and his brothers swam in Gibraltar Bay or in the island's small lagoon where the water was

warmer than in Lake Ontario itself. This was the first opportunity
that the younger Thompson boys had found for swimming since it
was not allowed elsewhere on the city's waterfront. Then, while
his brothers fished for perch or catfish, Seton watched the bird life.
The reed beds along the northern edge of the island and in the
marsh at the mouth of the Don River were inhabited by marsh
birds he had never before seen or even heard of, and the eaves of the
boathouses and summer shacks along the shore housed thousands
of songbirds. At the western end of the island he found hundreds of
pairs of sand swallows nesting in holes in the clay bluff.

In the early winter of 1872–73 Seton became acquainted with
Bill Loane, a "grand old sportsman" who made his living as a
gunner on the marshes, providing game birds for restaurants and
institutions.[2] Seton met him after one of his friends at the Victoria
Street School suggested an expedition to watch the trap-shooting
on the Don Flats. The following Saturday, Seton watched while a
group of men took turns shooting birds as they were released
from "traps," small cages which collapsed when a string was
pulled. The birds, mostly snowbirds with a few redpolls and
shorelarks which had been accidentally netted, flew up to escape
as soon as the cage fell away around them. They were immediately felled by gunshots. At least fifty birds died or were badly
mutilated in this way while Seton watched "in a daze of strange
feelings, horror and disgust now strongest."[3] After the killing was
over, the dead birds were gathered up to be taken to the hospital
where they would be made into soup. This gesture, explained Bill
Loane, who had provided the birds for the trap shoot, was
intended to keep the authorities happy. There was always the
danger, he said, that some do-gooder might begin agitating to
stop the slaughter.

For fifteen cents Seton bought three of the birds still awaiting
execution: two redpolls and one shorelark. At home he installed
them in his bedroom in a cage made of mason's laths. The redpolls soon adjusted to this environment and accepted a preparation of pea meal, olive oil and egg yolk, sometimes taking the
food from his fingers. After a while he was able to turn the
redpolls loose in his bedroom, and they learned to sit on his
shoulder while he fed them.

Meanwhile, the shorelark had been unable to adjust to captivity
and ran back and forth on the cage floor, crying unhappily. As

spring came, the lark's behaviour became even more frenzied, and Seton, having tamed the redpolls, decided to give the lark the freedom of his bedroom as well. The bird emerged timidly from the cage when the door was opened, then, realizing that it was free, rose straight up into the air, smashed into the ceiling and fell dead at the boy's feet. Once more Seton had learned the lesson that wild birds are not intended for cages. In sadness, he opened the bedroom window and shooed the redpolls out into the spring air. This was his last attempt to domesticate a bird or animal of any kind; from this time on he observed them carefully, sometimes by keeping them in captivity, but never by making pets of them.

Seton visited Bill Loane and the other marsh gunners many times over the next few years, though he never again watched a trap shoot. Loane often shot rare birds in the marshland — this was referred to as "taking" or "collecting" — and sold them to collectors; in one day alone he shot seven eagles. By tagging along on the gunner's expeditions, Seton was able to absorb the bird lore the man had acquired in his years on the marsh, and the boy became more and more determined that he would devote his life to ornithology, though he would not give up his interest in other wildlife.

The second important contact he made in these years was Dr. William Brodie. Brodie's son, William Jr., was two years younger than Seton; the two boys had met through the similarity of their interests after the Thompsons moved to Mutual Street. Brodie was the eldest child and only son of the doctor, and it was the father's intention that the boy would become a professional naturalist. Dr. Brodie himself was a naturalist by avocation only; he supported his family by dentistry. From boyhood, however, he had been studying the birds and animals of Ontario and collecting the specimens that would become the basis of a collection eventually housed in the Ontario Provincial Museum. As the result of his research, he also became one of the first to recognize the importance of parasites in protecting plant life from insect pests.

When Seton met him, Brodie was forty-two and already respected as the fount of natural history wisdom by the young people who came to him for advice. He was invariably patient with them and enthusiastic about their projects. Even in his

seventies he continued to amaze all his protégés with his youthful-
ness and the originality of his ideas.

Shortly after first meeting him, Seton captured a rat and took it
as live food for the four rattlesnakes the doctor kept in a basement
cage. When introduced into the cage, the rat attacked the rattlers;
when the battle ended, all five combatants were dead. Writing of
this event in his memoirs, Seton describes Dr. Brodie as a
"grizzly old naturalist" with "bony hands" and eyes that
"gleamed with animal joy," and implies that the doctor was
somewhat demented.[4] This does not square with the facts of
Brodie's life, however, for he was sane enough to be elected
president of the Toronto Naturalists Society when it was formed
in 1879; he became the first president of the Liberal Party's
Toronto Reform Association, and in 1899 was appointed to the
post of biologist for the Ontario Provincial Museum.

Seton went to Brodie for advice on many occasions during
the next fifteen years, especially when he needed help in identifying specimens. He also allowed Brodie to promote him for
the vice-presidency of the Toronto Naturalists Society in 1882,
and to attempt to get him an appointment as naturalist to a
government expedition to Hudson Bay. Seton, however, found
it very difficult to give credit to those who helped his career
along — perhaps in fear that this would diminish admiration for
his own accomplishments — and in his memoirs he often
resorts to unwarranted ridicule of his former instructors and
friends.

During these early years in Toronto, Seton also found new
friends of his own age. After he was admitted to the Collegiate,
he met boys who shared his interests, not only in wildlife but also
in reading matter and in games. They were all fourteen- and
fifteen-year-olds, but less adult than modern boys of that age,
mostly because their parents and teachers still considered them
children and treated them as such. Unlike the toughs at the Elizabeth Street School, most of these boys still dressed in knee pants;
they had not yet discovered sex, and they only fought one another
for sport. Their pastimes were inspired by the books they read:
*Swiss Family Robinson, Animated Nature, Robin Hood, Robinson
Crusoe* and Mayne Reid's *Scalp Hunters* and *Boy Hunters*. With the
woods only a half dozen blocks away, it was easy for them to
make-believe the adventures they found in these stories.

When Seton entered this group, he had just discovered the world of the Indian. He had never met an Indian, nor had he even seen one, but he had just read James Fenimore Cooper's *The Last of the Mohicans* and had recognized the adventure potential of the Indian as a make-believe character for himself. It would be many more years before he would recommend the life of the ideal Indian as the model for white men's lives, but at fourteen he celebrated the beginning of his interest in the Indian's character by concocting a play for his friends to perform in a neighbour's loft. The play followed the exploits of a villainous Indian — played by Seton — who, contrary to tradition, ended up victorious.

After the play, Seton attempted to organize an Indian tribe among his friends, but they favoured becoming a Robin Hood band. Seton then manoeuvred himself into the role of Robin Hood. Trouble arose almost immediately when Little John claimed that he, and not Robin, should blow the horn used to summon the Merry Men. When the band was asked to vote on it, Robin lost. A short time later, the Merry Men were discovered trying to excavate a "secret cave" under the Thompson house and were dispersed by Seton's angry father.

With Seton as its leader, the band could not have survived much longer in any case since he was constantly battling the other members of the group for control. Of all the boys in the group he was probably the most imaginative and most capable of leading them, but they were not willing to accept him as their controlling genius, preferring instead government by consensus. At fourteen, Seton knew nothing about co-operation, and whenever he could not be leader, he opted for solitude, or at least for situations where he could work independently. Most of the excavation under the Thompson house had been done by Seton alone, and most of his expeditions into the woods or the marsh were solitary adventures. He had little to do with his brothers by this time, and though he sometimes took his younger brothers on Saturday afternoon expeditions into the Don Valley, "they soon wearied of the far tramp, with no reward but 'trees and things.' "[5]

It was while on one of these "far tramps" up the Don Valley in the summer of 1874 that Seton found his private paradise. Although the city of Toronto had already straddled the Don Valley in its lower reaches, farther north the city's rim coincided with the Necropolis and St. James Cemetery. Beyond these was a wilderness of ravines and forest richly inhabited by wildlife. Each Saturday, Seton's explorations led him deeper and deeper into these woods until one day he found himself in a small, heavily wooded ravine which had been carved by one of the Don's tributary streams. Here, against the hillside, he built a crude cabin, using discarded cedar fenceposts for the walls, and brushwood, clay and grass laid over poles for the roof — as Yan does in *Two Little Savages*.

Then, in a curious foreshadowing of his life on the prairie ten years later, having built a shelter for himself that utilized the basic pioneer techniques, he began playing Indian there instead. He became the lone member of a mighty Indian band, silently skulking through the forest tracking "game." He stripped off his clothes so that the sun would turn his skin bronze, made himself moccasins and put feathers in his hair. He was supremely happy in his secret paradise, however much he still longed to be the leader of a fierce tribe of braves.

While the snow lay on the ground in the winter of 1874–75, the cabin on the Don held little allure, but when spring came again, Seton returned every Saturday afternoon to continue his fantasy. Then one Saturday, "after one of the worst beatings given by [his] father," he fled to the cabin to find that three tramps had taken possession of it. Years later Seton wrote: "I tottered off a couple of hundred yards; then prone on a bank I fell, and sobbed hysterically: 'Oh, God! Oh, God!' My spirit was wholly broken now."[6] When the tramps moved on, they left the place wrecked, and Seton, his paradise contaminated, abandoned it forever.

He plunged into his studies, but while it had required little effort on his part to be the brightest student at the Elizabeth Street School or the head boy at Victoria Street, at the Collegiate there was keen competition for the top places. By term's end in July 1875, he had made himself ill, probably less from his hours of study than from his fear of failure. With their usual pragmatic approach to the health of their sons, his parents decided that a month in the country would restore him. They made arrangements for Seton to visit the Blackwell family who had bought The Elms.

There were six Blackwell children, ranging in age from eighteen-year-old George to a boy of nine, but Mrs. Blackwell had plenty of motherliness left over for the thin fifteen-year-old who arrived on her doorstep that summer. Seton's eyes, however, were all for her husband, William, a big, rugged man who, though largely uneducated, was a shrewd trader in livestock and a very successful farmer. He had made The Elms profitable where Joseph Thompson could not. Blackwell in his turn was very impressed with Seton's learning, often posing mathematical questions just for the pleasure of hearing the boy's swift responses. On one occasion he took Seton to a school board meeting to have his help on the estimates for a new school building. Seton soon worshipped Blackwell, always arranging to do chores that would keep him near his idol, and secretly, "at first with shame and self-rebuke, but later quite frankly," wishing that William Blackwell had been his father.[7]

The Blackwell children were easygoing and generous, quite willing to accept Seton into their lives on his own terms. Consequently, it was not long before he revived his dream of a make-believe Indian tribe. This time his tribe was composed of the Blackwell boy nearest his own age and a handful of boys from the surrounding farms, less sophisticated than Seton's city friends and less knowledgeable about democracy. It is the romanticized adventures of this new tribe that make up the bulk of *Two Little Savages*.

When he returned to his family in August, he found himself more out of step than before, and he became convinced once again that he was a foundling. At this time there were definite physical dissimilarities between him and his brothers, who were all square, stocky young men, vigorously healthy. He alone was wiry and undernourished-looking — he weighed less than one hundred pounds — and rather short for his fifteen years.

Now he worked even harder at his studies, ignoring the marsh and the Don Valley, remaining aloof from his friends of the previous year. He was determined to win a scholarship to the university so that he could leave the family home, and he began preparing for the five days of Christmas exams with a single-mindedness that bordered on fanaticism. After writing the third day's exams, he went to his bedroom to study for the next day and found himself "staring at the wall, everything black and whirling about [him]."

"I can't study. I can't study!" he sobbed in despair and collapsed.[8]

One of his brothers, unimpressed with this latest drama, suggested that a beating might cure him, but when his mother found
he had a fever, she called the doctor. It was now decided that his
lungs were "affected" — a euphemism for tubercular — and that
he must be sent to the country immediately. For Seton, except for
his brother's lack of sympathy, this was a replay of his deathbed
fantasy of earlier years, and in spite of the knowledge that he
could not return to school, he had a definite sense of satisfaction.

The next morning his mother walked him to the train station,
and he returned to Lindsay. A neighbour gave him a ride to the
Blackwell's gate. With a fine touch of drama, he left his bundle at
the gate and "crawled up the lane to the door," telling the
Blackwells that he had been too weak to carry it.[9] Once more
Mrs. Blackwell took him in and mothered him, but, according to
Seton's memoirs, after a week she sent for Alice Thompson with
the message: "You better come; he is not long for this world."[10]

When Alice arrived, the two women went down on their knees
at Seton's bedside and prayed, his mother begging for forgiveness
for neglecting her son and beseeching God to restore him to
health. When she arose, crying but happy, she announced that
God had heard and had told her to take her son home at once. The
following day they rode the train back to Toronto and hired a cab
for the trip from the station to the house. Seton was now petted
and pampered and treated to the best of food. Every day Alice
knelt at his bedside to pray.

Seton's illness had effectively ended his schooling. He knew
that once he was well again he must launch a career of some
kind, but jobs were scarce. The depression that had hit the
United States in 1873 had come to Canada in 1875, and already
the Thompson family could feel the effects. There was little
work in the construction industry for William, Joseph Jr. and
Arthur; Enoch's real estate and brokerage business had come to
a standstill; Charlie had returned from Glasgow and was unem-
ployed.

Seton lay in bed for a month; then one day in March, as he
stood at his bedroom window, one of the last great flights of
pigeons flew over Toronto on their way north. For most of the
day, the sky was dark with them. As Seton watched, he longed
for a gun of his own so that he could "take" specimens and begin
a collection of stuffed birds like the one he had seen in Foley's

store nine years earlier. Convinced that his father had denied him a gun in the past in order to discourage his interest in natural history, he did not approach him directly now for permission to own one. Instead, he convinced his mother that he should be allowed to have one when he got well; he left her to deal with his father. Joseph relented, but only on condition that Seton buy his own gun as his brother Arthur had done.

By the time Seton was on his feet again, puberty had at last set in and by early summer, instead of short and thin, he was tall and even thinner. By the fall of the year, he would be six feet and built like a lath. In an effort to develop some muscles on his gangling frame, he began making regular trips with some of his friends to work out at the YMCA's new gym. There was no instructor; the boys simply experimented with the available apparatus.

One evening Seton tried to shinny up the gym's thirty-foot upright pole, but halfway up realized he could not go all the way. He gave one last try that took him a little higher; at the same moment he felt "a bursting hurtful sensation" in his groin.[11] The family doctor explained that it was a hernia and prescribed a truss. Seton was not incapacitated in any way by the hernia or the truss, but he regarded this thing hiding under his clothes as a "loathsome reptile" clinging onto his flesh.[12]

In June 1876 Seton returned to the Blackwell's farm and began collecting specimens. While at the Blackwells he was invited to visit the farm of one of his father's old farmhands, north of Sturgeon Lake. He was assured that he would find plenty of game on which to use his new gun, but at the farm he contracted malaria and spent most of the month of August in bed. When his mother learned of his latest calamity, she came to fetch him once more, and he was escorted home with "the beauty of new hope and mother love . . . in [his] soul."[13]

6

Blood Will Tell

In 1877 Joseph Logan Thompson's older sister Ann Lee came to visit the Thompson family in Toronto, and in the course of her stay she brought up a subject which would fire her imaginative nephew with a new project. It was Ann Lee's conviction that her brother Joseph was the true Lord Seton, Earl of Winton, and she was insistent that he lay claim to the titles, reminding him that it had been their Grandmother Logan's dying wish — nearly forty years earlier — that he claim them and restore the family to its rightful place in the peerage.

Just as Joseph Thompson had made no move to claim the titles after his grandmother's death, he did not do so after his sister's exhortations. This was not because he was indifferent to exalted status; like most middle-class Victorian gentlemen, especially those in North America, he was not immune to the mania for finding family ties to the ancient nobility of Europe. But Joseph already knew a great deal about his family tree.

On his father's side he could trace his lineage back to a great-great-great-grandfather named Alan, or Evan, Cameron, reputed to be a foster brother and cousin to Lochiel, Chief of Clan Cameron. This was probably not the famous Sir Ewen Cameron of Lochiel (1629–1719), but his grandson Donald Cameron (1695–1748), known as Gentle Lochiel, who became head of the clan in 1719 and who was therefore a contemporary of Alan Cameron. In 1745, after the battle of Culloden, Alan Cameron fled for safety to the Tyne River valley and settled in the town of South Shields. There, in order to hide his identity from the English, he assumed the most common name in the district: Thompson. And by that name his descendents had lived in the town and district ever since, prospering as shipping men and merchants.

Alan Cameron was of fine Highland heritage, brave and well educated, but he brought no titles with him to hand down to the family. However, Joseph Logan Thompson's mother could claim the Setons as ancestors, and it was the Seton titles that Ann Lee wished her brother to inherit.

While all the young Thompsons knew they were connected to the Seton family, this was probably the first time it had been suggested that there were titles involved, or that those titles might be within reach. In fact, Seton understood his aunt to imply that his father could have them simply by making representations to the proper courts. That he had let forty years go by without doing anything to obtain his "rightful" inheritance seemed only to prove to Seton that the man was a complete sloth.

When Ann Lee visited the Thompsons, four of the sons were out of town. William and Joseph Jr., unable to find work in Toronto, had gone as carpenters to St. John, New Brunswick, to help rebuild the city, recently devastated by fire. Arthur was in Manitoba and Harry was on his way to New Zealand. Two of the remaining six were minors and could not take action without parental permission. Of the other four, Enoch, Charles and George reacted to her news by taking Seton as a middle name. The eighth Thompson resolved to begin calling himself Ernest Evan Thompson Seton, vowing to change his surname legally as soon as he was of age.

Although Seton wrote in his memoirs that his father had "cordially approved" of this name change,[1] in the "life forecast" which he prepared in 1881 he noted that he expected to have "trouble" with his family when he changed his name officially. Joseph could not have approved of the change because he must have known he could not go into court over the titles. He must have been aware, for example, that even if he was descended from the first Earl of Winton through his mother and grandmother, he could not inherit the earl's title, for while many

The Family Tree of the Setons and Thompsons
with Specific Reference to the Claims to Family Honours, Lands and Titles

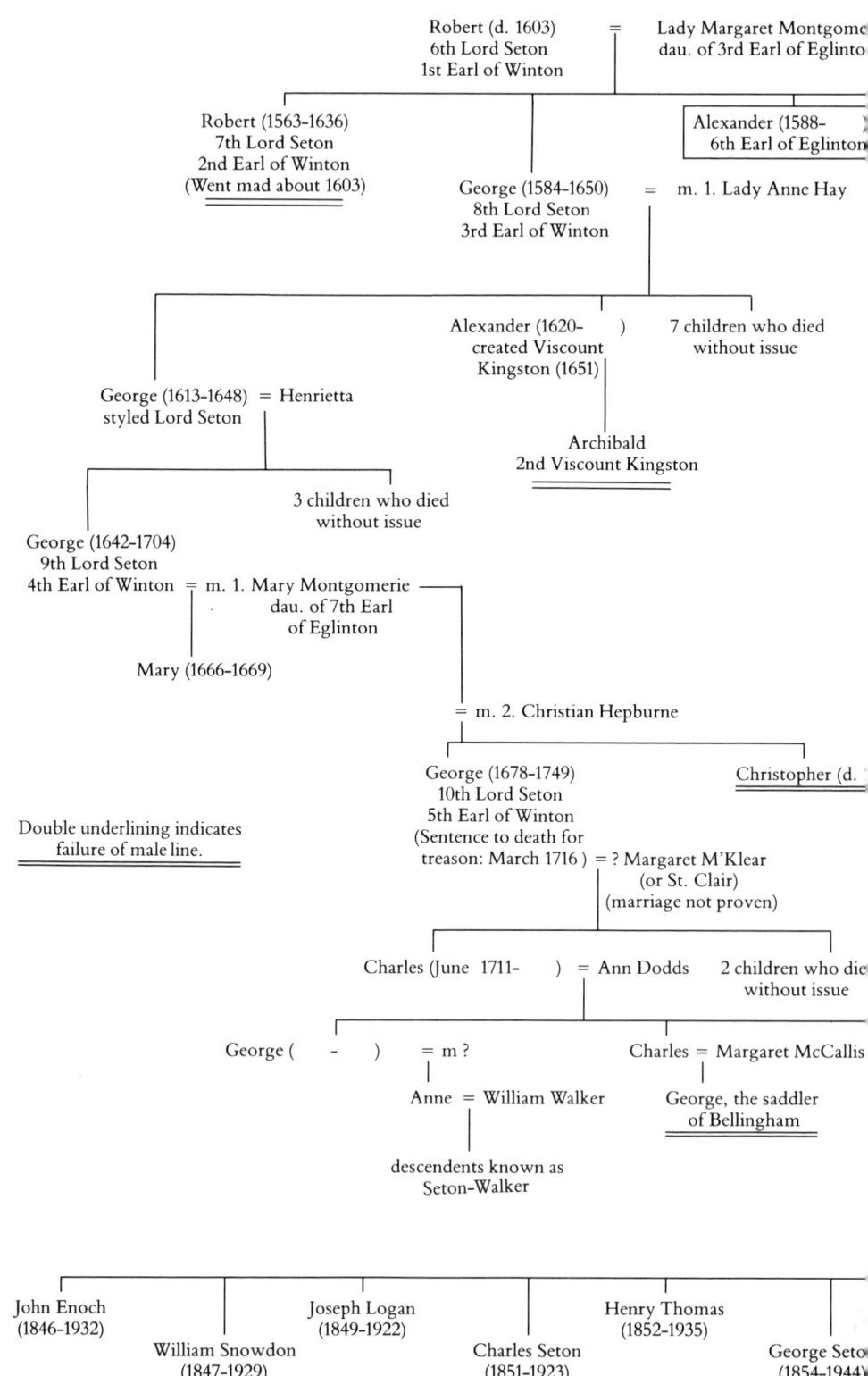

Robert (d. 1603) = Lady Margaret Montgome
6th Lord Seton   dau. of 3rd Earl of Eglinto
1st Earl of Winton

Robert (1563–1636)
7th Lord Seton
2nd Earl of Winton
(Went mad about 1603)

Alexander (1588–
6th Earl of Eglinton

George (1584–1650) = m. 1. Lady Anne Hay
8th Lord Seton
3rd Earl of Winton

Alexander (1620–   )   7 children who died
created Viscount   without issue
Kingston (1651)

George (1613–1648) = Henrietta
styled Lord Seton

Archibald
2nd Viscount Kingston

3 children who died
without issue

George (1642–1704)
9th Lord Seton
4th Earl of Winton = m. 1. Mary Montgomerie
dau. of 7th Earl
of Eglinton

Mary (1666–1669)

= m. 2. Christian Hepburne

George (1678–1749)   Christopher (d.
10th Lord Seton
5th Earl of Winton
Double underlining indicates   (Sentence to death for
failure of male line.   treason: March 1716) = ? Margaret M'Klear
(or St. Clair)
(marriage not proven)

Charles (June 1711–   ) = Ann Dodds   2 children who die
without issue

George (–   )   = m ?   Charles = Margaret McCallis

Anne = William Walker   George, the saddler
of Bellingham

descendents known as
Seton-Walker

John Enoch   Joseph Logan   Henry Thomas
(1846–1932)   (1849–1922)   (1852–1935)

William Snowdon   Charles Seton   George Seto
(1847–1929)   (1851–1923)   (1854–1944)

John (succession failed with grandson) | 2 children who died without issue

= m. 2. Elizabeth Maxwell

John (1639-1686) created baronet (1664) known as Sir John Seton of Garleton = m. ?

Robert (1641-1671) created baronet (Jan. 1671) known as Sir Robert Seton of Wyndygoul (died without issue)

10 children who died without issue

George (1665-1720) 2nd Seton baronet of Garleton = Barbara Wauchope

John (1668-1715) = Francis Neale

8 children who died without issue

George (1685-1769) 3rd Seton baronet of Garleton (Sentenced to death for treason, 1716. After death of 5th Earl in 1749, was styled Earl of Winton)

Ralph (1702-1782) heir to the 3rd baronet (known as Sir Ralph Seton)

John (1707-1775) = Mary Newton

John (1755-1796) recognized as head of House of Seton after death of Sir Ralph Seton, 1782 = Mary Hughes

Mary Catherine (1796-1870 = John Broadbent

3 children who died without issue

James Seton-Broadbent = Sophia Francis Lee (1828-1907)

Thomas George Seton-Broadbent (1855-) considered head of House of Seton

Ann (1763-1840) = Joseph Logan

Mary Ann Logan = Enoch Donkerly Thompson

Jane (married a Mr. Robertson)

Ann (married Harry Lee)

Evan (died without issue in 1863)

Mary (married a Mr. Hanzell)

Joseph Logan Thompson = Alice Snowdon (1820-1902) (1823-1897)

Mary Ann Snowdon (1856-1862)

Arthur Septimus (1859-1944)

Ernest Evan (1860-1946)

Walter (1862-1941)

Alan Cameron (1864-)

Scottish titles can be passed on through a daughter when the male line dies out, the charter for the earldom of Winton specifically bars female descent.

In 1600 Robert, sixth Lord Seton, was created first Earl of Winton by King James VI of Scotland (who would in 1603 become James I of England) in recognition of the hospitality and aid that Seton had given to James's mother, Mary Stuart. The charter provided for the new earl's lands and titles to descend to his heirs-male. Accordingly, when the first earl died three years later, his son Robert assumed both of his father's titles to become seventh Lord Seton, and second Earl of Winton. But that same year, Robert, who had always been somewhat unstable, went mad; he was forced to resign his titles and lands to his next youngest brother, George, who became eighth Lord Seton, third Earl of Winton. Along with his new titles, George was given a new charter for the earldom of Winton which specifically defined the line of inheritance. The title thereafter was to go to "the heirs-male to be lawfully begotten of his body, whom failing, to his brothers in succession and the lawful heirs-male of their bodies, whom failing, to his nearest and lawful heirs-male."[2] This meant that when George's own direct male line died out, his titles would revert to his next youngest brother, Alexander, or to Alexander's male descendent. In the meantime, Alexander had been made heir to his cousin Hugh of Eglinton and had thereby become the sixth Earl of Eglinton.

George, eighth Lord Seton and third Earl of Winton (1584–1650), married twice; his first family consisted of five boys and four girls, but only two of the boys and one girl survived infancy. Of the boys, the eldest, again named George (1613–1648), was designated heir; the second, Alexander, was created Viscount Kingston in 1651. Of the third Earl of Winton's second family of twelve, only two boys survived to manhood: John was created a baronet in 1664 and was known thereafter as Sir John Seton of Garleton, the name of one of his father's estates. His brother Robert became Sir Robert of Wyndygoul — another estate — in 1671, but he died the same year without issue. The third earl, therefore, had three possible ways of continuing his male line and preventing loss of the titles to the issue of his younger brother Alexander: the title could descend through his sons George, Alexander or John.

The odds narrowed in the next generation. Son George (1613–
1648) died before his father, but left three sons: another George
(1642–1704), who would become ninth Lord Seton and fourth
Earl of Winton, Alexander and Christopher, but the latter two
died without issue. Meanwhile, Viscount Kingston's heir also
died without issue. Sir John Seton of Garleton, however, did have
an heir who became Sir George Seton of Garleton. This left only
two possible direct heirs to the third earl: two grandsons named
George.

The ninth Lord Seton and fourth Earl of Winton married a
distant cousin, Mary Montgomerie, daughter of the seventh
Earl of Eglinton. They had one daughter who died at three
years of age. In 1667 the Countess of Winton left her lord,
complaining of his open infidelity, but, while suing him for
divorce, she died. Her kinsmen, however, did not forget the
earl's offences to her. Shortly after this, a lady named Christian
Hepburne joined the earl's household and in 1678 became the
mother of a son whom she named George. The earl acknowledged the boy as his progeny, but he did not marry the child's
mother until 1679. A year later she gave birth to a second son,
Christopher.

When the fourth earl died in 1704, he had one legitimate son
and one illegitimate son, but the legitimate one died less than a
year after his father's death. George, the illegitimate son, now heir
to the titles, was on the Continent where he had been working as
a journeyman blacksmith for four years. It took him three more
years to come home to claim his estates, and another three before
the courts declared him legitimate and recognized his right to be
tenth Lord Seton, fifth Earl of Winton.

He did not impress the gentry with his blacksmith manners.
In 1715 the diarist Lady Cowper complained that "his natural
Character is that of a stubborn, illiterate, ill-bred Brute. He has
eight 'wives.'" Another commented that he was "mighty subject to a particular caprice, natural to his family," presumably a
reference to his numerous lady friends.[3] According to *The Scots
Peerage,* "he seems to have been looked upon by his contemporaries as eccentric, and mentally somewhat deficient, but spirited, courageous and determined. He was a zealous Protestant,
but being, nevertheless, suspected of Jacobite views, he was
summoned to Edinburgh in September 1715, and failing to

appear was declared a rebel, and shortly afterwards sentenced in absence to escheat, a fine of £500, and imprisonment for a year."[4]

The fifth earl showed his resentment of this treatment by arming his servants and a party of "domestic gentlemen" and heading south to join the rebel Scots. He was taken prisoner at the Battle of Preston on 14 November 1715, confined in the Tower of London, arraigned for high treason and sentenced to death. While awaiting execution, he escaped (probably with the connivance of the government), but he had forfeited all his lands and titles. He went first to France and later to Rome, where he died on 19 December 1749.

Meanwhile, the only other direct descendent of the third earl, Sir George Seton of Garleton (second baronet) had produced a son — alas, another George — who became the third baronet. This George was *also* taken prisoner in 1715; he also forfeited all his lands and titles, escaped from the tower and took refuge in France. After the death of the fifth Earl of Winton in 1749, this Sir George Seton of Garleton (third baronet) "was styled as the Earl of Winton," an expression simply meaning that he was considered to be the heir to the title since he was the next in line for it, but that he had not or could not legally assume it, in this case because the fifth earl had forfeited it.

So now there was only one heir to all three titles, Earl of Winton, Lord Seton and Baronet of Seton, but all three had been forfeited. When the third baronet, the heir to all these titles, died unmarried in Paris in 1769, his heir was his cousin Ralph, who was thereafter accepted as the head of the House of Seton. After Ralph's death in 1782, this designation was accorded to his nephew John Seton. From this point onward the lineage descended through females, but all members of the family in the direct line added Seton to their family names. In Joseph Logan Thompson's day, the head of the House of Seton was John's grandson, James Seton-Broadbent, a man who had no claim to the title of Earl of Winton, but could, perhaps, have successfully sued for the title of Lord Seton.

After a general amnesty for the rebellious Scots was declared in 1823, one George Seton, a saddler from the town of Bellingham, Northumberland, appeared before the courts to petition for the titles of Winton and Seton. This George claimed to be

the great-grandson of the blacksmith earl (the fifth) through that
earl's marriage to a lady named Margaret M'Klear, or St. Clair,
the daughter of an Edinburgh physician, about the year 1710.
According to the saddler, this union had been blessed with three
children: two girls who died in infancy, and a boy named Charles.
When the fifth earl had fled to the Continent, he left his family
behind. Margaret, fearing for the safety of her children, did not
divulge the name of their father. Her son, Charles, grew to manhood and fathered two boys — George and Charles — and a girl,
Ann. This George was the father of one child only — a girl.
Charles had a son, George, who became the saddler of Bellingham. The daughter, Ann, married a man named Joseph Logan;
they had a daughter, Mary Ann Logan, who married Enoch
Donkerly Thompson and became the mother of Joseph Logan
Thompson.

Unfortunately for the saddler, he could not produce the marriage certificate of his great-grandparents, but because he bore an
almost uncanny resemblance to a well-known portrait painted by
Sir Antonio More of George, the fifth Lord Seton, it was the
decision of the court on 1 May 1824 that he should be granted the
title of Earl of Winton. At this point there came a protest from a
member of another family line. The thirteenth Earl of Eglinton,
the direct male heir of the third Earl of Winton's brother
Alexander, claimed the Winton title and petitioned the courts to
overturn the award on the grounds that no true marriage had
taken place between the fifth earl and Margaret M'Klear, and that
the lady had indeed been only the earl's mistress. Circumstantial
evidence was on Eglinton's side because of the fifth earl's numerous lady friends and because his own legitimacy had been questionable. Therefore, on 22 December 1840, the courts disallowed
their earlier award to the saddler and declared the thirteenth Earl
of Eglinton to be the lawful male heir to the fourth Earl of Winton
(the fifth earl having been attainted). And in 1859 the Earl of
Eglinton was officially installed as the Earl of Winton. He had not
sued for the Seton title, probably because it was a secondary title
with no lands or privileges attached to it.

Joseph Logan Thompson must have been aware of these facts
since the final events had taken place in his lifetime, and he had
wisely refused to be prodded into action by either his grandmother or his sister. A man who had seen his tangible assets

dwindle into nothing as the years went by, he still clung with tenacity to his dignity and social station, and had no desire to scramble through the courts after a title which he had not the faintest hope of acquiring. The charter specifically denied inheritance to any except heirs-male, and even if it had not, he could not have proved the fifth earl's marriage any more than the saddler had been able to prove it. The only thing he could accomplish by a court appeal was another airing of the family skeleton, for if the saddler was not considered a legitimate descendent, neither was Joseph Logan Thompson. Therefore, if he had thought it necessary to do anything at all about his inheritance of names and titles, he would have changed his surname to Cameron since Thompson was only an assumed, not a legal name. But Joseph was content to let sleeping dogs lie.

Seton, on the other hand, blamed his father's failure to act on his "constitutional dislike of effort." However, he could do nothing to make Joseph claim the title, so he had to abandon all hope of becoming the son of an earl. In any case, he could never have inherited that title from his father unless something happened to his seven older brothers, and since they were a remarkably healthy lot, there was little possibility of advancement in that direction. So Seton concentrated his efforts on the family's right to the Seton surname, which he would insist to the end of his life was the "real" family name. It was another twenty years before he had any evidence to corroborate his claim, and then it came in the form of a recommendation from Archbishop Robert Seton of New Jersey, the Seton family historian, who announced that "all the Setons were sportsmen and had literary tastes and gifts. . . . Blood will tell. You are a true scion of the line and impelled by its best traditions and interests."[5]

On 1 February 1883, exactly as he had vowed at the time of his aunt's visit, Seton notified the world via the *Winnipeg Tribune:* "The undersigned hitherto known as Ernest Evan Thompson of Toronto, art student, gives public notice that he has assumed their ancient family surname of Seton."

From that time on, he signed all documents with his new name: E. E. Thompson Seton. This continued until 1887, when Alice Thompson prevailed upon him to change it back again. In his account of this event, he wrote:

. . . she put her arms around my neck and kissed me; then invited me to kneel with her and pray for heavenly guidance. She prayed as few but my mother could pray; then rose and said: "Oh, my boy, I want you to give up the name of 'Seton,' and be known as 'Thompson' as long as I am alive."

Thus I was attacked in the weak spot of my wall.[6]

Seton was convinced that his father had pressured her into making this appeal; it is far more likely, however, that Alice Thompson was experiencing the same embarrassment that her husband and her other sons were feeling. Seton, of course, could never refuse his mother and therefore agreed that he would revert to the surname Thompson, but use the nom de plume Seton-Thompson on his published work until after her death. So from 1887 to 1897 he signed his letters "Ernest E. Thompson" but signed all of his artwork with the name "Ernest Seton-Thompson."

After Alice Thompson died in 1897, Seton did not immediately revert to the name of his choice, probably because he had married in the meantime and his wife was legally known as Mrs. Thompson. But he did begin signing his work with his reversed nom de plume, "Ernest Thompson-Seton."

In 1901, after he moved to the United States, having confused people for long enough, he applied to the Supreme Court in the county of New York to legally change his name to Ernest Thompson Seton and this was granted on 24 October of that year. Then followed a barrage of letters to publishers and distributors to have his name changed on the cover and title page plates used for reprinting his most recent books. Later, he asked to have his name changed on all the signed plates in his books.

It is impossible to tell whether Seton knew the facts about the family's descent either at the time of his original decision to change his name or in later years. Certainly, in the last century it was no simple matter to research the facts, as there were no omnibus genealogical guides to Britain's peerage. It may be that he consulted one of the hundreds of self-styled genealogists who were quite willing to "prove" their clients' descent from any crowned head in Europe; if so, he would have been assured that his claims were correct. In any case, after 1900 he never wavered in his conviction that Seton was his real name.

Naturally, he had a perfect right to change his name to anything he fancied, but the object of his name change was the acquisition of a noble family tree and the status that came with it. He had to believe the name was his by right of descent. His new name was, of course, far more distinctive than either Ernest Evan Thompson or Ernest Evan Cameron would have been on a book jacket, but his stories, drawings and paintings would have been just as compelling and just as enduring by any other name than Ernest Thompson Seton.

7

High Realism

In November 1876 Seton was apprenticed to John Colin Forbes, the Toronto portrait artist. He had spent weeks carrying his animal sketches and an oil painting of a sharp-shinned hawk around to the studios of all the city's artists in turn, but only Forbes had shown any interest. Consequently, Seton accepted the two-year apprenticeship that was offered, even though he would receive no pay.

Joseph Thompson was well satisfied with this apprenticeship. He had made up his mind ten years earlier, when he watched the boy making his cork-and-feather chickens, that Seton would become an artist. Each new sign of creative genius after that confirmed his decision. In the family workshop Seton had carved animal figures from chunks of basswood and constructed treasure boxes of white pine with perfectly fitted sliding lids, shadow boxes decorated to simulate woodland scenes, and finely detailed model ships. In the winter of 1870–71, after the family moved to Toronto, Seton had accepted his brother George's challenge to carve a block of fancy lettering as expert as one he had seen in the newspaper. With the help of some secondhand engraving tools presented by his brother Enoch, who had watched him struggling to carve with a jackknife, he did such a creditable job that George took his letter-block to the printer's shop where he was apprenticed and made a number of prints. One of them was sent to Grandfather Thompson in England, who was sufficiently impressed to reward the boy with a "valuable" book on the art of engraving. With his first box of water-colours, Seton had painted woodland scenes and bird specimens; then, after a few lessons from a neighbour, he had begun working in oils. Even the quick sketches he made on his rambles in the marsh or in the Don Valley showed promise, and at all his schools, even the Collegiate, he was always the best student in his art classes.

Had Seton won a scholarship to the university, there is little likelihood that Joseph would have moved to prevent his accepting, as he was certainly not a wasteful man; but he had never approved of natural history as a career for his son, simply because he did not believe Seton could earn a decent living collecting birds and writing treatises on their habits. On the other hand, he was confident that an art apprenticeship would fully exploit his son's remarkable talents and that even if he never became one of the highly paid portrait artists of the city, he would be in demand as an illustrator for newspapers and journals.

In true Victorian fashion, Joseph considered it his duty to see his sons settled in careers. His own father had assumed that responsibility for him, and though the sea would have been his own first choice, he had not been unhappy with the career in which his father had settled him. When the time came, Joseph chose careers for his own sons, and was confident that he had made suitable choices. He had sent Enoch to his uncle's ship brokerage office in Newcastle to begin his career, and now Enoch had his own real eatate, brokerage and insurance business in Toronto. William had spent two years in his father's office as assistant bookkeeper and two years learning carpentry, and in his later life went into real estate, buying up land and building houses for resale. Harry had been apprenticed in dry goods and remained in that business all his life, while George spent his in printing. Arthur was probably the only one whose apprenticeship was wholly inappropriate, though in 1876 Joseph could not yet know that the son he had apprenticed to his older carpenter brothers would eventually become a doctor.

By apprenticing himself to Forbes, Seton seemed to be acknowledging the end of his dream of becoming a naturalist. In fact, he had always known that to obtain the scientific training he needed to be a naturalist he must win the scholarship, but he had always thought of art as an alternative career. In any case, he had no intention of giving up natural history entirely; he simply planned to enter the field via another route. If he could not be a naturalist known for his artistic illustrations, he was determined to become a wildlife artist known for the scientific authenticity of his animal and bird portraits.

John Colin Forbes was thirty years old and already an acclaimed artist when Seton went to work in his studio. He had begun painting in his boyhood, and won attention for a marinescape exhibited at a provincial exhibition while still in his teens. He had studied abroad, first at South Kensington and later at the Royal Academy in London, then returned to Toronto in 1871. In the years that followed, he made his name with a series of portraits of famous men and women, including the Earl of Dufferin, Sir Wilfrid Laurier and Sir John A. Macdonald. Later he returned to London to paint the Prince and Princess of Wales (Edward VII and Queen Alexandra) and Prime Minister Gladstone. Forbes was a founding member of the Ontario Society of Artists, and in 1880 would become a charter member of the Royal Canadian Academy.

In his memoirs Seton is careful not to name Forbes, whom he describes as producing "a long and dwindling series of pot-boilers, made wholly for the sake of the cash, and dropping ever lower and flatter as the years went by. . . . I think I learned all there was to be learned there in the first three months. It was strictly a life of routine and mass production. . . . The real world of painting and art culture was one that my teacher never entered, and had no knowledge of." And he wrote to a friend: "If ever Potherb thought itself a Pine, it is he."[1]

Forbes was apparently working with the new American technique for portraiture that made use of a photographic negative projected by a magic lantern onto the canvas. Seton was given the task of drawing the projected outline on each canvas ready to be filled in by the artist, and of preparing his master's palette. Although he claimed to have learned nothing from Forbes in the two years he worked in his studio, Seton was indebted to the portrait artist for introducing him into Toronto's art community and for insisting that he take night classes at the new Ontario School of Art and Design.

Founded in 1876 as the teaching arm of the Ontario Society of Artists, the school at that time was housed at 14 King Street West. Both daytime and evening classes were given, the latter attended by students who held daytime jobs, some of them in photographic studios colouring portraits, some as artists' apprentices and some in purely menial tasks. George Reid, for example, who enrolled a year after Seton and became one of his friends, worked in a foundry by day.

Classes were given three nights a week in basic drawing and outline techniques, drawing from inanimate models, the fundamentals of design, and "antique drawing" — the process of sketching from casts of famous antique statuary. There were no life classes, for Canadian art teaching followed British custom; flesh and blood models were an innovation of the French schools. The classes were organized as workshops, each student pursuing his own project and receiving criticism and coaching from instructors. There were no exams; instead, students were given certificates for each term of classwork completed, as at the Royal Academy, and at the conclusion of the spring term the best work was displayed in the OSA salon, with medals awarded for outstanding submissions.

In Seton's day, all of the instructors at the Ontario School of Art were British trained, and their teaching emphasized the discipline and craftsmanship of close realism. Of all of his teachers — J. A. Fraser, Marmaduke Matthews, T. Mower Martin and Charlotte Schreiber — only Schreiber commanded his undying regard and affection. Unfortunately, the tribute to her influence on his life and work, which he had planned to include in his memoirs, was cut out when they were reduced from two volumes to one.

Charlotte Mount Brock Morrell Schreiber (1834–1922) was the daughter of an Essex clergyman and claimed descent on her mother's side from the same Brocks of Guernsey from whom Sir Isaac Brock, the hero of the Battle of Queenston Heights, was descended. Her father, recognizing her artistic abilities, sent her to study at Mr. Carey's School of Art in London and even allowed her to take anatomy lessons from a Mr. Scharf, who appears to have been an unsuccessful surgeon. From their instruction, she graduated to the studio of John Rogers Herbert (1810–90) of the Royal Academy, whose sacred and historical paintings had earned him commissions to paint many of the frescoes in the House of

Lords. Herbert was a leader among the high realists of his day, and as a result, he insisted that his students concentrate on draftsmanship and exquisite detail in their work.

Charlotte Morrell, as she was then known, was an apt pupil, and as her own historical paintings and carefully finished scenes of everyday life became popular, she was allowed to exhibit at the Royal Academy. Herbert then encouraged her to submit a series of drawings illustrating Chaucer's story of the Red Cross Knight to the London publisher Cundall, and they were published with the text in 1871. She also illustrated a special edition of Elizabeth Barrett Browning's *The Rhyme of the Duchess May,* published in 1874.

In the midst of this mounting success she married her cousin, Weymouth George Schreiber, and settled with him in Toronto. Her new husband was a widower, and at forty-one, Charlotte became the mother of his half-grown family. Her success in this new role was primarily due to her wholesome, commonsense approach to life. When Seton met her in 1877, her hair was already greying, but her face was youthful and sweet. Tall and spare, and in robust health, she enjoyed tramping around the family estate in all weathers to observe the birds and animals. Near the house she kept a menagerie of birds, rabbits, squirrels, cats and dogs, and often used them as models for her paintings.

Charlotte Schreiber had been teaching at the School of Art for a year when Seton joined her oil painting classes, and she was able to offer him exactly what he needed next in his training as an artist. Her expertise as an animal painter and her study of anatomy enabled her to give him comprehensive groundwork in these areas, but it was her emphasis on realism that was most important to the type of animal illustrations he was attempting at this time. She had no patience with impressionism and told an interviewer: "The human hand, the fingernail, the foot, every portion of the living body, the parts of a flower, are divinely beautiful. It is a joy to paint them as they are in reality. Is it not better to do so than to use that method which gives any structure when viewed near at hand the appearance of an indistinguishable blotch?"[2]

Of equal importance to the professional instruction was the personal attention she gave Seton. In her he found the same motherliness that he had found in Mrs. Blackwell, though the two women had little in common except the warmth of their personalities and their ability to recognize the young man's desperate need for love and attention. But while Charlotte Schreiber felt enormous pity for him as he told of his brutal, insensitive father, she also believed that Seton's calling was to be an artist, not a naturalist.

Soon after Weymouth Schreiber brought his new wife to Canada, he built her a home at Springfield-on-the-Credit (later called Erindale), and it was to this house that she invited her protégés from the art school. Mount Woodham was set on a hill at the end of a long winding drive through private woodlands. To the north of the house stood a background of tall pines; to the south the land fell away in a sheer drop of nearly two hundred feet to the flats bordering the Credit River. A stream running through the property had been dammed to form a large, picturesque fish pond, and close to the house were carefully tended gardens, but the rest of the estate had been left wild.

Seton was first invited to Mount Woodham in the early spring of 1878, and he set up his easel next to his teacher's in the large studio her husband had built for her. Here, with her other students, he painted the models who came to sit for her, and on several occasions posed himself for one of her narrative pictures. The walls of this studio, like those of the hallways, morning room and drawing room, were almost completely covered with paintings; in time, one corner of the morning room would be devoted to the work of her favourite protégé, Seton.

He was enormously impressed with Mount Woodham and would use it as his model years later when he built a home of his own; still, he was happiest roaming the woodlands to observe the wildlife or lying beside the stream with his sketchpad. On some of these days, his teacher accompanied him and the two would sketch together. He repaid her for the privilege of visiting her home by creating "contrivances" to please her, such as a flight of rustic steps up the side of a ravine where she frequently walked.

However, Seton's visits to Mount Woodham were not entirely sublime. Although he would later claim that in time he "came and went as one of the family,"[3] he was always regarded by the artist's stepchildren as an outsider. All three were close to his own age — Lisle, the eldest, was just two years older than Seton — but they belonged to a social set from which he was excluded. Although the Thompsons had never lost any of the traditions or manners of their better days, Seton's present poverty and his lack of social graces set him apart from the Schreibers. When he became enamoured of Susie Grahame, one of the younger sisters of Lisle Schreiber's fiancée, Ottilie, he discovered that she scarcely noticed he existed.

In mid-April 1879 Seton's fourth term at the Ontario School of Art came to an end, and he submitted his best work of the preceding winter for the spring exhibition in the OSA gallery. When the submissions were adjudicated, Seton's work was awarded the Gold Medal; the *Toronto Mail* of 19 April found his studies for the antique "particularly creditable."

The awards were presented at a ceremony at the school presided over by the Honourable Adam Crooks, the minister of education who would attempt to close down the school the following winter by cutting off its funding. Seton's parents and seven of his brothers attended the ceremony and heard the minister praise his talents, then watched as Seton was handed the medal which symbolized his success. Just before he left the platform, Seton was given a whispered instruction to "slip behind the chairman and quietly lay the medal on the table again" because the real thing was "not yet received from the hands of the artificer."[4] Seton never did receive the medal, and it was not intended that he should. Joseph made a number of enquiries at the school but was always put off with excuses and finally let the matter drop.

For Seton the medal was only a small part of the award; his two years at the school had opened doors to a network of artists and art patrons which would be invaluable to him in the coming years. He had also taken the first step toward the level of society on which the Schreibers and Grahames lived and had seen there a way of life he was determined to have for himself. From this time on, though he still ridiculed his father's squire-of-the-manor attitudes, he would dream of a Mount Woodham of his own.

Winning the award convinced Seton that the instructors of the Ontario School of Art had nothing more to teach him, and that he must go abroad to study. Of the three cities that could provide further training — New York, Paris and London — the first was out of the question, for even though a good school had developed in New York, Seton would still have to go "abroad" at some later date to be respected as an artist at home. Charlotte Schreiber had already convinced him that Paris could only teach him to paint "indistinguishable blotches" in the impressionist style. This left London where Schreiber had trained and exhibited in the Royal Academy, and where Seton's other instructors — Fraser, Matthews and Martin — had all attended art school.

London was entirely suitable as far as Seton was concerned. Ever since his Aunt Lee's visit, he had been convinced that his destiny lay in England, and he was prepared to add further glory there to his noble family line. He was also fully aware that it would be easier to convince his father to give him the money for study in London rather than in the immoral city of Paris. When approached on the question of financing study abroad, Joseph was not unwilling that Seton should go, but he was hesitant about providing the funds. According to Seton, his father's response was "I'll send you to London for a year at least. I will talk it over with your mother and brothers, and see what we can allow you. But it will surely be the least possible you can live on, and must be considered merely a loan to be repaid later."[5]

Joseph had reason to be cautious. His four oldest sons were all married and having their own financial problems in the depressed times: George had taken a job with a printer in Chicago; government posters announcing free homestead land in Manitoba had lured Arthur west to make his fortune; Harry had quarrelled with his uncle in Leeds and gone off to New Zealand. And Joseph, having lost his accountant's job, was supporting the three youngest sons, Polly Burfield and his wife on the reduced salary of a bookkeeper.

When Seton pressed his father to find out exactly how much he would receive as an allowance, and Joseph would not be specific, Seton complained to his mother and she promised that he would receive twenty-five dollars a month "if we can possibly spare it."[6] Convinced that if his mother made a promise, it was as good as cash in his hand, Seton made plans to travel to London.

On 12 June 1879 he boarded the *Algerian* for the journey from Toronto to Montreal where he would transfer to the *Samaritan* bound for Liverpool. He was now almost nineteen years of age, gangling and awkward in his movements, except when he was creating with paints or carving tools. He was morbidly sensitive to criticism of his person or his work, yet arrogant and condescending to those he considered his inferiors. Convinced that he was the object of persecution, he railed against his tormentors with such sincerity that many of those who heard were persuaded of the bitterness of his life and truly pitied him; yet he thoroughly enjoyed his self-imposed martyrdom. He was well on the way to becoming a confirmed hypochondriac, yet revelled in outdoor life and long, invigorating tramps in the woods. At last aware of his own sexuality, he was extremely responsive to beauty, but was just as easily touched by sentimentality and melodrama.

Therefore, it was an extremely immature boy who stood, with tears in his eyes, at the rail of the *Algerian,* watching the figures of his parents dwindling, his mother's white handkerchief waving, waving until distance swallowed it. "Something told [him] it was a final good-bye,"[7] but it certainly was not, for he and Joseph Thompson would stage many more battles on the family hearth.

8

The Cost of Living

Seton was seasick for most of the *Samaritan*'s voyage, as he would be almost every time he crossed the ocean for the rest of his life, prompting him to complain later to a friend that he would "rather go to jail than to sea."[1] As a consequence, he was even thinner and less healthy-looking than usual when he was met in Liverpool on 23 June 1879 by his father's sisters, Ann Lee and Mary Henzell, and their husbands. Uncle Lee had a ship chandlery business near the docks; Uncle Henzell seems to have been an exporter. Seton was driven to Alfred Villa, the Lee's comfortable home on the London Road, to recuperate from his voyage.

Two days later he set off for South Shields to stay with the Tates and revisit the scenes of his childhood. Aunt Mary Tate was the sister of Alice Thompson and no friend to Joseph Thompson, possibly because Joseph had attempted to persuade her husband to emigrate with him in 1866. Seton found in her a good friend and a source of much lurid information that added fuel to the bonfire of hate he was building for his father. Aunt Mary Tate was the "authority that would surprize you" cited in one of Seton's letters to his brother William nearly twenty years later, an authority who accused Joseph of being "a worthless lout, a petty swindler, a wife beater, a child murderer and many other pious things."[2]

Seton stayed a week in South Shields, then went to London to investigate art schools. When he found they were closed for the summer, he returned to the Tates and remained more than a month. At the end of August he was back in London. The memoirs which he published in 1941 describe a confident young man finding rooms for himself and determinedly setting out to qualify for entry to the Royal Academy of Arts by submitting a "large and satisfactory drawing of an antique figure." To accomplish this, he headed for the British Museum "without losing a day"[3] and set up his easel among forty or fifty other students who were all attempting to produce a work which would secure for them one of the half dozen scholarships offered by the Academy.

Fortunately, Seton came from a family of journal-keepers: William had kept one on his journey on the *Marathon* and for most of the remainder of his life; Harry kept one on all his overseas travels; Enoch kept one when he became consul for Spain and set off to see the country he represented, and Arthur kept a journal during his homestead years in Manitoba and later during his medical career. Seton had also been encouraged to keep a journal by Dr. Brodie, who stressed the value of noting scientific data. He began his first journal on 12 June 1879 as the *Algerian* was leaving Toronto, and continued the practice for the rest of his life, never making daily entries and often writing only one or two almost illegible words to record wildlife sightings. In spite of his obvious intention to make these primarily natural history documents, they are an excellent source of data on his daily life, and often provide a far more satisfactory account than can be found in his memoirs.

For example, Seton's journal reveals a far less assured young man-about-London than his memoirs depict. He did not, for instance, simply march out and find himself lodgings; he stayed first in the flat of Fred Hayward, a childhood friend from South Shields who was travelling on the Continent, then shared lodgings with his cousin Kit Tate. It was the late spring of 1880 before he found lodgings of his own.

And far from not losing a day on his drawing project, three months passed before his first drawing was ready. It was a sketch of "Hermes," and was rejected by the Academy. However, he had not wasted these three months. In addition to visiting relatives just outside London and contacting J. R. Herbert, who was to act as his sponsor for the Royal Academy, he had been extremely busy. On 27 October he bought a dog's corpse at the "Dogs' Home" and spent a week dissecting it "muscle by muscle" and making a clay model of it.[4] And about this same time, he discovered the library of the British Museum and applied for a reader's card. When the clerk at the main desk told him that no one under twenty-one was allowed readers' privileges, he asked to see the chief clerk. Again he was told that he was too young to be given a card, so he demanded to see the chief librarian, Sir Edward Bond. To Bond he poured out the story of his thwarted dream of becoming a naturalist and the absolute necessity of having a reader's card so that he could have access to the library's enormous collection of natural history books. Bond explained that the rule had been made to exclude all but serious students, then told him that if he wished to appeal the ruling, he would have to write to the trustees: the Prince of Wales, the Archbishop of Canterbury and Lord Beaconsfield. That night Seton mailed letters to all three and promptly received acknowledgements from them, with promises to consider his case. Two weeks later, he was invited back to Bond's office where he was given not merely a reader's card but a Life Member's ticket.

From this time on he spent every evening in the library. It was here that he became acquainted with the works of John James Audubon, and to his disappointment learned that the clamp he had invented back in Toronto to support his sharp-shinned hawk while he painted it had already been invented by Audubon fifty years earlier. He read Alexander Wilson's nine-volume pioneer work on American birds, *American Ornithology,* and Thomas Nuttall's *Manual of the Ornithology of the United States and Canada,* and as he read he began to realize the full extent of the errors in Ross's *Birds of Canada* for which he had so carefully saved his pennies a few years earlier. He found Elliott Coues's recently published *Key to North American Birds* the first real attempt to apply the botanical "key" system to zoology; but when he compared this work to the "Key to Birds of Prey" which he had worked out on the blank pages at the back of his copy of Ross, he decided that Coues's system was artificial and based on trifling details, whereas his own system was far more natural and dealt with the most important features of the birds.

Since the day in Toronto when he first realized that Ross's book was defective, Seton had toyed with the idea of preparing his own

key to the bird families of Canada. Now, with Coues's text
before him as a pattern, he started work on this project and completed it in a few weeks. He arranged his key so that identification
of each family could be made by reference to his pen-and-ink
illustrations of the essential features, and these he supplemented
with a short nontechnical text. The completed project lay in manuscript form until 1895, when he contributed it as an appendix to
Frank Chapman's *Handbook to the Birds of Eastern North America.*

Seton spent Christmas 1879 with the Porteous family at Saffron
Walden. George Porteous, husband of Polly Burfield's older sister, was a senior official in the local bank. One of his juniors was a
young man named Robert Miller Christy, and since Christy's
interests matched Seton's own, Porteous arranged that the two
should meet. Thereafter, on bank holidays and summer week-
ends, they tramped through the countryside together, rising at
five in the morning to see as much of the woods and fields as
possible before the day ended. Christy had developed a much
broader background than Seton from reading books on ornithology, botany and even archaeology, and therefore became both
friend and teacher; and Seton, who had an infinite capacity for
absorbing ideas and details, would rush back to the British
Museum library with each new morsel of information that
Christy provided in order to read more about it.

George Porteous was also responsible for introducing Seton to
another family friend, a Dr. McKelham, with whom Seton discussed his hernia problem. After an examination, the doctor concluded that the rupture was a simple one which an operation
could easily correct, but he cautioned Seton that, as he was in
poor physical condition, he should build himself up before under-
going the surgery.

Seton's exercise regimen should have ensured at least reasonably good health, in spite of his long hours in the library and at his
easel. He hiked vigorously around the countryside with Christy,
went on three-day walking tours with his Tate cousins and always
tramped about London to save himself fare money. He even
clocked himself and found that his long legs could carry him at
five miles an hour on long hikes, and six miles over short distances.

His diet, however, was not adequate to maintain this output of
energy, especially since he had grown so much taller in the two

years prior to his arrival in London. Breakfast was porridge and milk, ersatz coffee and a slice of bread and butter. Lunch was white beans, "occasionally varied with a few raisins or dates"; supper was bread and milk.[5] He had given up meat and fruit because he found them too expensive. Whenever he visited his cousins, he was given three good meals a day and ate them ravenously, but these brief banquets were not enough to offset the deficiencies of his regular diet.

His poor mental health also contributed to the decline in his physical condition. He was lonely. Life in Toronto had not prepared him for the size and impersonality of London; in the past he had always been able to find a few cronies who were willing to overlook the peculiarities of his personality for the sake of common interests. Now he could only visit his friend Christy and his cousins on holidays; except for an occasional excursion with Fred Hayward, the rest of the time he lived a solitary existence.

Since his rejection by Susan Grahame, he had moved warily where girls were concerned. His one female friend was Harriet Hatton, a Londoner a few years older than he, who had been struggling for acceptance to the Royal Academy when Seton first arrived in London. They had worked at adjoining easels, talking whenever they took breaks from their work. She seems to have been in some way connected with the world of the arts and letters, and it was she who directed Seton to the British Museum library. She overlooked his gaucheness and shabby clothes, and encouraged him in his work; for this Seton was humbly grateful.

He did not press Harriet Hatton for more than this platonic kindness, however, for he had become convinced that he was sexually abnormal. Puberty had arrived for Seton while he was at the Ontario School of Art, but the full force of it did not come until he was in London, where he awoke every morning "in a state of violent sexual excitement." This excitement recurred at intervals throughout the day with erections occurring for no apparent reason, much to his horror and embarrassment. With no one to confide in, he became terrified that others would become aware of his perversion and his "lustful imaginings," and he determined to conquer them. He placed two drawing boards on top of his mattress to punish his body, and splashed cold water on "his parts" several times each day.[6] He walked blocks out of his way to avoid passing the print shops which displayed suggestive pictures, and whenever he was in the National Gallery or the British Museum, he averted his eyes from works of art that depicted unclothed women. He studied the life of St. Anthony, and, taking a leaf from his mother's book, began making fervent offerings to God night and morning, awaiting a message that would lead to a cure.

In time, the cure came as it would have in any case, for Seton was simply going through a normal phase made more acute by his anxiety. But the regimen he imposed on himself coupled with his inadequate and unbalanced diet produced another dividend: he began to have visions.

The sweet peace that possessed me in the early morning as I lay on my hard boards was my exceeding reward. Each morning it came, and with growing power. Then I began to hear the Voices, weird ecstatic mumblings at first; then, after a month or more, these mumblings took intelligible form. I heard my name, and strange words. The first clear utterance came in tones of my mother's voice, and all it said was: "Remember, it is for eternity."[7]

Seton grew quite accustomed to his Voices, and seems to have welcomed them as if they were friends entering his essentially lonely life.

By December 1880 he had finally completed a new drawing to submit to the Royal Academy. This time he had chosen Michelangelo's "Satyr" as his subject, and on Christmas Day he learned that he had been accepted as a probationer at the Academy. He was one of six chosen from the year's applicants, and automatically became entitled to seven years' free tuition as long as he passed his probationary exams and his yearly progress exams.

The drawing of the Satyr seems to have been the only tangible piece of art work he produced in the year 1880. He did, however, earn a little money during this time by making black-and-white illustrations for the publishers Cassell, Petter and Galpin, to whom he had probably been directed by Charlotte Schreiber. The remainder of his year had been dedicated to natural history, either in the British Museum library or in the field.

On 18 January 1881 he began his studies at the Royal Academy. As a probationer he was required to spend his day from 10:00 A. M. until 4:00 P. M. in the Antique School, and from 4:30 to

6:30 P. M. in the Life School, Monday through Friday. As at the Ontario School of Art, instruction took the form of criticism by a succession of Royal Academicians, each one making two visits a week for four weeks. Those who inspected Seton's work in his Antique classes are unknown, but his life drawings must have been criticized by Lawrence Alma-Tadema, whose historical idylls were at the height of popularity, and by two lesser Academicians — P. H. Calderon and H. S. Marks. Seton has left no comment on any of them, either in his memoirs or in his journals.

Having finally been admitted to the Academy with seven years of tuition-free schooling ahead of him, Seton should have been supremely happy, but he was not. On 7 March 1881 he sat down to forecast his future, and his forecast did not include seven years at the Royal Academy.

The Plan of My Life by Ernest E. T. Seton

I, Ernest Evan, eighth son of Joseph Logan Thompson, whose right surname is Seton and who is the sole and lawful heir of George Seton, Earl of Winton, being of sound mind, though not of robust body, do hereby outline and forecast my own life in the light of my knowledge of myself and my surroundings.

This coming spring I shall exhibit a picture at a Royal Academy exhibition.

I shall return to Canada for the winter. I shall there undergo a dangerous operation for the radical cure of the rupture that now distresses me and shall be perfectly and happily cured. I shall undertake this against the advice of all of my friends.

On my twenty-first birthday I shall publicly resume our proper family name of Seton and thenceforth be known as Ernest E. T. Seton. In doing this I shall have trouble chiefly with my own people.

I shall spend a year in writing and illustrating a book on the birds of Canada with Joseph McP. Ross. This book will give me great pleasure. It will make for me a local reputation and it will bring me some money. I shall then go to New York to make my way as an illustrator and painter of animals.

In 1890 I shall marry an English woman or of English extraction. She will have light hair and blue eyes, be of medium or small size, inclined to be stout; that is, in all ways the reverse of myself. Mentally she will fill the gaps where I fail. God grant that I may know her when she comes, that I may waste no time in following others.

We shall have three children, two boys and a girl. The first boy will be a source of sorrow, but in the other two we shall find much happiness.

In 1905 I shall by God's help have made a comfortable fortune by my pen and pencil also by judicious speculation. I shall then return to England, buy a small estate in Devonshire and a house in London.

In 1915 I shall be knighted by the king in recognition of my work as an artist-naturalist.

In 1924 I shall die in my London home of a bronchial trouble in the spring of the year, being then in my sixty-fourth year.

This is my destiny: to restore in some measure the ancient family of Seton of which my father is the rightful representative, and whensoever I shall turn aside from this plan I shall have great trouble. And such deviations shall always be brought about by the active interference of my own immediate family. Therefore, to be safe I should avoid them. Nevertheless, my heart cleaves to my own people.[8]

In spite of this forecast, when he was admitted to the Painting School of the Royal Academy on 8 April 1881, Seton accepted the appointment and began classes. In this discipline, the instructors for the term were led by Sir Hubert von Herkomer, who would influence art education with the Herkomer School of Art founded in 1883; the others were J. Pettie, H. S. Marks and W. F. Yearnes. No attendance records were kept for this period so it is impossibe to tell whether Seton attended classes regularly, but by this time his attention had been diverted to a new interest. Acceptance by the Academy had entitled him to free admission to the Regent's Park Zoo, which at that time housed one of the most extensive animal collections in the world. It now became Seton's daily practice to set up his easel outside the animal cages so that he could draw and redraw the captives within. In June two of his bird drawings were accepted and exhibited in the Dudley Gallery; although it was not the annual Burlington House Exhibition that he had predicted for himself, it was a good start.

By the term end at the beginning of July, Seton had definitely resolved not to continue at the Academy, but to follow his forecast and return to Canada by the winter. He knew this decision was correct because his Voices were quite insistent by now that he should go to live on the Canadian prairies, have his hernia repaired and then set off for New York to make his fortune. Some of his Voices had probably been prompted by letters from home telling of Arthur's adventures on his Manitoba homestead; the rest were simply the voices of homesickness and emotional torment — potent influences on an imaginative young man like Seton.

The only problem remaining was how to return home without appearing to have failed. His ego would not allow him to write home saying he was ill, though subconsciously he knew that illness would trigger the necessary response from his mother. His problem was resolved after he was examined by Dr. McKelham on 25 June at George Porteous's home at Saffron Walden. Struck by his poor physical condition and knowing of his earlier lung trouble, McKelham suggested to Porteous that Seton should be sent home where his family could care for him. Porteous then wrote to Alice Thompson, and in September Alice wrote telling her son to come home.

On 26 October he embarked from London on the *Erl King* bound for Montreal. He did not ask his family for the fare, and was only able to afford a steerage ticket. He was seasick for most of the voyage and arrived home after sixteen stormy days, his body crawling with lice.

Once settled into his old room and given three square meals a day, he was soon in improved health. Gun in hand, he returned to his bird collecting on the Toronto Marsh, in the Don Valley and in the open country north of Bloor Street. Nearly every day, though it was now almost Christmas and the weather was bitterly cold, he shot and carried home birds to draw and dissect — pigeon hawks, crows, juncos, shrikes and waterfowl — lamenting later that he had not saved their skins. But Seton's main interest in them was for his forthcoming book on Canadian birds. These "birding" expeditions continued throughout the winter, with Seton often setting off alone, though he spent much of his time in the company of Dr. Brodie, his son, Willie, or the former art school friend Joseph McPherson Ross, with whom he planned to write his book.

Then, several weeks after he arrived home, he was invited into his father's study for a talk. Exactly what transpired there is unknown, but in the version given in Seton's memoirs — he did not record the meeting in his journal — his father showed him an itemized bill for $537.50. This amount covered all monies paid out on his behalf to that time, right from the "doctor's fee for bringing [him] into the world" to the cost of his London adventure.[9] According to Seton, after his father showed him "page after page in the cash book," he explained that while he had not charged interest so far, he must henceforth charge six percent per annum. He then asked his son to begin repaying the money as soon as possible, and suggested that it was time Seton struck out on his own.

Seton was "utterly staggered." "Oh, the blackness of that moment!" he wrote in his memoirs. "Twenty-one years of age, nothing achieved, no progress in life, not a cent of money, no prospects of any — nothing but a millstone of debt bearing heavy interest; broken in health, ordered to leave and swim for myself."[10]

Seton acknowledged in his memoirs that Joseph Thompson had advanced him four hundred dollars of this amount during his two years in London. The remainder must therefore have been the costs incurred over the first nineteen years of his life. If this $137.50 was indeed charged against such fundamental items as the doctor's fee, then Joseph's actions were certainly reprehensible, but it is a fact that none of Seton's brothers were ever asked to pay for such things. All had been born with a doctor in attendance, so that all would have been liable for the one-guinea accoucheur fee.[11] And the first six sons would also have been liable for their boarding school fees and perhaps for their passage from England.

The four hundred dollars seems to have been a legitimate debt, because Joseph had told Seton it was to "be considered merely a loan to be repaid later." In asking for repayment at this time, Joseph Thompson probably felt fully justified, for Seton had not completed his art training and had spent most of his time in England pursuing his natural history interests. Since his return home he had done nothing about finding a job as an illustrator, a career for which even his abbreviated training would have fitted him. Instead, he had shown every intention of remaining under the parental roof forever, making daily forays to collect specimens, and perhaps eventually writing a book about birds.

The main reason for Joseph's request for repayment was a more fundamental one, however: he needed money. At sixty-one he was past his best earning years. He was just a bookkeeper and he would remain so until he could no longer work. From this time onward the financial plight of the elder Thompsons would become the concern of the entire family; in fact, when Seton arrived home from London, the family was in the throes of carrying out what they hoped would be the ultimate solution. In the early spring the house at 17 South Pembroke was to be sold, and their parents and Polly Burfield (who had never married) were to go to Manitoba to join Arthur on his homestead.

Regardless of whether the interview took place as Seton described it — or even whether it took place at all — Seton's belief that the money *had* been demanded from him, and that it constituted the entire cost of raising him to manhood, released him from any pretense of respect for his father and gave focus at long last to the hatred that had been building within him for so many years. If his father wanted him to strike out on his own, he would do so. With only weeks to go before Christmas, he landed a commission from a printer for the preparation of a set of one dozen Christmas cards, and for these he was paid sixty dollars. He contemplated giving some of this to his father, then, remembering that he "was to be thrown on his own resources,"[12] changed his mind. His Voices promised him that he would go west; therefore, he would use the money for his journey and escape the tyranny of his father forever.

It would be nearly eight years before he paid off the money which his father claimed from him, and there is nothing to show that he paid interest on the outstanding balance during that time.[13]

ABOVE: A view of Lindsay, Ontario, 1865 (Archives of Ontario).

LEFT: Archibald MacMurchy, principal of the Toronto Collegiate, c. 1875 (Archives of Ontario).

ABOVE: The Thompson family, Toronto, 1889. Standing: William Snowdon, second son; Arthur Septimus, seventh son; Charles Seton, fourth son; Ernest Evan Thompson (Seton), eighth son; Joseph Logan Jr., third son; Harry Thomas, fifth son and George Seton, sixth son. Seated: Mary Ann ("Polly") Burfield, adopted daughter; Alan Cameron, tenth son; Alice Snowdon Thompson; Joseph Logan Thompson; Walter, ninth son and John Enoch, first son (Courtesy of Beverly McKie).

OPPOSITE: Charlotte Schreiber at Mount Woodham, 1890 (Courtesy Seton Village).

TOP RIGHT: American Bison, sculpted by Seton in 1883 when he was studying with William Sartain at The Art Students League of New York, and cast in bronze for the first time in 1983 (Property of the Seton Estate, Santa Fe, New Mexico).

BOTTOM RIGHT: Arthur Septimus Thompson and Ernest Thompson (Seton), 1883 (Courtesy Seton Village).

ABOVE: *Awaited in Vain*, painted in 1892 (Courtesy Seton Village).

RIGHT: Two animal studies — *Wolf*, 1890; *Marmot*, c. 1900 (Courtesy Seton Village).

OPPOSITE PAGE: Self-portrait in London, England, 1879 (Courtesy Seton Village).

Grouse study, c. 1885 (Courtesy Seton Village).

9

The Winnipeg Wolf

Seton had never looked to his brother Arthur as a role model during their adolescence, but he was impressed with his success as a Manitoba homesteader. Arthur had claimed land southwest of Portage la Prairie in 1879 and now had full title to it. By the fall of 1881, when his thirty-year-old brother Charlie joined him, he had already constructed a log shanty and barn and had begun to establish a herd of cows. Together the two men had made a start on the construction of a six-room frame house which was to accommodate the senior Thompsons, Polly Burfield, Charlie's wife and child and the two youngest Thompson brothers, all of whom planned to move west in the spring.

In spite of the expected family invasion, Seton decided that Arthur's De Winton Farm would make an excellent staging area for his own future. He would homestead land of his own nearby, farm and carry out naturalist studies, then sell his property at a profit and move on to New York where he would become rich and famous. At no time did he see himself as a farmer on a permanent basis. He was far too romantic to find any lasting appeal in such day-to-day drudgery, especially the kind he recalled his older brothers performing on the Lindsay farm. But he thrilled to the concept of the pioneer adventurers of the prairies, joyfully "going forth to possess the land. . . . every eye ablaze with the light of hope. . . . Every furrow struck, every post-hole sunk, every sod house temporarily built, . . . prompted, planned and completed, roofed in with the glamor of glowing expectation for the future, a magic that turned squalor into freedom, . . . hardships into a joke. The sun came up and sank each day on a world of newborn hopes."[1]

Seton's total capital in March 1882 was the sixty dollars he had made drawing Christmas cards and another fifteen dollars earned drawing trademarks for a collar company. From these funds he paid out twenty-five dollars for a rail ticket to Manitoba and, on Arthur's advice, spent thirty dollars on sixty chickens and a few geese and turkeys. He set forth on his new adventure with Willie Brodie, who was being sent west by his father for some practical field study. Young Brodie had been supplying specimens to the Smithsonian Institution in Washington for several years and had contracted to supply more from the almost unknown Canadian prairies.

The two young men had tickets on the 16 March "farmers' train" — a dozen stock cars and one day coach — from Toronto via Chicago and St. Paul to Winnipeg. (It would be another four years before a Canadian rail line was pushed through north of the Great Lakes and onto the prairies.) After paying fifteen dollars for space for his poultry in a cattle car, Seton had five dollars left, an ample sum for meals and other incidentals on the five-day trip.

The train reached St. Paul, Minnesota, on the third day, but could go no farther because of a blizzard raging across the plains to the north. After waiting two days in the train, which had been shunted onto a siding, Brodie and most of the others who had no livestock to care for transferred to a northbound passenger train that was awaiting a break in the weather. When this break finally came, Seton's "farmers' train" was hauled another ten miles along the line by a decrepit engine before it broke down, blocking the main line just as the blizzard resumed. The farmers on board were given shovels and invited to dig the train out while they awaited a rescue engine. When it arrived late in the day, it pulled the train north once more with the blizzard howling around it.

In the middle of the night, with the train chugging along at twenty miles an hour, Seton opened the rear door of the car to get fresh air; attempting to step onto the platform of the following car, he found that it was no longer there. Seton clung to the rail beside the door, his feet bumping on the ties below. In terror, he hauled himself back into the car, convinced that he had been only moments away from death. His mother, when told of the adventure later, cried and told him that God most certainly had work for him to do.

At Fergus Falls, about fifty-five miles southeast of Fargo, the rescue engine shunted the train onto another siding and here it remained for four days. Fortunately, the farmers were able to buy food here for themselves and their livestock. On 27 March, eleven days after leaving Toronto, Seton and his poultry headed north once more, but each time the blizzard began again, snowdrifts would block the tracks. They finally crossed the border into Canada on 30 March.

By this time the blizzard had subsided and the train made steady progress toward the city of Winnipeg. Through the window, Seton stared at mile after mile of thick poplar forest. Then suddenly, when the train was only minutes from the outskirts of the city, he caught a brief glimpse of a scene which would stay in his mind for the rest of his life and mark the beginning of a fundamental change in his attitudes. In a clearing not thirty yards wide stood a lone wolf ringed about by dogs. As the train passed slowly through the clearing, the dogs attacked, but the wolf defended itself successfully: "... *chop, chop, chop,* went those fearful jaws, no other sound from the lonely warrior; but a death yelp from more than one of his foes, as those that were able sprang back, and left him statuesque as before, untamed, unmaimed, and contemptuous of them all."[2]

In his memoirs Seton identified this animal as the "Winnipeg Wolf," or "le Garou," a timber or grey wolf that prowled just beyond the city limits, preying on dogs. A few years later, on one of its forays into the city, it was killed and its carcass mounted and displayed in the Hine brothers' taxidermy shop. In 1893 it was exhibited at the Chicago Exposition.[3]

Seton was fascinated by the battle in the clearing and found himself hoping the train would become stuck in a snowdrift at that moment so he could witness its outcome. "All my heart went out to that great grey wolf," he wrote. "I longed to go and help ... that rare and wonderful creature." In the instant of identifying with the wolf, Seton began to change his own self-image. He had seen himself as vulnerable and abused by an insensitive world;

now he began to see himself as he saw the wolf — untamed, unmaimed and contemptuous of them all. He became obsessed with the need to know more about wolves, to understand them, to track them down and inevitably to pit himself against them. After a few years, this obsession was recognized by his friends who nicknamed him "Wolf," and by this name he became more and more generally known.

On the evening of 1 April, Seton caught the westbound Portage, Westbourne and Northwestern train and in the middle of the night was deposited in the snow at a tiny station labelled De Winton. A mile from the track he found his brother's cabin. The following day, Seton and Willie Brodie, who had arrived a few days earlier, set off with their guns under their arms on their first prairie hunt for specimens. Seton carried his copies of Coues's *Key to the Birds of America* and Jordan's *Manual of Vertebrates,* while Brodie carried in his head the vast store of information he had received from day-to-day field work with his father. Each day they brought their specimens back to the thirteen-by-sixteen-foot cabin where, to the disgust of Arthur and Charlie, they dissected them and wrote up their findings in their journals.

A few days after Seton arrived on the farm, the crates of chickens that he had been forced to leave behind in Winnipeg were deposited at De Winton station. All of the chickens survived the journey, but the turkeys and geese apparently had succumbed to the cold. Seton sold six hens to a neighbour for thirty dollars cash, the price he had paid for all his poultry in Toronto less than six weeks earlier. Within a week the weather had improved enough that Arthur and Charlie were able to resume work on the house, while Seton built a henhouse. On 11 May, leaving Brodie in charge of the farm, the three brothers set off toward the southwest to look for homesteading land.

The Land Act of 1872, which set down the provisions for homesteading on the prairies, was patterned after similar laws in the United States. It provided that the prairie land should be surveyed into townships commencing at the international border and moving northward, each township to be six miles square and divided into thirty-six sections of 640 acres each. Any family head or person twenty-one years or more could claim a quarter section (160 acres) on payment of a ten-dollar registration fee, and gain full title on proof of three years' residence, cultivation of the land

and certain specified improvements. The homesteader could also pre-empt the adjoining quarter section of land by paying a small sum per acre to the Crown over an extended period. Finding good homesteading land, however, was complicated: the Hudson's Bay Company had been given title to two even-numbered sections in each township, the railways had been deeded alternate sections in a twenty-four-mile-wide belt on either side of their rights-of-way, and two odd-numbered sections in each township were set aside for the support of the schools. This left barely one quarter of the fertile belt in the southern prairies available for homesteading.

The Thompson brothers' land search took place about a year after the high point of the brief Manitoba homestead boom, which had resulted from government advertising overseas. Would-be homesteaders had been encouraged by the formation of an internationally funded syndicate pledged to complete the Canadian Pacific Railway from coast to coast by 1891. This meant that farmers establishing themselves on the prairies could be guaranteed of eastern markets within a few years. But the boom collapsed when the railway company faltered, and by the summer of 1882 only a handful of immigrants were out land-hunting, compared to thousands the previous year.

Although Charlie was the eldest of the three brothers, it was Arthur who acted as head of their land-hunting expedition. He was also driver of the farm team which pulled the light wagon they loaded with their camping gear and oats for the horses. Arthur had been on the prairie for five years by this time and had become thoroughly independent. A short, stockily built man, brusque and brief of speech, he appeared far more mature than Seton, though he was only twenty months older. Seton accepted Arthur's leadership without complaint during this early stage of his Manitoba experience, but as he became familiar with the new environment, he became far less willing to take his brother's advice, and in their final year together their relationship was very strained.

This first expedition took them south of Brandon into the Pembina valley, but all the land there had been staked the previous year. For Seton, however, the trip was not wasted: he found the prairie alive with wildlife, and made notes on badgers, ground squirrels, skunks and foxes. He saw flocks of brown cranes, occasional pairs of white cranes, wild geese winging their way north in great V-shaped bands and prairie chickens on every grassy knoll.

On 26 May the Thompsons returned to De Winton Farm to find that the rest of the family had arrived from Toronto. With them was a young Englishman, Fred Calvert, who had come from England to join Brodie for a year of specimen collecting, and within a few days Brodie and Calvert set off on a collecting expedition. Seton, who was committed to helping on the farm, had to remain behind. He was assigned the task of milking three or four of the cows, a chore which caused his hands to swell so badly that for the first month he had to massage his fingers each morning before he could get them to move at all. Although he hated milking the cows, he enjoyed bringing them in from the fields for milking because then he could examine the nests of the seemingly endless variety of birds which spring weather had brought back to the prairie. And he had no complaint about being sent to the field to plough. The soil here had few rocks or roots, so it was a simple matter to guide the horse and keep the plough upright while he studied the antics of the crows that followed him, hopping to within a few feet of the horses to scavenge in the freshly turned earth, or wheeling and calling overhead. From his vantage point behind the team, Seton watched flocks of ducks, geese and prairie chickens alighting on the stubble fields, and thousands of blackbirds settling in the leafless trees, then rising in dense black clouds into the sky. And every evening he made notes in his journal of what he had seen.

Meanwhile, just beyond the fences of De Winton Farm, changes were taking place. The tiny railway station that had been designated De Winton because of its proximity to the farm had been moved a half-mile east on the line in May, and another half-mile in June and was finally dismantled altogether. On its final location a more elaborate station was being built, intended as the principal stop between Portage la Prairie and Brandon. Within months a school, post office and shops had been constructed near the station, and the entire settlement was christened Carberry after Lord Elphinstone's estate in Scotland. It was to this town of Carberry that Seton would return in later years to be treated as the "local boy who made good."

After the crops were planted in late June 1882, the brothers began their second search for land. This time it was Arthur, Walter and Seton who set out together for the upper Assiniboine valley, stopping at the office of the government agent in Birtle to get a list of farms which could be claimed. These were homesteads and pre-emptions that had been staked a year or two earlier and abandoned, usually because the settlers had been unprepared for the realities of homesteading. The three men remained together until 12 July, when Seton returned to De Winton. His journal notes that he was stricken with "rheumatics," but the real cause seems to have been disagreements with Walter. The other two continued the search while Seton walked thirty miles to the railway line and caught the train back to the farm to resume his wildlife observations. On 1 August Walter and Arthur returned, their search unsuccessful.

Although he made notes on all animals he saw during that summer, Seton concentrated his field studies on the birds, for he was still determined to publish his book on the birds of Canada in spite of the fact that Ross was no longer interested in collaborating. That spring, shortly after the snows disappeared, Seton had seen the prairie chickens' spring dance ritual for the first time. By constructing a blind for himself, he had been able to watch from a few yards' distance while the birds stamped across their "dancing mound," fluttering their tails and uttering "a sort of bubbling crow."[4] Again and again throughout May and June this ritual was re-enacted as Seton watched and made notes. He caught young birds and kept them in captivity while he measured their growth and flying ability. The careful notes he took were not wasted, for they became the basis for a twelve-hundred-word article, "The Life of the Prairie Chicken"; it was published in *The Canadian Journal* in February 1883, Seton's first scientific work in print.

By the time Seton came to Manitoba he was still not an exceptional marksman, but he was able to hit his targets often enough that he soon had a sizable specimen collection. When he shot a Brewer's grackle, he counted each feather on its body with painstaking care and noted that there were exactly 4915 of them. He "collected" a nesting *Philadelphicus vireo* when he correctly suspected that its nest and eggs were unknown to science; unfortunately, the eggs were accidentally crushed before he could package them for shipment to the Smithsonian Institution. He was more successful with a pair of Connecticut warblers and their eggs, which arrived safely at their destination. He climbed trees to examine the nests of Swainson's hawks, entering in his journal a list of the materials that made up their nests, and the size, shape and colouring of their eggs. He found a flicker nesting in a hollow oak, and made experiments with the nest of a Baltimore oriole to determine its strength. And he began mapping the identifying marks and flight habits of the local birds. He had been making this kind of sketch since his early hikes in the Toronto Marsh, but now he approached mapping more methodically so that the sketches, when compared, would instantly reveal the differences between the birds.

That fall, when most of the birds had left the prairie to go south, "yelping like an uncountable pack of dogs,"[5] Seton gave closer attention to the wild life of the mammals. He gathered information about the behaviour of foxes, striped gophers and ground squirrels, but his real interest was the wolf population. The prairie wolves, or coyotes (*Canis latrans*), in the Assiniboine area were much smaller than timber wolves, weighing between twenty-five and forty-five pounds. Once the snows came, these animals moved closer to the settlements where they often came into conflict with farm dogs. Once it became local knowledge that Seton was interested in these animals, he was always called when one began hanging around a neighbour's farm, but though he went after them with his rifle on many occasions, he was never successful and all his field notes had to be made on animals that had been killed by poisoned bait.

As the winter deepened, the temperature dropped to minus twenty degrees Fahrenheit and stayed there for weeks. This extreme cold was too much for the elder Thompsons, and after Christmas, just seven months after their arrival, Joseph and Alice Thompson and Polly Burfield returned to the east. Polly went to live with George and his new wife in Chicago; Joseph and Alice moved in with Joseph Jr. in Toronto and Joseph Sr. became an "architect" for his son. Charlie took his young family to Portage la Prairie a few months later.

To celebrate his father's departure from the land he had staked out for himself, in February 1883 Seton advertised in the *Manitoba Tribune* that henceforth he would be known by the "ancient family surname of Seton."[6] None of his brothers followed his example. According to the schedule laid down in his Life Plan, he was a year and a half late.

He was also late for another item on his list: his hernia operation. His physical condition was now excellent so that the time was ripe for surgery, but more importantly, his mental health had improved to the point that he no longer *needed* to be physically ill. Part of this improvement had been forced upon him: it was simply too difficult to get sympathy for his illnesses in this new environment — no one had the time to listen to his complaints. Another part of this improvement was the result of the recognition he was receiving for his work in natural history. On 15 February Spencer Baird of the Smithsonian Institution had written inviting Seton to become a "correspondent in natural history." Baird's letter was prompted by Elliott Coues for whom Seton had offered to collect specimens in spite of his reservations about Coues's "key" system. Seton had also achieved a degree of recognition from the acceptance of his article by the *Canadian Journal,* and, through Christy, he had published an article in the *Herts and Essex Gazette* on the delights of life in Manitoba.

But by far the greatest improvement had come about because of the change in his self-image. He had not forsaken his persecution complex — that would be part of his emotional equipment throughout life — but now, instead of seeing himself as vulnerable and misunderstood, he saw himself, like the Winnipeg Wolf, as untamed, unmaimed and contemptuous of all those by whom he was misunderstood and persecuted. He had simply learned to ignore those ordinary people, including his family, who did not understand him. Furthermore, in the course of his year at De Winton Farm, he had discovered that being physically fit brought him much more attention than being ill had ever aroused. At twenty-two-and-a-half he was tall and well-built, with the stamina to outwalk anyone else in the township, and, though there was still a certain petulance in his face, he had become an exceptionally handsome man.

On 15 March 1883 Seton went to Chicago for his hernia operation. His brother George and Polly Burfield met him there. Next day these two took him to the weekly clinic of Dr. Moses Gunn at the Chicago City Hospital, and there he was exhibited as one of a long string of "cases" before an assembly of medical students.

Seton's hernia was a simple reducible one, requiring a type of surgery Dr. Gunn had performed a hundred times, but the doctor evidently realized that he had a very impressionable young man before him, and took the time to make sure that Seton had made his peace with his God.

As Seton was not a Chicago resident, he could not be admitted to the City Hospital; he was told he could pay six dollars a week for a ward bed in St. Joseph's Hospital and have his surgery done for free. The operation was performed on 20 March; in late April Seton was discharged and he returned to Carberry physically fit. It was not the last illness in his life, but it was the last time that illness would form an integral part of his self-image.

On 21 May 1883 Willie Brodie drowned in the Assiniboine River near Fort Pelly. He was crossing the river by canoe when it overturned, and though he began swimming strongly for shore, he was apparently seized by a cramp and disappeared. Fred Calvert, who watched helplessly from the shore, recovered the body the next day. For Dr. Brodie the loss of his only son was an enormous blow, not only because of the strong relationship between them but also because of his belief that his son would achieve the renown he had not won for himself. After a year's mourning, however, Brodie returned to his work and became the mentor of a long list of young naturalists.

Seton did not learn of Brodie's death until ten days after it occurred. His reaction is unknown; his journal states only that he had been advised of the death.

Alan and Walter Thompson were back in Toronto by the time Seton returned from Chicago. This left Arthur with only the help of "the Naturalist," as he now referred to the younger brother "who was more interested in nature study than farm work." Arthur seeded forty acres that spring "without help."[7]

Late July brought Christy from England for a visit to the prairies, and he and Seton spent their time investigating the lake country to the north and the bogs and forests to the south. Christy's knowledge of English plant life helped Seton identify many of the Manitoba plants, but Christy's greatest contribution to Seton's scientific education was his knowledge of Darwin's theories of evolution. It was an area of study that Seton would investigate much more fully in the next few years.

But Seton's idyll was coming to an end; he had a schedule to keep. "Time is passing," he wrote in mid-August;

> My time in this land is drawing to a close. I must start soon but the idea of leaving these fair flower starred bird enlivened prairies for horrible crowded smoky miserable New York is simply loathsome. I think at times I'd rather be a farmer and stay, but then again I know it would be no use. In a year or so I would be stung to misery by the saddest of thoughts of what "might have been."
>
> There is no limit to the possibilities of him who *wills*. I feel I cannot give up cherished hopes, I will go to New York and labor in the galleys for a year or two, and hope that the time is near ahead when I shall leave cities for good, on that hope I must live and work (as an illustrator I suppose). I often feel gloomy when I put my thoughts long on this outlook. But I never lose faith in the maxim: *All things are possible to him that wills.*[8]

Seton's decision to go to New York was not motivated entirely by his recognition of the passing of time. Arthur Thompson had enrolled in the University of Manitoba's Faculty of Medicine and would begin classes as soon as the harvest was over, so if Seton stayed on at De Winton, he would be there alone. On the other hand, he was not really prepared to leave immediately, as he had not completed the research for his bird book, nor had he fulfilled his dream of claiming a homestead for himself.

On 1 October he set off with two young men from Carberry to make one final attempt to find land before winter set in. Arthur had by this time despaired of help from his brother and hired a greenhorn from South Africa to lend a hand with the harvest, so Seton was not missed. He and his friends headed much farther north than previous searches had taken him, into the semi-wooded country just west of Duck Mountain, an area that is now part of Saskatchewan. Here their expedition found rich soil, and when Seton discovered a small lake fed by a clear stream, he decided he had come far enough. For himself he claimed the southwest quarter of Section 36, Township 28, Range 31 West of the 1st Meridian, and he pre-empted the adjoining southeast quarter which included the lake. For Arthur he staked the two northern quarters, even though there was little likelihood that his brother would ever make use of the claim.

That night, after the Carberry men had rolled up in their bedding beside the campfire, Seton watched the moon rise over the prairie. Suddenly, he realized that it had been exactly two years since he had stood on the Thames Embankment looking at the moon, and he was overwhelmed by the drama of the moment. Convinced — and somehow quite content — that he would never see London again and that he was done forever with the world of art, he opened the bag that was attached to his belt and dumped all the mementos of those years, including his Life Pass to the library of the British Museum, into the fire. At the last moment he rescued a letter from his mother and the ivory ticket which represented his right to seven years' tuition at the Royal Academy. Later he would regret this melodramatic ceremony, but at the time he found it enormously satisfying.

Having chosen his land and filed his claim at the Birtle land office, Seton returned to De Winton Farm in the third week of October. There had already been serious frosts in the area and Arthur, who had lost his entire crop of Red Fife wheat, now sold off his cattle and took his horses to winter on a neighbouring farm. On 11 November the temperature dropped below zero and the first blizzard of the winter began. When it ended on 14 November, Seton packed his belongings and boarded the eastbound train.

He arrived in New York with only a few dollars in his pocket, but within a week he settled into lodgings with Charles Broughton, an acquaintance from art school days in Toronto, and soon found himself a job. He had brought a portfolio of his drawings with him to show to prospective employers. In those days, the New York publishers of newspapers, magazines and books employed batteries of artists to draw illustrations on boxwood panels which were then handed over to similar batteries of engravers whose job it was to carve the pictures in relief ready to be electrotyped. Most of the illustrators were hacks who would never be known outside the drafting rooms they worked in, but some of them became famous, particularly the ones who specialized in cartoons. During the 1870s Thomas Nast's cartoons in *Harper's Weekly* were credited with the defeat of William Tweed's political machine. Frank "Chip" Bellew became the star of *Life* magazine, and the Beard brothers achieved such popularity that they set up their own studio as free-lance illustrators — Dan

Beard was the original illustrator for Mark Twain's *A Connecticut Yankee in King Arthur's Court*.

Seton's portfolio won him a place in the drafting room of Sacket, Wilhelms and Betzig, a publishing firm that specialized in lithography. There he churned out advertising illustrations for twenty dollars a week, which was enough to allow him to live reasonably well, pay off monies loaned to him by George and Enoch and begin putting money in the bank.

In London he had been denied the pleasures of the city because of his poverty; now New York was open to him because of his comparative wealth. He had kept in touch with Harriet Hatton and, after her arrival in the city, began escorting her to art galleries and lectures. With Charles Broughton and another Toronto friend, Jack Willing, he attended the theatre and saw Edwin Booth in the role of Shylock, and Lily Langtry in *Peril*. Seton's solvency brought him new confidence in the business world, too; he marched into the office of W. Lewis Fraser, the art manager for *Century Magazine,* and sold him a picture of a tanager.

Money also made it possible for Seton to tell Broughton to move out when he decided his roommate's constant talking was interfering with his own concentration. Seton actually welcomed conversation when he was drawing or painting, but now he wanted to use his spare time to write. With Broughton gone, he spent his evenings preparing accounts of his wildlife observations. Some of these were strictly factual reports intended to establish his reputation as a naturalist; others, such as "The Snowshoe Rabbit," were more popular science than scientific because he introduced personal comment that went beyond the factual and observable. An even more important development in his writing that winter was his first nature story, "Benny and the Fox." For this piece he altered his style slightly to appeal to a more youthful readership by exploring the personality of an individual animal rather than the habits of a whole species. From this beginning would develop the animal adventure stories that would not only make him famous but would also threaten to destroy his credibility as a naturalist.

In January 1884, encouraged by Charles Broughton who was already a member, Seton joined the Art Students League of New York. The League was a rendezvous for young artists, and also provided classes where they could upgrade their talents. The instructors were all recognized artists, with a strong element of the radical among them, but it was the influence of the Munich schools of art that predominated in League classes, as both Walter Shirlaw, who taught composition, and William Chase Merritt, the painting and drawing instructor, had trained in that city. The Munich schools specialized in the technique of drawing directly on the canvas with paint, a method that allowed more spontaneity of expression than the British or Paris schools, which demanded careful and accurate drawing. However, there were also Paris-trained instructors at the school, and Seton, whose approach to art was still essentially cautious, chose one of these as his instructor. William Sartain had studied in Paris under Boulanger and Bonnat, both of whom were known for their portrait painting in the academic tradition, and as a result, his own style was founded on meticulous technique. Sartain's life drawing class was the first that Seton had attended — life drawing at the Royal Academy had meant live hands, feet and heads — and he was delighted when, within weeks of enrolling, Sartain selected one of his drawings for special praise.

At the end of March 1884 Seton advised Sacket, Wilhelms and Betzig that he planned to return to Manitoba because "the Call of the West" had become too strong for him to resist.[9] While it is true that he would always prefer the open spaces of the west to the cities of the east, the irresistible call he heard had actually arrived in the form of a reminder from Arthur that unless he returned to help with the spring planting at De Winton Farm, he could not expect help building his claim shack on the Duck Mountain homestead. Although Seton knew that he would never become a real farmer, ownership of the homestead was important to his self-image. As a "frontier naturalist" he felt he had to be a man of the land, not just another visiting amateur scientist, and he could only stake Manitoba as his own natural history territory if he could legally claim some small part of it as his own. Building his cabin, therefore, was not just a legal requirement for ownership of the land but a symbol of the fulfillment of the promise he had made himself to strike out on his own. To his friend Jack Willing he wrote:

> I know that if I fix my mind on such a thing and am willing to pay the price and determined to attain to it there is no adversary power can stop it. So it *must* be ever with any that *wills*. For will is the

greatest power under the sun. There are only three (secularly speaking): Money, Knowledge, and Will. The last controls the 1st and 2nd, and 2nd controls the first. The first controls neither of the others, and he who wills can be both wealthy and wise to the fullest. [10]

There was no doubt about Seton's willpower, and he was acquiring knowledge and filing it away in his journals. Wealth would take a little longer, but by the time he left New York on 14 April 1884, he had repaid all borrowed monies, except that owed to his father, and had put by one hundred dollars for the future.

Seton had been back at De Winton Farm for nearly three weeks when Arthur arrived to begin the spring ploughing. Once the crops were planted, they set out for the new homestead claims at Duck Mountain, arriving there 8 June. On Seton's land they prepared a shallow well close to the stream and then began felling trees for the cabin. In this operation, Seton acted as helper; Arthur was an expert with the broadaxe and could not only fell a tree on the exact spot he wished but also could hew planks with it as neatly as if they had been sawn. The finished cabin was eight feet by twelve feet. Woodstrips were nailed into the cracks between the logs and then plastered with clay for windproofing. The roof had a shallow pitch formed by resting rafter poles on a thick central ridgepole; on top of the rafters they spread a layer of wild prairie hay, then a six-inch layer of clay from the stream bed. Finally, Arthur created a plank door, and in the lintel over it Seton carved: E. T. Seton, 1884.

Had he really intended to farm, Seton would soon have realized the drawbacks of the land he had chosen for himself; it would never produce crops like those on De Winton because it was too far north. For a budding naturalist, however, the Duck Mountain homestead was ideal. Exulting in the cabin's completion, Seton wrote to Willing:

Stand upon the hill with me, the hill whereon now is a white-washed shanty with my name on the lintel. It is early morning now, so early that it is yet dark. The yellow stars are still bright in the smooth blue-purple sky, all below is dark. But in an hour or two it is changed. All above is bright and all below is a firmament: the broad prairie in the rising sun like a golden sky spangled with blue-purple stars, the reverse of the sky-flowers are these prairie stars, — but just as many. They are lavished on every side, shapely six-rayed stars — we call their kind stargrass — books call them blue iris, and mingled with them are as many of the golden orange Puccoon blossoms, gilding the land in places. I thrust my hand into the grass once and plucked and counted the Puccoons in that one handful. 175 perfect blossoms and buds innumerable! And over there [amid] millions of purple and orange flowers there are thousands of purple and orange butterflies, and all this lavish beauty is nothing to what you may see.

The Prairie rolls away and higher on the next ridge are wild roses — you cannot see them from here, but you note a pink mist along the broad hillside and catch the smell of their sweetness. I have read of Persian roses and seen some noble garden displays but all that I ever saw or read of sinks into meanness when compared with the unsullied loveliness of the spotless burning intensity of these Roses of Assiniboia.

And the prairie rolls away and rises to the Duck Mountain and in a deeper hollow whence comes a cold spring stream — "sown in a wrinkle of the monstrous hill" — is a tamarack swamp. . . . The burley plants of the plain are barred from this place, the loud harsh birds of the open have learnt to shun the spot. Here we find the delicate Droserae and the many dyed pitcher plants, the Solomon's seal and the primrose, and orchids rare are everywhere. While in the upper boughs the rarest of the golden warblers move about at home, and the veery's soul and the hermit's hymn are heard from the distant solitudes. . . .[11]

Even as Seton catalogued the wild beauty of his new farm, he knew that cultivating it — as he was required to do in order to earn legal title to it — would destroy the very beauty that had drawn him to the spot. In fact, it took less than ten years for the southern Manitoba prairie as he knew it during these years to disappear. On a visit to Carberry in 1892 he found that the lakes had become marshes and the marshes farmland. The prairie birds were gone, and of the animals, only the yellow gophers, which burrow deep into the ground, and the coyotes, which have learned to exist in the shadow of man, had flourished. But for Seton "the biggest change of all was that made by the plough.

The rich old level prairie, with a myriad of sweet and delicate flowers, was gone — wholly gone — turned into farmers' fields of grain. The sweet sandflower, pasque flower, crown of the springtime, was gone . . . replaced with Canada thistle, Russian thistle, tumbleweeds."[12]

Construction of Seton's claim shanty took only a week, and then, since Arthur had no interest in building a cabin on the land that Seton had claimed for him, the two men began the return journey. They set off by way of the Cotai Indian country to the northwest so that Arthur, who was keenly interested in geology, could examine some land formations he had heard about. When they came to the upper reaches of the Assiniboine River, they attempted a crossing and would have lost both team and equipment except for the help of an Indian who came to their rescue. He was a Cree named Chita.

When the man joined them at their evening campfire, Seton, who until this time had only met Indians coming to buy supplies at the Carberry general store, decided to find out if it was true that Indians, out of politeness, would always mimic the manners of their hosts. He found that Chita carefully followed his example when he went through an elaborate ritual with his tea cup, and did the same when he used his knife and fork in an eccentric way; Seton would have experimented further, but Arthur indicated that he was to stop.

The return trip took them three hundred miles out of their way so that they did not arrive in Carberry until 26 June. During the entire three weeks they were away, the two had not held a single conversation. Arthur used speech only when absolutely necessary, expressing himself instead with Indian sign language or the occasional monosyllable. For the rest of the summer the two men worked side by side in utter silence from dawn to dark; then, by lantern light, Arthur pored over his medical texts while Seton worked at his easel or dissected specimens. Seton regarded his brother's silence as an eccentricity; it never occurred to him that he had done anything to irritate him, yet Arthur's memoirs make it clear that Seton's work habits were a continual source of annoyance.

Seton could still find time to observe birds and small animal life even while ploughing out potatoes or stacking sheaves, and each night he made one or two careful drawings or prepared the skins of rodents or other small creatures. He now had a recipient in mind for both drawings and specimens: the secretary of the American Ornithologists Union, Dr. C. Hart Merriam. On his return journey from New York that spring he had gone to visit Merriam at Locust Grove in the Adirondacks. Merriam had heard of Seton from Spencer Baird of the Smithsonian, and had written to him at Carberry; when his letter caught up with Seton in New York, the two men arranged a visit. Merriam, only six years older than Seton, was a medical doctor who came from a wealthy, politically prominent family, but his primary interest was in natural history. When Seton gave him a demonstration of his gift for animal drawing, Merriam had been so impressed that he ordered fifty more drawings, but in June a letter arrived in Carberry from Merriam saying that Seton's first submissions, although beautiful, had too much detail and shading to be reproduced economically. Seton accepted the criticism and thereafter made his drawings simpler, concentrating on the creature's outline and identifying characteristics. He also reduced his asking price, for Merriam had protested that his pictures cost too much.

The harvest was late that year and the two brothers were still working in the fields when the first heavy snow fell on 26 October. Seton had made up his mind that he would culminate his prairie experience with one final success: he would shoot a deer. Until this time, though he had often spotted deer tracks around De Winton Farm, the only wild deer he had ever seen had been the one shot by his brother Joseph on the Lindsay farm. Now, with fresh snow on the ground, he decided to follow the tracks that led across his brother's farm and into the nearby woods. For a week he went out each day, and though there were plenty of tracks, he still saw no deer. Then, early in November, while in Arthur's company, he saw seven deer in a single day, but was so fascinated by their effortless leaps as they bounded gracefully into the distance that he forgot to fire at them.

The next afternoon he wounded a deer, which ran away. Following its track, he met a Cree Indian who was also tracking it. It was too late to continue the hunt that night, but the next day when he again went after the deer, the Indian and his companions had already killed it. Seton demanded to know why they had taken his deer, and the Indian told him that a wild animal belonged to the man who killed it. Intrigued by the man's calm logic, Seton invited himself along on the Indian's hunting expedition.

His name, Seton learned, was Chaska. He was as tall as Seton but more powerfully built, and dressed in the usual Cree blanket and leggings. Like many of his people, he was a poor marksman, but his tracking skills were so refined that he found at least twice as many opportunities to shoot as most white hunters did. Seton had tracked animals on many occasions and had learned to interpret each variation in the pattern of tracks: he understood a fox's hunting methods and could see where a mouse had become prey to a hawk. But Chaska's knowledge of deer tracking was such an exact science that he could even anticipate the animal's future movements. Seton, always eager to learn more about animals, became Chaska's devoted student; in the end, though, the subject he studied most carefully was the Indian himself.

Seton's pleasure in finally getting to know an Indian was increased by the fact that the man seemed to have come straight out of a James Fenimore Cooper "good Indian" mould. When neighbours that he met in the Carberry general store assured Seton that Chaska was not a typical Indian, Seton continued to think of the average Indian as the crafty, scalp-hunting savage of his boyhood's storybooks, rather than as an individual like Chaska, with a distinct and valuable culture worthy of his investigation. It was only as he became more disillusioned with the benefits of pioneer life that he gradually began to look to the Indian people for a solution to the white man's problems.

Although Seton watched while Chaska bagged deer, he was unsuccessful himself; in late November, however, he and a friend found themselves on the trail of a moose. After three days of tracking they shot it, only to have it claimed by a Sioux Indian. Now Seton had an opportunity to view one of the "notoriously quarrelsome" Sioux[13] at close hand and make comparisons with the noble Chaska. While his friend went for a sleigh to bring the carcass out of the woods, Seton held the Indian at bay and argued over possession. At length the man disappeared into the woods, threatening to bring his friends to take the moose; fortunately, the sleigh arrived before the Indians.

Having "killed the grandest beast of chase that roams America's woods," Seton was temporarily jubilant, but his pleasure soon faded to remorse. He had transformed this "superb animal . . . into a pile of butcher's meat for the sake of a passing thrill of triumph."[14] Once more he made a vow — reminiscent of his vows after the deaths of the baby crow and the shorelark — this time that he would never again lift his rifle against any of America's big game as long as extinction threatened them. The new vow left him free to kill wolves, foxes and other mammals, as well as birds, but it was the first step in a process that would change him into an outspoken conservationist.

This final adventure in Manitoba became the story "The Hunting of the Moose," which in turn became the inspiration for *The Trail of the Sandhill Stag,* published in 1899. In dedicating the book to "The Old-timers of the Big Plain of Manitoba," Seton was also dedicating it to himself and to a time when the stargrass and puccoons had still blossomed on the plain, for he considered these the best days of his life, his "Golden Days."[15]

Arthur did not regard his brother's moose with any pleasure whatsoever. He had been visiting with Charlie and his family in Portage la Prairie and returned, as he wrote in his memoir,

> late one bitter cold day to find the most disorderly state of affairs in the house that could possibly be imagined. The hard frozen carcass of the moose had been skinned in the kitchen, the frozen hide lying on the floor which was littered with moose hair, chips of frozen meat, the table covered with dirty dishes mixed with scraps of bread, etc., writing materials, the couch a common resting place for blankets, dirty socks, boots, etc., very little firewood, altogether a welcome home I have no wish to experience a second time.[16]

The moose hunt marked the end of Seton's Manitoba experience, twenty-five months that would prove to be the most productive in his evolution as a naturalist. Here he was working in virgin territory as far as natural history was concerned, a territory which provided him with a foundation of information no other worker in the field could match. He would make the mistake of assuming that because he possessed this information he had become a naturalist, and he would misinterpret some of his information because of his lack of training; nevertheless, he had moved much closer to his desired goal.

Seton never returned to his Duck Mountain land; once he had made the symbolic gesture of building the cabin, the homestead held little further interest for him. He was also beginning to realize that the pioneer who ploughed up the land and drained the swamps was anathema to the naturalist, and that only the way of the Indian could preserve the wildlife of the west.

On 15 January 1885 Seton left De Winton Farm for the last time. Arthur had already departed for medical school in the final week of November — in those days starting dates were delayed to accommodate the harvest — and, having no further need for the farm, had sold it to a neighbour. He would finance his remaining years at medical school with scholarships, and in the summer of 1885 would be employed as a field dresser with the troops called out to quell the Riel Rebellion. By disposing of the farm, Arthur was also spared his brother's inroads upon his privacy.

10

The Bones of
Contention

Seton, who had left Toronto in March 1882 vowing that
he would never return to his father's house, returned there — or
at least to his brother Joseph's house where his father and mother
were living — at the end of January 1885. He brought his bird
collections and the mass of notes and journals that he had accumulated for a book he intended to write on the birds of Manitoba,
and he settled down to twelve- to eighteen-hour days preparing
his work for publication. Throughout the spring and on into the
summer, he laboured over this project, taking time off only to
join collecting forays in the local countryside.

The bird book was still far from complete when Seton left
for New York on 17 September. He complained that "the home
government" — his brother Joseph in this case — had suggested
that he and his collections were too much for the household,[1]
but Seton had intended to go in any case because in New York
he would be much closer to Merriam and Coues. He had also
begun to realize that the data he had collected were inadequate
for a volume with which he hoped to impress the scientific
community.

When he returned to New York this time, instead of looking
for a job in a drafting department, Seton set himself up as a free-
lance illustrator. He obtained his first commission by turning up

with a drawing of a mule deer at the *Century Magazine* office of W. Lewis Fraser, the art manager to whom he had sold the picture of the tanager in the fall of 1883. Shortly after this, Fraser asked Elliott Coues to edit the biological entries in the new six-volume *Century Dictionary*. Coues agreed on condition that his young protégé, Seton, would be hired to make the one thousand or more drawings necessary to illustrate his entries. This commission provided Seton with a steady income for more than a year and still allowed him to accept other commissions.

By the time the American Ornithologists Union met at the Museum of Natural History on 18 November, Seton was already on close terms with three of the leading members — Coues, Merriam and Baird — and at the meeting he was introduced to Joel Allen, Frank Chapman, William Brewster and Robert Ridgway, all respected scientists who would play important roles in Seton's future. Allen was the new curator of the bird collection at the Museum of Natural History; Chapman was his assistant. Brewster had succeeded to Allen's former position as curator at the Harvard Museum of Comparative Zoology, and Ridgway was curator of birds at the Smithsonian. To Seton's delight, he found that this distinguished company accepted him as one of their own, mostly on the strength of recommendations by Baird and Coues, but also because of the detailed accuracy of his illustrations for Merriam. Since he was already established as an illustrator of birds and animals, it seemed to Seton that he would only have to publish *The Birds of Manitoba* to be recognized as a naturalist as well. Unfortunately, before he could do that, there were those one thousand drawings to prepare for the *Century Dictionary* and a set of illustrations to make for Merriam's new book on American mammals.

Seton worked steadily for the next eight months in the attic rooms he had taken at 51 East 9th Street, only pausing to make forays to the New York and Philadelphia zoos to check details of the animals he was drawing. For a man accustomed to Manitoba's open plains, this was a long time to be cooped up in the city, and when he received a request from Toronto that he take his brother William away while he recovered from a serious illness, Seton packed his bags and headed north. The two men left Toronto on a fine October day on the CPR's *Arthabasca* headed for Port Arthur. In the Lake of the Woods area, Seton collected specimens and took notes while William followed, impressed by his younger brother's "indefatigable energy." Seton was "always busy," William wrote. "Even during the evenings he would be preparing his specimens or else getting his traps ready."[2]

Seton went on alone to Carberry, but on 23 November, while on a collecting expedition five miles beyond town, his right knee suddenly became rigid and painful. He hobbled back to Carberry where the local doctor treated him for muscle strain; the knee, however, continued to give him pain and made further long field trips on foot impossible. Many years later, Seton would be told that this attack was acute arthritis; in any case, it provided a reason for a change in his mode of travel in the future.

On his return to Toronto in January 1887 he was confronted by the elder Thompsons who were now determined to resolve the family name problem. Seton had been the only one of the brothers to actually change his surname, and the family was intent on persuading him to change it back again. Alice Thompson made the appeal. Convinced that his mother must be obeyed in all things, Seton agreed to resume the Thompson surname except on his published material where he would use, as a nom de plume, the name Ernest Seton-Thompson.

Then, apparently to compensate him for giving up his chosen name, and possibly to indicate the family's approval of his budding career as an illustrator, Joseph Jr. offered Seton the post of caretaker on a development estate he was buying near Port Credit on Lake Ontario. In return for his caretaking duties, Seton would be given a studio cabin rent-free and have the freedom of eighty-six acres of wooded land abounding in wildlife. The arrangement was similar to the one he had enjoyed at De Winton Farm, except that his duties at Port Credit would be far less onerous and he would not have to share his living quarters. His new home also had the advantage of being close to Toronto and within a day's travel of New York. In spite of these benefits, Seton might still have returned to New York but for the fact that his brother's property was only a short walk from Mount Woodham, the home of Charlotte Schreiber. Although it was eight years since he had worked at his easel in her studio, she still regarded him as her protégé and encouraged his visits.

Seton moved into his new quarters in May 1887 and remained in residence there for two and a half years. The bulk of his time was spent on the completion of *The Birds of Manitoba,* but he also took on illustrating commissions, some of them for popular journals, and prepared articles from his field notes for such periodicals as *Auk* and *Field and Stream.* His most important accomplishment during this period, though he did not consider it so at the time, was the drafting of his first real nature stories: "The Springfield Fox," "Dabbles the Coon" and "Molly Cottontail." He also collected most of the data on which he based "Bannertail the Squirrel," "Why Does the Chicadee Go Crazy Twice a Year?" and "The Song of the Golden-Crowned Thrush."

Seton would probably have been content to remain in this retreat indefinitely, but events occurred which somewhat soured the idyll. In returning to Charlotte Schreiber's circle, he also renewed his contact with her stepchildren. Lisle was now married to Ottilie Grahame and had built his own home, Ivorholme, on the family estate. Susie Grahame, who had spurned Seton when he was an art student, was a frequent guest there, and an even more frequent one at Mount Woodham, so inevitably Susie and Seton became reacquainted. Having forecast a marriage for himself in 1890 to a girl of Susie's qualifications, Seton renewed his suit and for a time appeared to be in favour with the lady. Charlotte Schreiber, in anticipation of the impending marriage, painted a picture of Ottilie, Susie and Seton together, but no engagement took place. (A few years later, when Susie did marry, her new husband asked Charlotte to paint Seton out of the picture. She did so, substituting a portrait of another Grahame sister, Vio, in his place.)

Annie Wood became Seton's next love. Her father was the owner of the prosperous wholesale dry goods company, Gordon Mackay Limited; her brother James was its manager. Annie's description exactly fitted the wife Seton had forecast: light brown hair, blue eyes, neither too tall nor too thin, and of English parentage. She was calm where he was mercurial in temper, stoical and sweetly trusting where he was convinced that he was the victim of persecution. They were mismatched in only one thing: Annie was a devout evangelical Presbyterian and Seton had by this time completely rejected religion. To please his mother he attended church when he was in Toronto, but his life in the open had nurtured his unavoidable rebellion against her rigid Calvinism. The pantheism with which he would eventually replace the religion of his boyhood had not yet become structured in his mind, though he was moving toward a recognition of God-in-Nature that would underlay his later work with boys, a philosophy in direct conflict with Annie's evangelism.

Their romance seems to have begun in 1888 and ended in late 1889: Seton complained bitterly that she had cruelly rejected him; Annie lamented that he had not fought for her when "pappa . . . said we could never be happy."[3] But the crux of the matter seems to have been the disparity in their religious outlooks. Annie eventually made a career as a street corner evangelist and, as the honorary secretary of the Christian Police Association of Toronto, did welfare work among policemen's families and the poor. To the day of her death, however, Seton was "the only man [she] ever loved."[4]

In the end, it was business problems that decided Seton's next move. Joseph Thompson had envisioned his park as a resort area in the manner of Hanlan's Hotel on Toronto Island or Duck's Hotel and Pleasure Grounds at the mouth of the Humber River, and he planned to take advantage of the excursion boats that shuttled between the city and Lorne Park, which adjoined his property, to transport his clientele back and forth. His troubles began when the Lorne Park Company objected to sharing their dock facilities and refused to allow charter boats destined for their landing to service Thompson clientele. In the meantime, Joseph Jr. had built a new home for his father — Glen Cottage, at 86 Howard Street — and then overextended himself by building a new home for his own family. Unfortunately, he had invested all his money and the savings of several of his brothers in the Port Credit property, and this money was all lost when the mortgage was foreclosed in December 1889.

There was none of Seton's money in this venture; instead, all his earnings from illustrations and articles had been invested in real estate within the city. When forced to vacate his studio in the park, he sold his real estate interests, paid his father the last $450 of the amount still outstanding on his "life bill," bought himself a steamer ticket to England and, in June 1890, with twelve hundred dollars in his pocket, departed from Toronto.

Ever since his return from London and his confrontation with his father in the fall of 1881, Seton had been striving for recognition as a naturalist, all the while supporting himself as an illustrator for others in the field. But two and a half years in close proximity to Mount Woodham and the coterie of Canadian artists who frequented it had revitalized an old ambition. In London he had forecast a career for himself as an artist-naturalist, not just an illustrator-naturalist, yet, except for a few months of night classes at the Art Students League in New York in the winter of 1883–84, he had done nothing to enhance his prestige as an artist. He could see that many of his paintings were better than some that were hung in the Ontario Society of Artists gallery, but he could also see that the most acclaimed pictures there — and in the galleries of New York and Chicago — were those painted by artists who had trained abroad. He had, of course, attended classes at the Royal Academy for a few months, but by 1890 it was the art schools of Paris, where impressionism had originated, that dominated the world art scene. All of the younger artists, such as George Reid and Paul Peel, had studied in Paris, and it was soon obvious to Seton that the key to their artistic prestige was their Salon training.

He arrived in England on 11 June 1890, visited with his relatives in South Shields, then crossed the Channel on 23 August. When he found the art schools still in summer recess, he returned to London "where at least [he] could study animals in the zoo."[5] He learned from another young artist that Joseph Wolf, the prestigious German painter of animals, lived only a few blocks from the zoo, and Seton introduced himself by taking some of his own drawings to the old man's studio. This "genial old Santa Claus" received Seton in his home several times during the next three months, and Seton "always came away helped and encouraged."[6] "Wolf," he wrote in a letter to a friend, "told me that I would not find anyone in Paris who could teach me anything about animals."[7]

At the end of November he returned to Paris, and after a few days in transient hotels found himself a small apartment on the top floor of a residential hotel on the rue Croix des Petits Champs. He was in complete disharmony with the city at first, partly because of the language barrier and partly because of his intensely British upbringing and experiences. He visited the Eiffel Tower and concluded that his "pocket was the worse for the trip and I don't know that I'm any the better."[8] He stood outside the Palais de Justice and the Cathédrale de Notre Dame and, though they were both open and free to the public, felt no desire to enter them, but a little farther down the street he enjoyed a half hour watching two dirty cocksparrows fighting for possession of a horseball. He wrote to his friend Henry Steele, "I feel well enough in body but oh so miserably homesick. . . . I am sick of this wretched much belauded village."[9]

Once he set about enrolling in classes and learning the language, much of the strangeness dissipated, though he was never completely comfortable in these alien surroundings. He could appreciate the informality of life in Paris, yet found it unacceptable that churches and brothels could exist there side by side, and while he heartily endorsed the Frenchman's lack of piety, he was forever amazed at the pornographic literature sold openly in the shops.

Seton did not apply for admission to the prestigious Ecole des Beaux-Arts, possibly because he was unwilling to waste time on the long application process and possibly because most of his friends in the art world had taken their training elsewhere. Both Peel and Reid had attended the Académie Julian, and it was here that Seton also enrolled. Julian's was nothing like the Ontario School of Art or the Royal Academy and only roughly similar to the Art Students League. It was, in fact, not a school but rather a number of attic studios, each under the "sponsorship" of a professor from the Ecole des Beaux-Arts. In each studio the art students set up their easels every day except Sunday, with a live model as the usual subject, and once a week the professor would visit the studio to criticize the work they had done. Although there were no examinations to be passed and no regular attendance requirements, the students laboured at their easels conscientiously because those enrolled at the Académie Julian were allowed to submit their paintings for the juried exhibition held each spring at the Salon. The jury members were all teachers at the Ecole des Beaux-Arts, and many of them also gave instruction at Julian's.

The noise level in the attic studios was deafening during the fifty-five-minute periods in which the model posed. There was "loud talking, . . . chorus singing, even guitar playing, though all were supposed to be working at their easels."[10] Seton complained to his friend Steele, "All day long, . . . we swap smut and sing hymns of the Beecham's Pills order."[11] Pandemonium broke out whenever the model took a five-minute rest break, with practical jokes and fist fighting taking over from art. Seton, who had enrolled at the studio where Bougereau gave instruction, was required to justify his entry into this company of artists on his first day, and when given a choice of dancing, singing, fighting or buying drinks, chose to buy wine for the thirty artists working there.

In spite of the racket and total disorganization, Seton learned much that was "never hinted at" in his previous training,[12] and the series of nudes that he drew during this period at Julian's show a mastery of the human form that had so far eluded him. Most of the models were peasants from the countryside around Paris so that there is a coarseness in the muscular forms depicted in Seton's drawings; there is also, however, especially in his female nudes, definite grace and strength of line. Surprisingly, the most exciting nude portrait that he did at this time is an oil painting of himself, which not only reveals his mastery of technique but also the muscular perfection of his body.

As Wolf had predicted, Seton did not find anyone to teach him animal painting in Paris. Jean Gérôme, then one of the foremost French realists, while praising his animal sketches, told him to forget about animals for a while and take a course in figure drawing. Gustave Wertheimer, to whom he was introduced by the *Century Magazine* representative in France, looked over his sketches and announced that he could teach him nothing about animals. "You are my master now," he told Seton, "but I can teach you something about painting."[13] With such tepid encouragement, Seton was forced to continue his animal painting on his own. Since he was only enrolled for morning classes at Julian's after his first term there, he was free to sketch in the Jardin des Plantes Ménagerie each afternoon. Here he discovered a number of wolves, and one of them, a beautiful grey specimen, took a nap at almost the same time each day. Seton would position his easel outside the cage and wait until the animal settled itself, because it obliged him by taking almost the same position in the same spot every time.

Although he had become very familiar with coyotes, or prairie wolves, in Manitoba, it was still the timber wolf that intrigued him most, and he had only once seen a specimen in the wild. The caged creatures were obviously his best hope of studying and painting the species at close range, and in spite of their captivity they proved to be more than adequate for his purposes. They were well fed and in no way tamed, so that even in sleep the power and ferocity they possessed in the wild was still evident.

Seton delivered his painting of "The Sleeping Wolf" to the Salon on 20 March 1891. Then, in the company of his artist friend, Robert Henri, and other students from Julian's, he set off to join the parade of students marching happily down the Champs-Elysées. They were led by a famous red-haired model named Sara Brun, who unfortunately chose to use her red parasol as a baton. The police, interpreting this as a flag of anarchy, arrested her and dispersed the parade.

"The Sleeping Wolf" was not only accepted by the Salon jury, it was also hung at "waist level," not "skyed" as often happened to the work of new painters. This was quite a coup for Seton, especially since the jury included Gérôme who had been so apathetic about his animal studies. However, it is possible that the jury excused the subject matter because of the artist's mastery of a painting technique that was reminiscent of Gérôme's own work. Robert Henri's submission was rejected because he had begun experimenting with impressionism in his work and Gérôme regarded this as "filth."[14]

The success of the wolf painting gave a tremendous boost to Seton's morale. In late January he had received the first copy of his *Birds of Manitoba* and was extremely disappointed. Originally, it had been submitted to a number of Canadian publishers, but was rejected even after repeated revisions. Finally, just before Seton went abroad in 1890, Spencer Baird of the Smithsonian Institution agreed to publish it as repayment for Seton's contributions from Manitoba. It was arranged that Robert Ridgway, the Smithsonian's curator of birds, would edit the work, with Seton stipulating that he wanted the right to proof the galleys before they went into print. The manuscript, however, had been sent directly to the printers after Ridgway was finished with it. Seton claimed in his memoirs that the book "came out overflowing with errors and misprints that have made it one of the dark spots in my memory,"[15] but correspondence that passed between Seton and Ridgway at the time the book was published indicates that Ridgway and Baird had serious doubts about the value of the manuscript. In answer to complaints about his editing, Ridgway replied that "the manuscript was, without exception, the worst

I ever saw," and he explained that he had cut large portions from it because Seton had used excessive repetition of trivial and irrelevant details.[16] Seton reacted by angrily declaring that he was sorry he had wasted his time writing the thing.

The main problem with the book stemmed from Seton's lack of scientific training. In a foreword to a 1980 edition of *The Birds of Manitoba*, C. Stuart Houston marvelled that Seton's observations were so remarkably accurate.

> These were the days before good field guides and good binoculars, and more than half a century before the production of good bird song records. There were no experts from whom one could learn. Coues's *Key* required a specimen in the hand; to key out the hawks, for example, one would count how many primary feathers were notched. Seton carefully sent his specimens to the Smithsonian Institution for verification, and the only apparent error in identification of specimens is the "Acadian Flycatcher." Others who published books about birds in western Canada at this time made more errors than did Seton. . . .[17]

For many of the scientific community the book failed because Seton had begun to develop the anecdotal style which would later make him America's most popular animal story writer. *The Birds of Manitoba* is rich with incidents of Seton's relationships with the creatures he was observing. Had he enlarged on these anecdotes and published it as a popular volume on bird lore, it might have been a commercial success. As it was, this venture into publishing only provoked one of his more petulant responses, and he turned away from ornithology to concentrate on the study of mammals. It also caused him to regard all future publishing contracts with suspicion.

The success of "The Sleeping Wolf" following so closely on his book's lukewarm reception led Seton directly into one of his most humiliating experiences. Having pleased the Salon jury with his wolf picture, he set out to woo them with an animal painting on a far grander scale, a painting that would also include the kind of narrative in which the Académie members specialized. In the French newspapers at this time was a horrendous tale of a woodsman in the Pyrenees who had been eaten by wolves. The man had apparently been responsible for slaying a number of these animals in the past and the newspapers capitalized on this by ascribing his death to the animals' revenge. Seton, as the champion of the persecuted wolf, determined to paint the scene for his next Salon entry, and to call it "The Triumph of the Wolves."

On 6 January 1892, encouraged by his artist friends who insisted that such a grand theme required an enormous canvas, he prepared one nearly four and a half by seven feet, and began making detail sketches for the painting. Next, having found a suitable landscape in a park five miles outside Paris, he constructed a mock-up of the scene as he envisioned it, using several wolf skins, a skull and some human bones he acquired from a medical school, peasants' clothing and sabots, and a bucket of blood which he bought at a nearby slaughterhouse. When all was ready and he had set up his easel, two forest rangers pounced on him, convinced they had stumbled on the scene of a murder. He was released from custody only after lengthy explanations.

Seton carried out the rest of his preparations for painting his masterpiece in a more circumspect manner, each day setting off into the January dusk to make tone, value and colour studies, and each evening, with dead dogs as models, making sketches for the wolves. In late February, when he was finally ready to paint, he found that his canvas was too large for his own meager studio and was forced to rent space in the studio of friends. The painting took a month to complete, and all that time while Seton painted, the art community of Paris dropped by to watch and pass judgement on the work. From the admiring comments that he heard, Seton came to believe that he had a Salon winner.

When the picture was almost complete, one of his friends convinced him to change the title from "The Triumph of the Wolves" to "Awaited in Vain." The new title, however, transferred the focus of the picture from the wolves and their retribution to the pathos of the family, waiting for the woodsman in the cottage just over the brow of the hill. At the same time, it changed the quality of the narrative from grim drama to Victorian melodrama. Seton was absolutely confident of success. The jurors, however, rejected the painting; Seton was shocked to learn that they had described it as offensive and horrible.

A month after the rejection he was back in Manitoba for the summer, visiting his old haunts and collecting specimens. Again he was disappointed, for the prairie he loved had become farm-land, and as the grasses were ploughed under and the marshes and lakes were drained, the creatures of the prairie were disappearing. Seton himself felt old. At thirty-two he already wore glasses for his close work, yet his eyes still pained him. Since his knee injury, he could no longer stride across the prairie as he had ten years earlier, and was reduced to renting a horse and buggy for his sketching expeditions. He felt that "the joy of youth was gone."[18]

That summer he made one contact which would shortly prove extremely useful. In Winnipeg he called at the taxidermy shop of Will and Calvin Hine, and there met a man named Scott who had been appointed by the Manitoba government to prepare an exhibit for the great World's Columbian Exposition which was to open in Chicago in June 1893. Scott was looking for mounted specimens of Manitoba animal and bird life and was pleased when Seton offered his help in making a selection from the local taxidermy shops and from the provincial museum.

In Toronto in mid-September, having learned from Scott that Manitoba's premier, Thomas Greenway, was at a conference there, Seton called on him at his hotel to make a proposal: Green-way was to name him official naturalist to the provincial govern-ment without salary but with a modest per diem rate and expenses when on government business, and in return Seton would prepare a unique natural history exhibit for the Exposition. Both Greenway and Seton knew that Scott had almost completed the overall provincial exhibit which already included natural his-tory specimens; nevertheless, the premier agreed to the proposal, and on 2 November 1892 a provincial government order-in-coun-cil confirmed Seton's appointment. With provincial funds in his pocket, he then began buying specimens from Toronto taxider-mists.

Busy with his new task, Seton found it convenient to return to the family home once more. This time his mother charged him board at three dollars per week, but he "voluntarily raised it to $5."[19] Alan and Arthur were also living with their parents: Alan was promoting a new real estate development; Arthur had built up a small medical practice and on the side was working with a partner examining properties for mining companies and doing assay work. Seton invested several hundred dollars in their schemes.

Soon after Seton moved into Glen Cottage, George Reid called to say that Seton's name had been put before the OSA for membership and that he had been accepted. Then Reid encouraged Seton to enter the Royal Canadian Academy's juried exhibition to be held in April of the following year, as a selection from that exhibition would be displayed at the Chicago Exposition. In order to drum up popular support for their paintings, most of the OSA members were renting gallery space for public showings before they submitted their work to the competition; Reid suggested that Seton should do the same. Pleased that his rejected wolf canvas would have another chance, Seton had it sent from Paris and on 15 November put it on display in his parents' drawing room along with "The Sleeping Wolf," a half dozen pictures from his Port Credit days, several studies of Manitoba deer and other prairie animals, some of the Rosedale Ravine, and two or three he had painted in Fontainebleau Park.

The show was rewarded with an unprecedented number of newspaper reviews, most of them complimentary about the whole exhibit but somewhat ambivalent about "Awaited in Vain." *Saturday Night* featured a photograph of the painting on its 3 December front page. This publicity brought so many people to see the painting that Seton was forced to move his show from his parents' home to a gallery at the rear of J. E. Ellis's Jewellery on King Street. In this new location, reported *Saturday Night,* it attracted "thousands of people and all pronounce it a work of genius. . . . If it is not sent to Chicago the public will regard it as something worse than a blunder."[20]

One of those who came to see the paintings during their month-long showing was Prof. James Mavor, the controversial Scotsman who had taken over the chair of Political Economy at the University of Toronto just months earlier. Mavor, although educated as a scientist and economist, was deeply involved in promoting cultural activities, and saw a great need for his efforts in a country where culture seemed to be "a kind of craze."[21] He made it his business to encourage artists and soon became Seton's good friend and patron.

Another of those who came to see the show was the poet Pauline Johnson who had embarked on a career as a recitalist the previous January. The daughter of an English woman and a Mohawk chief, she had achieved enormous popularity as

"Tekahionwake, The Mohawk Princess." When George Reid brought her to the Ellis Gallery, according to Seton, "she seized both my hands in both of hers, and said: 'I know that we are kin. I am a Mohawk of the Wolf Clan, and that picture shows that you must be a wolf spirit come back in human form.' "[22] Later she sent him a silver talisman in the shape of a wolf. Seton accepted her pronouncement as confirmation of an identity that he had always believed lay hidden within him.

In January the OSA opened an exhibition of members' work that was to be considered for the Chicago show. Each artist was allotted a section of wall space to hang as many paintings as there was room for. Because of the massive size of "Awaited in Vain," Seton only had room for a few of his smaller pictures; he did not enter "The Sleeping Wolf." On 20 January the Royal Canadian Academy jury chose 24 oils and 18 watercolours from nearly 150 in the exhibition, but since some of these would be eliminated after a selection was made from a similar show to be held in Montreal, the jury refused to release a list of the paintings chosen. *Saturday Night,* not suffering from the same delicacy of feeling, printed the names of the winners; "Awaited in Vain" was on the list.

On 21 February the exhibition at Montreal's Gallery of Art opened with all of the Montreal Art Society's entries on display plus those selected from the OSA. By 1 March Seton knew that "Awaited in Vain" had been one of the paintings eliminated in the Montreal round of judging. He was thoroughly crushed by this second rejection.

The OSA executive, however, reacted with outrage, but not for Seton's sake alone. At stake was the control of the RCA. The jury that had chosen the paintings for the Chicago show had included two Toronto artists — George Reid was one of them — and three artists from Montreal, all three of whom voted against inclusion of "Awaited in Vain" on the grounds that the subject matter was "ghastly and loathsome,"[23] particularly in the foreground area where the remains of the woodsman had been painted in exquisite detail. This criticism prompted Robert Gagen of the OSA to dub the painting "The Bones of Contention," and this bit of black humour renewed the interest of newspapers and periodicals. *The Week,* which had commended Seton for his "magic mastery of art" and his "romantic idealism," now demanded "fair play for Mr. Thompson";[24] *Saturday Night* expressed the hope that the artist would accept his rejection as a sign that the public wanted "more pleasing subjects."[25] Meanwhile, the OSA executive, having encouraged Seton to enter his painting and having voted for it, felt that the Montreal jurors' decision was a comment upon the artistic judgement of the OSA, and they demanded that the decision be reconsidered.

When Seton realized that he had allies in his cause, he took heart. Recalling his successful campaign to get a reader's ticket at the British Museum library in 1879, he began asking influential people to put pressure on the Montreal jury members to reverse their decision. Below the letterhead of the Manitoba government, of which he was now an official, he sent off letters to any official of the federal government who might have some power over the jury. The recipients of these letters included several senators and members of parliament, the director of the Dominion Geological Survey, government biologists, the minister of agriculture who was nominally in charge of the Chicago exhibit, and the executive commissioner who actually organized the display.

Unfortunately for Robert Harris, the president-elect of the RCA, most of these people directed their letters to him because it was generally felt that he would be able to redirect the jury. Harris, however, refused to intervene and advised Seton that, like the artists of all the other rejected canvases, he would find that his future success would make up for the "slight disappointment" of this rejection. He wrote:

> Don't imagine for a moment that you are alone in feeling aggrieved. You are however alone in having sought to force the matter out of the jurisdiction of the professional jury appointed to select the pictures. There is no reasonable grounds for any man who acts on the jury than this: to do his best to decide justly in every case which comes up and to agree to a decision of the majority. On what grounds do you assume that it is fair for you to attempt to influence the judgement of the jury or apply for reconsideration that do not apply to the author of other unaccepted pictures?[26]

Seton argued that his picture had not been rejected on artistic grounds, but that the jury had been afraid that potential tourists would get a "false idea of life in Canada." His picture, he insisted, was no more "ghastly and loathsome" than pictures of the

Laocöon and the Serpents, or those of Christ on the cross since it depicted a real event also. Next, he suggested that he would submit "The Sleeping Wolf" instead of "Awaited in Vain," and when this proposal was refused, he announced that he had repainted the foreground area that had caused all the trouble. By this time the jurors had been badgered for nearly a month, and desperate to escape the battlefield, they agreed to accept the altered picture, and Seton's "Awaited in Vain" was rushed off to Chicago. (Whether he really did repaint it is debatable; the foreground of the final version appears identical to that on the *Saturday Night* front page of 3 December 1892.)

Although Seton did have exceptional knowledge of animal behaviour, his understanding of human behaviour was always seriously flawed. He was unable to see the difference between putting pressure on a salaried employee of the British Museum library and forcing the hands of a group of unpaid and very independent jurors. Consequently, when he arrived in Chicago on 23 April to set up the Manitoba natural history exhibit and went to see the RCA exhibit, he was dumbfounded to find that the jurors had taken their revenge upon him: they had "skyed" his painting — hung it so high on the gallery's wall that it could only be seen by contortionists.

Defeated in his artistic endeavour, he prepared to mount his natural history exhibit, but again he was ambushed. Since Seton's appointment as government naturalist, Scott had hired the Winnipeg taxidermist Calvin Hine to mount a natural history display. Naturally, Hine refused to take orders from Seton, who was determined to mount the display which he had promised Greenway. To avoid duplication, Scott appointed Seton purchasing agent and gave Hine the job of setting up the display, whereupon Seton left Chicago in a huff.

He was deeply depressed. In the space of a few months he had been discredited as both naturalist and artist. His *Birds of Manitoba* had gone unnoticed by the scientific community, and his reputation as a naturalist had been scorned by the government of Manitoba. Both the Académie Française and the Royal Canadian Academy had snubbed his artistic endeavours. He decided it was time to rethink his future plans.

11

A Pine in Paris

After the disappointments of the Chicago Exposition, Seton returned to his father's home in Toronto to work on the illustrations for a proposed *Art Anatomy of Animals*. Ever since he had been commissioned to make the illustrations for the *Century Dictionary,* he had been faced with the problem of understanding the bone and muscle structures of birds and animals in order to paint their visible aspects. There were plenty of texts already available on the dissection and structure of dead animals; what was needed for the artist, sculptor and illustrator was an analysis of the living animal, a volume that would show proportions, muscles that controlled characteristic movement and poses, shapes of feathers and hair and how they were overlapped and patterned. During the spring of 1893, Seton conducted negotiations with the Macmillan Company of London and finally secured a contract to prepare such a book.

This project necessitated frequent trips to New York to consult with naturalist friends and to conduct research. On several of these trips Seton took the time to visit the Fitz-Randolph home in Plainfield, New Jersey. He had met Virginia Fitz-Randolph in Paris and travelled back to New York with her and her fiancé on the *Etruria* in May 1892. On the dock in New York they were met by her father, Louis Fitz-Randolph, a wealthy businessman with a cattle ranch in New Mexico. Seton had been invited to their home in Plainfield a few days afterwards and there Fitz-Randolph had told him about the wolf problem on his ranch. Eager to learn more about wolves, Seton listened carefully, then countered with suggestions for getting rid of the animals. Each time he returned to the Fitz-Randolph home he reopened the subject, and finally, in September 1893, his host made the offer that Seton had been waiting for: Fitz-Randolph would pay all his expenses to go to New Mexico and teach his ranch hands how to destroy the wolves, and in return Seton could collect the bounty on all the wolves he killed.

Seton had never been to the southwest and knew nothing about cattle-ranching, but he would have accepted an invitation to Siberia if it allowed him to observe timber wolves more intimately. However, he had another good reason for accepting the offer. His doctor had prescribed a holiday away from his easel to cure his headaches and eye strain. Seton had been wearing glasses for close work for nearly four years, but even with new stronger lenses, his headaches were increasing so that they interfered with the twelve- to sixteen-hour workday he imposed on himself. And he seemed to be constitutionally incapable of working less. Hamlin Garland would later write of him: "Until I visited him and saw him at his desk I thought myself a fairly industrious fellow, but in comparison with him I am a weakling. When he can no longer write to advantage he gets out his drawing board."[1]

Seton arrived in Clayton, New Mexico, on 22 October and caught a thirty-mile ride with the local mail carrier to Clapham post office. There he was met by a ranch hand from Fitz-Randolph's L Cross F Ranch and immediately taken for his first lessons in wolf hunting. He was shown the remains of a number of yearling calves that had been killed by wolves, and while examining them, his guide explained that because wolves attack only at night, guns are no use as a weapon against them; coyotes, on the other hand, appeared by day so shooting them could control their numbers.

Seton had ridden horseback in Manitoba but had never become an expert rider; he had taken so much joy in walking and greatly preferred it when tracking wildlife. Now, because of his knee injury and because the distances he would have to travel were too great, he had to ride. In the next three months he learned to ride like an old hand, even mastering the technique of lassoing his horse when he wanted to saddle up.

He began his second lesson in wolf hunting by consulting with ranchers who had successfully used poison against the animals. Then he worked out a system of leaving chunks of strychnine-injected beef along a pathway known to be used by wolves and coyotes. This way, when the animals died, Seton could easily find the carcasses and collect the bounty on them. Although the timber wolves carefully avoided this bait, he killed coyotes with it day after day.

Then one morning, as he was setting off to collect the previous day's carcasses, he surprised a coyote eating one of the baits, and he watched as the animal went into immediate convulsions. In an attempt to put it out of its misery, Seton raised his gun and fired, but the shot went wild. The coyote staggered to its feet, vomited up the bait and tried to escape. Its hindquarters were already partially paralyzed by the poison, however, and the beast turned again and again, snapping at the legs which were slowing down its flight. Seton fired repeatedly, but the shots only goaded the animal on until at last, having apparently worked off the effects of the poison, it was running almost normally, and disappeared into a gully.

About the same time, on a neighbouring ranch, one of the hands who had been suffering from a touch of fever had taken a spoonful of medicine from a bottle which he believed to be quinine. Within three minutes he had died in horrible agony while the other hands stood by helplessly. The bottle had contained wolf bait. These two incidents quickly put an end to Seton's poison campaign.

He was deeply affected by these events, and as a result moved one step closer to his ultimate conservationist position: "What right, I asked, has man to inflict such horrible agony on fellow beings, merely because they do a little damage to his material interests?"[2] He had been killing animals to learn more about them ever since he was a child, and in this pursuit he was no different from any other would-be naturalist of his day who emulated Audubon. Between them, they had been responsible for the deaths of thousands of birds and animals — some for dissection, some for mounting — yet most of the sacrificed creatures had helped in some way to advance man's knowledge of wildlife. The

growth of this knowledge, however, was gradually making specimen collecting less important, while at the same time the accumulated knowledge had begun to alert scientists to the serious need
for conservation.

Seton's own approach to the collecting and killing of animals
had been completely transformed since the days in Lindsay when
he was obsessed with the desire to own a stuffed bird collection
like the one in Foley's store. The Seton who watched one of the
last great pigeon flights over Toronto in 1875, and yearned for a
gun of his own, was not the same Seton who bagged a moose in
1884 and then vowed never again to lift a rifle against one of
America's big game animals. Yet wolves, and to a lesser degree
coyotes, were in a different category for Seton. It was somehow
necessary for him "to meet them and beat them,"[3] almost as if in
destroying them he could establish his own identity, prove himself their superior. It helped, of course, that wolves were anathema in cattle country, so that in killing them Seton could reap
approval and a bounty, but in spite of the no-holds-barred battle
developing between Wolf Thompson and the grey wolves of
New Mexico, he could not continue to use a weapon that caused
such suffering.

Having given up poison as a weapon, Seton turned to the use of
steel traps. The heavy, double-spring affairs used by the local
ranchers were toothless, so that when ranch dogs blundered into
them, they could be extricated without serious injuries. To avoid
contamination with human scent, the traps were never touched
by bare hands, and once they were buried, the dirt over them was
cleaned of human tracks with a piece of rabbit's fur.

By the time that Seton switched to using traps, his interest had
focussed on a particular wolf, an enormous male known locally as
Lobo. This wolf was extremely cunning, refusing to take bait or
be lured into the traps no matter how cleverly they had been laid;
he appeared to understand the human mind far better than
humans could fathom his animal mind. In the end, however, after
his mate had been killed, the big wolf himself was caught in a trap
that had been dusted with her scent. Seton attempted to keep the
animal in captivity, but Lobo died within a day even though he
had not been wounded in any way. After he was dead, Seton
wrote: "I took the chain and collar from his neck, the cowboy
came to help me. And as we raised his body, there came from the

near mesa, the long and mournful howling of the wolves. It may have been the ordinary hunting cry; but coming at that moment, as it did, it seemed to me a long, sad, faraway farewell."[4]

The old wolf's story became the most famous of all Seton's animal stories in the years to come, but his death seems to have brought an end to Seton's "collecting" phase. Almost all his future shooting was done with a camera.

A few days after Lobo's death, Seton was warned that he had been implicated in cattle rustling and that it might be wise for him to leave the area. There was apparently a certain amount of truth in the charge: in exchange for information on trapping techniques, he had designed a cattle brand for two local brothers who were now using it to "re-brand" their neighbours' cattle. Although Seton claimed not to have understood what they intended to do with the brand, the sheriff had prepared a warrant for his arrest. Seton was on his way to New York on 5 February.

The summer of 1894 saw him enrolled once again at the Académie Julian in Paris and once more preparing to enter a painting in the spring Salon. But the experiences of the past year had limited his subservience to the standards of world art and particularly to those of the Salon. On 22 December he wrote to his friend "Rufus" (Henry M. Steele):

> I have spent all afternoon at the Louvre and as I went from one great master to another and saw all kinds of peculiarities and extremes, yet all resulting in great pictures, there was this lesson that was impressed on me more and more: the man who does immortal work develops *himself.* Here have I living in Norway been trying to grow a palm tree because I saw that African palms were good and each fresh frost cut down my puny sprout. It has only recently dawned on me that I must grow my *pine.* It is the timber for my soil. What a noble tree I might have had now had I realized this ten years ago. This then is my theory: I have something that no one else in the world has. It may be a little thing but it is me. It is my pine tree and I shall grow it though it never exceed a foot in height, it will at least be always a living thing.[5]

For the next nine years, convinced that he had something unique to offer, Seton would grow his pine defiantly, and this period would be the most productive of his life. He began his revolt by preparing another wolf painting for submission to the Salon. In this one the narrative was slight: it was simply a view of a pack of wolves as seen from the back of the sled they are pursuing. There are no humans in the picture, only the sled tracks in the snow which suggest the fleeing humans. Some of the wolves have given up the chase and have dropped behind, but the wolves in the foreground, leaping powerfully toward the viewer, are symbolic of Seton's new defiance.

Preparation for the painting tied in quite neatly with his continuing work on the *Art Anatomy*, for besides diagrams of the bone and muscle structures of birds and of the common domestic and zoo animals, Seton decided to include diagrams of the wolf. While in New Mexico, he had prepared some of the necessary plates, but for the remaining studies he used the carcasses of dogs which he secured from the Paris dog pound. The book was also to contain motion studies, and for this he secured permission to use diagrams based on the photographs of Eadweard Muybridge, whose celebrated pictures of horses and dogs in motion had caused an upheaval in the art world. Although Seton must have been familiar with Muybridge's work through his massive *Animal Locomotion,* published in 1887, he had access to the man himself at the Chicago Exposition where Muybridge had used his patented Zoetrope to show "movies" of his animals in action.

Seton began his art anatomy project alone, but during the winter of 1894–95 he acquired an assistant. She was Grace Gallatin, a young woman he had met on board the S.S. *Spaarndam* while travelling to Europe the previous July. Seton had almost missed the boat; the gangplank was already being taken up when he raced onto the Jersey City pier, but his long legs had carried him across the intervening water and into Grace's life. She was travelling with her mother, and once in Paris, they turned to him for help in finding them accommodations in the Latin Quarter near his own tiny studio.

The Gallatins came from Sacramento. Grace's father was Albert Gallatin, the son of a Swiss father and an English mother. At the time Seton met Grace, Albert Gallatin was the president of the huge hardware, rail and steel corporation, Huntington, Hopkins Company, the largest of its kind on the Pacific coast. In addition, he was president of the Sacramento Electric Gas and Railway Company and first vice-president of the California State

Bank; he also owned more than fifty thousand acres of northern California ranchland.

Grace's mother was the former Clemenzia "Memie" Rhodes of Chicago, who had married Gallatin in 1865 and divorced him in 1883. The couple had three children, all of them born in the Gallatin mansion which, when sold to the state in 1888, became the governor's mansion. Grace, the youngest, had spent most of the years since her parents' divorce with her mother in Chicago and New York where they were included in literary and artistic circles.

In July 1894 Grace Gallatin was twenty-two years old, a graduate of the Chicago Female College and the Packer Collegiate Institute of Brooklyn, and she had come to Paris to learn more about art. Although creative, Grace was not an artist; she was a writer and had already sold stories to several American magazines. After she settled in Paris, her stories about the artists she met there soon turned up in both American and English periodicals, and, as she spoke French fluently, in French papers as well. Her prose was spare, well-organized and always touched by the dry humour with which she habitually met the world.

Seton was immediately attracted to her. Like Susie Grahame and Annie Wood before her, except for a little Swiss-French blood from her father, Grace had all the qualities he desired in a wife. In addition, she was what he described as "socially well placed" and very wealthy.[6] Outside of his career ambitions, Seton wanted nothing more than social position and wealth. His father had frustrated his chance to be the son of an earl and thereby acceptable to the British upper classes; his alternative was to become acceptable in the better circles of North America by acquiring wealth or a socially prominent wife — or both. Each of his love affairs had been, perhaps subconsciously, calculated to produce a wife with this necessary qualification: Harriet Hatton in London, Susie Grahame, Annie Wood. When Elizabeth Taylor, the daughter of the American Consul in Winnipeg, turned up in Paris in 1891, Seton courted her until she elected to become an Arctic explorer, setting off to follow the MacKenzie River the next year. He wooed Virginia Fitz-Randolph until another man won her, then wooed her prettier sister, Caroline. Each of these women was beautiful and charming, and each had the right social connections.

Not that his love affairs were cold-blooded — far from it. Seton's need for love and appreciation had been at the root of most of the illnesses of his youth, and it was only as he reached an age and appearance that appealed to younger women that he had gradually ceased manipulating his mother's emotional reactions. For at least ten years before he met Grace Gallatin, his good looks had inspired interest from a steady parade of young women, and serious speculation in the minds of their marriage-conscious mothers.

Grace had one further appeal for Seton — she was neither cowed nor submissive. She was, in fact, a strong feminist and a suffragette, and in the years ahead would become one of the stalwarts of the New York and Connecticut Votes-for-Women leagues. She did not believe that a woman's needs or interests should be subordinated to those of her husband. And Seton was pleased.

Once they were well acquainted, Seton found that Grace had excellent judgement in literary matters and with her help he was able to complete the text of the *Art Anatomy* before the autumn of 1895. His new wolf painting had been completed in time for the spring Salon of that year. "La Poursuite" was somewhat smaller than "Awaited in Vain" — only three and a half feet by five feet — as it had been suggested to him that the size of the earlier picture had also worked against its acceptance. Although he was once more assured by his instructors at Julian's and by his artist friends that his canvas was a Salon winner, he took no chances this time, and submitted his twelve preliminary studies for the wolves along with the picture itself. "La Poursuite" was rejected, but six of the studies were accepted and hung "on the line" — that is, at eye level — in the Salon.

For Seton this qualified acceptance was not enough. "La Poursuite" was the last pine he would grow for the world of art in Paris or anywhere else. He did not re-enroll in courses at Julian's after the spring of 1895, and when his pictures were released from the Salon, he packed one of the wolf studies off to the Ontario School of Art for inclusion in their spring Salon, at the same time advising them that he was resigning from the OSA as of the conclusion of the membership year. Ever since his first visit to New York in 1883, Seton had become more and more aware that his future lay in the United States; his resignation from the OSA was just the last deliberate move to cut his Canadian ties. The only things that remained were his Manitoba government appointment — which he retained for the rest of his life — and his bond with his mother.

At the end of March 1896 Seton and Grace returned to New York to be married. Seton still had little money, but the *Art Anatomy* was due to be released that summer, and as well Frank Chapman had asked him to illustrate his forthcoming book, *Bird Life*. As Grace had been born and raised in cities, she would have been quite content to settle in New York, but Seton had spent enough time in cities and wanted to return to the west. A compromise was arranged by Grace's mother. She had discovered a small estate for sale near Tappan, New Jersey, within a few minutes of the railway and just thirty minutes by rail from New York. Sloat Hall was a thirty-room, rambling, colonial-style house set in the midst of an old orchard on 235 acres of land. Both Grace and Seton were delighted with the house since it provided scope for her entertaining plans, and space for workshops and studios for him and a study for her. The cost, however, was prohibitive: fifteen hundred dollars down and the balance on a mortgage. Grace's mother solved that problem by providing the cash.

They took possession of the house on 30 May 1896. Two days later Grace Gallatin became Mrs. Ernest Seton Thompson, the name by which her husband was officially known, although his friends called him "Wolf" Thompson and his publishers knew him as Ernest Thompson-Seton. The bridegroom was thirty-six; the bride, twenty-four.

CLOCKWISE FROM ABOVE: Seton with skunks at Wyndygoul, 1908 (Courtesy Seton Village); Rabbit cartoon (Courtesy Seton Village); "Johnny Bear," the orphan of Yellowstone, 1897 (Courtesy Seton Village).

CLOCKWISE FROM ABOVE:
Wyndygoul, Cos Cob,
Connecticut, 1909 (Courtesy Seton
Village); Seton's Hollow Tree
under construction at Wyndygoul,
Connecticut, 1908 (Courtesy Seton
Village); Seton in his study "at the
top of the house among the
treetops" at Wyndygoul, 1909
(Courtesy Seton Village).

CLOCKWISE FROM ABOVE: Seton, Robert Baden-Powell and Dan Beard. The 1910 photograph that offended Seton (Courtesy Seton Village); Seton (extreme left) teaching Indian wrestling to a visiting "tribe" at Wyndygoul, c. 1910 (Courtesy Seton Village); Seton in Indian costume, 1917 (Courtesy Seton Village); Seton illustrating the making of an Indian drum, Wyndygoul, c. 1910 (Courtesy Seton Village).

RIGHT: Seton in 1922 (Courtesy Seton Village).

BELOW: Annie Wood, c. 1920 (Courtesy Seton Village).

OPPOSITE PAGE: Seton and Grace Gallatin Seton, c. 1925 (Courtesy Seton Village).

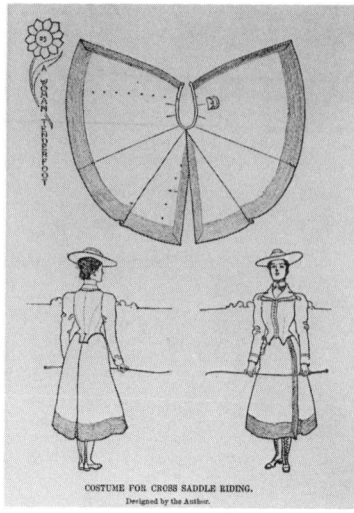

COSTUME FOR CROSS SADDLE RIDING.
Designed by the Author.

ABOVE LEFT: Grace Gallatin Seton designed her own costumes for mountain travel. This is one for cross-saddle riding. Unknown artist, in *Woman Tenderfoot in the Rockies*.

ABOVE RIGHT: Grace Gallatin Seton on the trail, 1907. Photography from cover of *Nimrod's Wife*.

BOTTOM: Grace Gallatin Seton on horseback. Drawing by G. Wright in *Woman Tenderfoot in the Rockies*.

12

The Nature Fakers

From June until August 1896 Seton spent all his days in his studio at Sloat Hall preparing illustrations for Chapman's book. Grace and her mother were busy organizing his social life, for while he had made friends and important contacts in New York since his first brief stay there in 1883–84, most of the people he knew belonged to the scientific or artistic communities. The Gallatins, on the other hand, were allied to the "old families" of New York and to the influential moneyed segment which controlled the banks, foundations and publishing houses. And although Seton would later characterize his wife as "ambitious,"[1] he was not reluctant to accept her social manipulations at the time.

In the first summer Sloat Hall provided just the right atmosphere for the newlyweds, but by November they found it impossible to heat, so they took a studio apartment at 123 Fifth Avenue in New York. In March 1897 Grace and her mother arranged for an exhibition of Seton's work in a small gallery nearby, and since the show concentrated on his detailed animal illustrations rather than his controversial wolf paintings, most of the reviews were positive. Possibly because the prices had been set rather high, few of the pictures sold. Even Theodore Roosevelt, who had been lured to the gallery by the Gallatins, announced, after admiring

"La Poursuite," that the price was "far beyond [his] means."[2] He compromised by ordering a copy of the study of the leading wolf in the picture.

The show did catch the attention, however, of G. O. Shields, the editor of *Recreation* magazine, who offered Seton a portion of the funds needed for an expedition to Yellowstone Park in return for stories and drawings for his journal. When shortly thereafter Macmillan offered Seton a commission to provide the illustrations for Mabel Osgoode Wright's *Four Footed Animals and Their Kin,* he realized that he could get material from the trip to Yellowstone for both assignments.

On 25 March Alice Snowdon Thompson died in Toronto at age seventy-five. The funeral was private with no flowers. Afterwards, Joseph Thompson and the seven sons who lived close enough to attend returned to the family home on Rose Avenue, and there a quarrel broke out between Seton and his father, possibly because Seton, who had arrived too late to see his mother before she died, had become convinced that his father had made "an attempt to poison [his] dying mother's mind against [him]."[3] In the course of the argument Joseph apparently called Seton "a 'disgrace to the family,' a 'good fornothing reprobate' and a 'liar.' " Seton left the house vowing never again to see or communicate with his father. Seven months later he wrote to his brother William, warning that if ever this "worthless loafer, a petty swindler, a wife-beater and a child-murderer. . . . tries to thrust himself on my notice, except in the dust and ashes of contrition and remorse, I'll publish his history as I learnt it from authority that would surprize you."[4]

Joseph never did attempt to contact his eighth son again, and after the old man's death in 1902, though Seton did not attend the funeral, he admitted to William that he "regretted his conduct to [his] father, and if he had to do it again would *act differently.*"[5] However, when Seton published his memoirs forty years later, he did include some of his father's "history"; the portions that his brothers persuaded him to leave out were published by his second wife twenty-seven years later.

Grace Thompson began her first wildlife trip with her husband on 2 June, when they left New York by train. They spent the first six weeks of the summer at a remote ranch on the Green River run by an elderly eccentric named John Yancey. Rather than put up at Yancey's main "hotel," Seton elected to make extensive repairs to a tumbledown log cabin across the creek and install himself and his wife in it. The Green River ranch proved to be an excellent base for animal watching, and Grace, in spite of being a tenderfoot who loved her "creature comforts, the tub bath, the warm dressing room, the . . . easeful bed,"[6] quickly adapted to outdoor life. Even Seton, writing in 1939 after their divorce and many bitter exchanges between them, had to admit that "as a camper she was a great success, never grumbled at hardship, or scolded anyone. She was a dead shot with the rifle, often far ahead of the guides, and met all kinds of danger with unflinching nerve; was always calm and clear-headed, no matter what the stance."[7]

After three weeks, Yancey raised his charge for board to nearly twice the price agreed upon, and when Seton protested, Yancey told him calmly that he had not expected them to like the place so well or to stay so long. Seton, though angry, was not put out enough to leave until the end of July, when the couple headed for Yellowstone Park to observe the bears. Their next stop was the Crow, or Absaroka, Indian Reservation on the Little Bighorn River. The painter E. A. Burbank had set up a temporary studio there while he painted Indian portraits, particularly that of Chief Plenty Coups. Seton planned to use this studio as the base for his own investigation of wildlife and Indian life in the area.

Since 1876, when Gen. George Custer had died on the Little Bighorn battlefield, Seton had been gathering information on the events of that day of battle, and this was his first chance to get the story first-hand. Soon after their arrival, he and Grace were taken over the field and shown the white stones that marked the places where each of the soldiers fell, and were told the terrible story of the slaughter. Later, Burbank introduced Seton to White Swan, who had been one of Custer's scouts. As his battle wounds had left him without the power of speech, White Swan spoke only in sign language, but Seton was able to communicate with him to a certain extent, having learned the rudiments of Indian sign language in Manitoba. This encounter was the starting point for his *Sign Talk Dictionary* published in 1918, but of more importance was its effect on his attitude toward the Indians. For the first time, Seton was given concrete evidence of the persecution of the Indian people, of the "unbroken narrative of injustice, fraud and robbery" that they had suffered at the hands of the white man;[8] even more specifically, he had evidence that Custer, who was held up to school children as a model of bravery and the victim of the Indians' treachery, was himself guilty of attempting to destroy an innocent people. With this information in hand, he prepared to debunk the Custer hero myth. That fall, however, he met Custer's widow and "felt it a high honour that he entertained her in his studio a number of times";[9] after their meeting he felt he could not deliberately wound this sensitive woman and until her death adroitly avoided public comment on Custer, even though his growing reputation would have given weight to his words.

Another curious example of his ambivalence regarding the rights and dignity of the Indian people was his participation in grave robbery. While on this same trip, Burbank offered to show the Thompsons a grove of trees which the Crow Indians had used as a burial ground. The bodies had been wrapped tightly in blankets, then hoisted into the trees and tied amid the branches. Burbank, Seton and Grace rode to the spot one afternoon, and Burbank was able to pull one of the more loosely tied corpses down to the ground. The trio found themselves looking into the mummified "but otherwise normal face of an Indian woman. . . . Seven brass rings were on her thumb and a carved wooden armlet encircled her wrist."[10] Burbank had just removed the bracelets and rings and given them to Grace when two Indians appeared on horseback in the distance. The three hastily emerged from the grove, managed to convince the Indians that they had only been out riding, and left the scene. Later, Grace wrote that she felt their actions had been "on a par with making up slumming parties to pry into the secrets of the poor."[11] Seton's writings contain no mention of the event.

On 6 September the Thompsons arrived at the Eaton Ranch on the Little Missouri River in North Dakota in time for a wolf hunt arranged by the three wealthy brothers who owned the ranch. Grace, the only woman among the dozen individuals who set off after Mountain Billy, the local equivalent of Lobo, lagged behind the party and was thrown from her horse when a rattlesnake crossed its path. Picking herself up, she found the remains of a rusted frying pan beside the trail and beat the rattlesnake to death before it could finish coiling to strike. She returned to New York with her trophy of snake rattles; the men in the party did not even set eyes on Mountain Billy.

Back in New York after their western adventures, Seton re-edited eight of his animal stories with an eye to publishing them in book form. These were "Lobo, the King of Currumpaw," "Silverspot, the Story of a Crow," "Raggylug, the Story of a Cottontail Rabbit," "Bingo, the Story of My Dog," "The Springfield Fox," "The Pacing Mustang," "Wully, the Story of a Yaller Dog" and "Redruff, the Story of the Don Valley Partridge." All had been previously published in *Scribner's Magazine* or *St. Nicholas*.

As magazine stories they had been very successful, mostly because they were completely different from any animal stories previously published. They were not like the anthropomorphic fairytales of LaFontaine or even of Kipling, and they were not like adventure stories where animals are included as adjuncts to human actions, nor were they philosophic essays on animals in their natural surroundings. In his new story form, Seton told a niece in 1926,

> the real life of the animal is portrayed from the animal's viewpoint. The human being is excluded wholly or reduced to a faint accessory. In this, an attempt is made to give the animal psychology, to show how it lives and thinks and feels. The adventures through which the hero passes are taken from life and every detail is made as true as possible to life, and yet the whole story must be considered fiction because the hero is really composed of several individuals and it ascribes to one the adventures which belong to others of the same kind. That is, it is a historical novel with an animal for a hero.[12]

Seton prepared a series of marginal illustrations to accompany the stories, then approached Charles Scribner's Sons with the collection. Encountering little enthusiasm, he offered to forgo royalties on the first two thousand copies, provided that the publishers pay him double the normal ten percent royalty on all copies over two thousand sold. In return, Seton promised to promote the book with lectures and lantern slides. The contract was signed on 1 July 1898.

This unusual contract was not really a gamble for Seton. Part of his confidence came from knowing that he possessed the physical attributes of a platform personality. "Tall, active and sinewy, with dark eyes and hair," wrote a *Toronto Globe* reporter, "he is often mistaken for a plains Indian because continual exposure to the elements has burnt his skin a deep copper colour."[13] Another part of his confidence came from knowing that he was an excellent raconteur. With his marvellously expressive voice and exceptional stage presence, he was already in demand as an after-dinner speaker, and at private affairs was always called upon to entertain with his stories. One of the most thoroughly documented of these affairs was a luncheon for playwright James Barrie in October 1896. Here, Seton with his wolf anecdotes outshone the guest of honour and won the applause of Theodore Roosevelt, *New York Times'* drama critic Brander Matthews, novelist Hamlin Garland, publisher Harry Kimball and artist Frederic Remington.

Seton had also learned that he could capture the attention of children; his visits to the home of James Mavor in Toronto always included storytelling sessions before the fire for the three Mavor children. Many years later the middle child, Dora (who became known to Canadian theatregoers as Dora Mavor Moore), would retell those stories to her own children exactly as she had heard them from Seton.

With nearly four months to wait between the signing of the contract and the release of the book in the middle of August, the Thompsons set off for the west once more, this time for the express purpose of studying bears in the area of Jackson's Hole, Wyoming. They approached their goal from Idaho Falls, travelling safely over the Teton Pass in a covered wagon, but while they were fording the Snake River, water swept into the wagon box and half of their possessions disappeared downstream. To add to their misery, after darkness fell their driver admitted that he was lost, and it was Seton, using his exceptional tracking ability, who found the ranchhouse that was their destination.

After a few weeks in Jackson's Hole with almost no bears to be seen, they travelled on to Yellowstone National Park. There, on the garbage dump behind the Fountain Hotel, Seton had the closest contact with bears that he had yet managed. For an entire day he lay "in a nest he had made for himself in a pile of rubbish."[14] At dusk, when his wife searched for him, she heard his voice issuing in a whisper from the garbage pile, warning her to keep quiet and not move as he was still making notes on the enormous grizzly finishing its evening meal nearby. From his "nest," Seton had been able to study as many as thirteen bears at a time, carefully noting their behaviour in his battered journal. Among them was an old she-bear, which he named Old Grumpy, and her sickly cub, Little Johnny, who became the protagonist of the sad story of "Johnny Bear." After the story was published in *Scribner's Magazine* in December 1900, the little bear was adopted by the graduating class of Bryn Mawr College, and the students had replicas made for themselves by Schwarz's toy store in New York. The bears quickly caught on with the public, but a few years later Theodore Roosevelt's celebrated encounter with a bear cub prompted the "teddy-bear" craze, and "Johnny-bears" were supplanted by the new hero.

In mid-September the Thompsons joined the pack-train of a friend from their Paris days, the portrait artist A. A. Anderson, an independently wealthy man who was on his way from Jackson's Hole to his ranch on the Greybull River. When they reached the Wind River valley, they found bears so plentiful that Grace and Seton elected to stay behind and set up camp there with the help of one horse wrangler and a cook. Within days the weather turned cold and snow began to fall, but the little party stayed on into early October so that Seton could complete his documentation on bears.

Wild Animals I Have Known was released in late October, and Seton immediately launched his first lecture tour. Within three weeks the first two thousand copies had been sold and before Christmas Scribner's had gone back to the printers three more times. Many of the copies sold were autographed by Seton on his extensive lecture tours, and most of those bore beside his signature the wolf paw print which he had adopted as his logo.

For the next three years this successful formula for promoting books was repeated. Every year a new collection was released, the stories chosen from those which had proved popular when they appeared in magazine format; thus, *The Trail of the Sandhill Stag* followed in 1899, *The Biography of a Grizzly* in 1900 and *The Lives of the Hunted* in 1901. As soon as each book appeared, Seton would set off on the lecture trail to promote it, and the resulting sales were unprecedented. But it was gruelling work. Rather than simply reading the stories to his audiences, Seton *told* them, enlarging on each tale with little anecdotes which were not in the book, and illustrating them with lantern slides of his drawings.

He also dramatized each story with appropriate animal cries. He was immensely proud of his ability to mimic animals so well; the naturalist Roy Chapman Andrews recalled Seton and the bird artist Louis Agassiz Fuertes sitting in a restaurant near the campus of Columbia University sometime in the winter of 1908–9 "debating" about the calls and cries of various animals and birds. "Each gave his version of a coyote howl, then began comparing macaw squawks."[15] Passers-by thought someone was being killed and called the police to investigate. On another occasion Seton, with the aid of a birch bark "horn" he had fashioned, produced such an authentic moose call that an immense bull moose tried to share his canoe.

Seton preferred audiences that were small enough to gather closely around him, for these groups responded most warmly to his personality, but as his popularity grew, he often found himself facing enormous crowds, largely comprised of enthusiastic children. In Toronto in March 1901 he drew an overflow crowd to Massey Hall. Officials had given out tickets to school children for double the number of seats in the hall because it was customary for only half the young ticket holders to show up. On this occasion about 3500 of them came to claim the two thousand seats, so that all the aisles were filled and many of the children were turned away. Seton began his lecture with a fox story, and then started on the story of "Johnny Bear." The *Toronto Globe* reported:

> He had been proceeding with great difficulty on account of the noise for in that great audience the least murmur became a roar, but when the children began to laugh at the funny pictures, getting them to be silent again became increasingly difficult. Each new picture showing Johnny Bear with his big ears and his little fat paunch climbing or hanging in some absurd position was received with roars of laughter and applause, very gratifying but no less perplexing to the lecturer, for in that audience the laughter would just begin to subside when other children would see the point and the laughter would begin anew.
>
> Mr. Thompson illustrates his lectures not only with the products of his brush, but also with his voice and he imitated the calls of vixen and mother bear to perfection, but when he got into the humorous part and began to imitate whining Johnny, the children, carried away by their unusual surroundings, began to copy the calls

and Johnny's whining yelps came from all over the hall. Then other children, who were anxious to have the lecture proceed, would shout "Order," "Silence," "Hush" until the hall was filled with a good-natured roar. The lecturer smilingly appealed to be allowed to continue, promising them that afterwards they would be allowed to practice as much as they wished, but . . . the spell had been broken and Mr. Thompson talked during the last half of the pictures amid a perfect babel of laughter, animal cries and the impromptu efforts of juvenile lecturers.[16]

While on a lecture tour in Washington, D. C., Seton stayed in a hotel that was hosting the national convention of an association interested in animal welfare. He demurred when asked to speak to the opening session, but after the lady in charge insisted, he agreed, at the same time warning her that what he had to say might not be palatable. It was not. When he told his audience that when the rights of animals and the rights of human beings conflicted, human rights must take precedence, there was an uproar. Then, as he was challenged from the floor, he pointed out the fur coats, leather shoes and silk dresses in the audience, which had all been produced at the cost of animal suffering.

Meanwhile, as Seton lectured, Grace assumed the responsibility of designing the covers and title pages of her husband's books, editing them and doing the general layouts. At the same time, she continued her own writing career, but while her earlier expertise had centred on the world of art, she now sold articles on the woman's view of outdoor life. In 1900 she published her first book, *A Woman Tenderfoot in the Rockies,* the story of her adventures on the 1897 and 1898 expeditions. Although it purports to be simply a guide for women who wish to follow their husbands on safari, from the very first word it subtly encourages female independence and quite clearly signals the beginning of the changes in the author which would eventually lead to her separate career as an explorer, big game hunter, lecturer and writer.

Each summer after 1898 the Setons went west to gather more wildlife information, always choosing slightly different territory to explore. In 1901 their goal was northwestern Colorado where they headed into the mountains in late August with John Goff, who had acted as guide for Theodore Roosevelt the previous winter. There were only a half dozen in the party, several pack animals and Goff's hunting dogs. This trip was intended as a general survey of Colorado animals, but Seton was also intent on resolving the question of the existence of the fan-tail deer, a tiny species reported to be found in this area though no specimens had actually been taken. In the course of their search for the fan-tail, they startled a cougar which had mortally wounded a blacktail doe; as Seton now hunted only with a camera, Grace shot the animal to put it out of its suffering. When at last Goff sighted what he believed was a fan-tail, Grace was told to collect the specimen, only to find she had shot the fawn of the blacktail doe killed earlier.

Three days later, their camp was visited by the game warden of Rio Blanco County, and Seton and Goff were placed under arrest, charged with baiting traps for mountain lions with venison and using dogs to drive deer. By paying one hundred dollars each, the men were permitted to proceed on their own to the settlement of Craig, where they were to be tried. There, Seton attempted to persuade the local newspaper editor to forget the story, but instead his pleas and threats acted like a red flag. When the case came to trial, both Seton and Goff were acquitted with the aid of a local lawyer, apparently more because the jurors realized that a conviction would be disastrous for the guiding business on which the town thrived than for any real concern for justice. By that time the story had appeared in every paper across the country, generally under the headline: SETON-THOMPSON ARRESTED!

This was not the end of the story. In January 1902 a taxidermist in Rio Blanco County attempted to ship to Seton in New York the hides of the animals Grace had shot. The shipment was intercepted by the Colorado Fish and Game Commission, and once again Seton's name was in the headlines as the Commission tried to have him returned to Colorado for a new trial. The attempt came to nothing and in time the hides were released. Seton dismissed the second threat as "nothing but a newspaper story, and while it was annoying for the time it really resulted in doing me good. The miserable creature who started it lost his situation and was very properly discredited for his action."[17]

In the midst of this crisis, the legal proceedings which Seton had instituted to change his name for the final time came before court, and on 24 October 1901 he was granted the right to change his name from Ernest Seton Thompson (and all the hyphenated variations by which he had also been known) to Ernest

Thompson Seton. Confusion continued to reign among friends and publishers for a few more years, but to most of them he was still "Wolf," no matter what surname he used.

By now Ernest Thompson Seton was a wealthy man. In four years he had amassed $200,000[18] by ploughing all his book royalties and lecture fees into "good, safe stocks and bonds."[19] "No big interest and poor security for me," he told his brother William; "I invest all my surplus funds in government bonds."[20] His friends were pleased with his success. Said the novelist Hamlin Garland, "He has something to give and the world is buying it. He is at once story-writer, naturalist and illustrator — and this triple activity has won a multiple success. No one can logically begrudge him his just rewards."[21]

All his life Seton had longed for land of his own. Even while he mocked his father's lord-of-the-manor aspirations, he had been planning his own estate — a mansion set amid untouched woodlands teeming with wildlife. In London at twenty he had planned that this estate would be in Devonshire; at twenty-two it had become a homestead in Manitoba; at twenty-eight he had been tenant-lord of his brother's resort lands. At thirty-six had come Sloat Hall, though it was a drafty old barn set amid cultivated fields, nothing at all like the wooded estate he had in mind. Field trips and lecture tours had left him no time to return to it after the summer of 1896, and he rented it out the following summer, then sold it a year later when he realized that he would soon be able to afford the estate of his youthful ambitions. On 25 May 1900 he found the piece of land he wanted at Cos Cob, near Greenwich, Connecticut. He wrote:

> For twenty-five years I had waited and hungered for this moment. Here at last were trees — 100 acres of splendid forest — a sparkling brook running down a rocky valley, which expanded into a marshy pond, then narrowed to quit the vale by a dammable gorge. Here were rocky hills, sloping green banks, noble trees, birds in abundance, squirrels in the woods, fish and turtles in the pond, a naturalist's paradise in truth and all was mine.[22]

(Some of the land was, in fact, Grace's property, but at this point in their lives, this was of little concern.)

To protect the wildlife on his new estate, Seton hired workmen to build a "horse-high, bull-strong, pig and rat proof fence" using wire mesh seven and a half feet high, with three rows of barbed wire above it, and another three rows attached to the oblique arms that were nailed to each post.[23] Almost as soon as this impregnable fence was erected, trouble began with the neighbourhood boys, who considered the land to be their playground. In a short time they found ways to break through the wire mesh, enter Seton's private park and paint obscenities on his gates. As threats had no effect on the boys, Seton went to the local schoolhouse in the late spring of 1901 and asked permission to speak at a school assembly.[24] In later years Seton told this story many times; the details varied from version to version, but the basic plot went like this:

He invited all the boys over twelve years of age to a picnic on his estate. The picnic would commence on the Friday after school was dismissed and finish on Sunday evening. His invitation was rewarded with dead silence, but when he singled out individual boys, they agreed to come, and the schoolmaster suggested that he should prepare for about twenty-four of them. Seton and his hired help prepared tents, made sandwiches and other provisions and waited; shortly after the appointed time, forty boys showed up, and Seton had to bustle around to provide more bedding and food.

For the first few hours after their arrival, the boys ran naked and swam in the stream and made so much noise that neighbours a mile away complained. At supper, they ate all the food that had been prepared for the entire weekend and Seton had to send out for more. Then, as it grew dark, they gathered around the campfire Seton had prepared and were quite agreeable when he proposed to tell them a story.

He talked about Indians, and when he was through, asked them if they would like to do their "camp-out" in Indian fashion. Not one demurred. Out of politeness, they would have accepted him as their chief, but he insisted that they elect chiefs and councillors from among themselves. They chose the biggest one of their number to be head chief, mostly because he could lick all the rest of them, and they accepted Seton as their medicine man; he adopted the name Black Wolf.

The weekend was a success far beyond anything Seton had expected; when the boys left the estate on Sunday night, each one had chosen a suitable Indian name for himself and all had become members of the "Senewauk tribe." In the course of the weekend, Seton and his Indians decided on rules for conduct in the park which, while successfully protecting Seton's land, also promoted an appreciation of the natural environment. The rules forbade trapping or harming wildlife, starting fires, damaging trees or flowers, betting games and disorderly conduct. (On future week-ends it became necessary to ban liquor from the park; some of the older boys had felt it was an indispensable item for a good time.)

As soon as the first tribe was well established, Seton approached Edward Bok, the editor of the *Ladies' Home Journal,* and convinced him that his magazine needed a boys' column. On 29 July 1901 he signed a contract with Bok to provide a regular section to be called "Ernest Thompson Seton's Boys" which was to commence no later than May 1902. The *Journal,* an exceptional forum for disseminating Seton's "woodcraft" message and for promoting new tribes, had a circulation of 800,000. The Senewauks, with whom Seton met whenever he was not lecturing or on field trips, provided him with a laboratory situation for developing the system of athletic challenges, campcraft and nature study projects, and the games that would become such an important part of woodcrafting.

In the meantime, work had begun on the mansion that was to be the focal point of Seton's country estate. By early 1901 he had been able to afford an expensive New York architect, to whom he gave carte blanche to design an "English style" house using fieldstone and other natural materials. After approving a watercolour sketch of his new home, he left on the ill-fated Colorado field trip, which he followed up with a promotional lecture tour. When he returned at last, he found the house well on the way to completion and realized that it was a monstrosity. He promptly fired the architect and supervised the removal of all the artificial timbers and beam-ends, dummy bolts and imitation ironwork, then stood over the workmen while they rebuilt the house to his satisfaction.

Damming the gorge took somewhat longer than anticipated because it became necessary to excavate to a depth of eighteen feet before the workmen found a solid clay bottom at the damsite. The finished dam was solid masonry, four feet thick, twenty feet high and three hundred feet long; it produced a lake a third of a mile long and twenty feet deep, dotted with fifteen islands. It bore little similarity to the fish pond at Mount Woodham which had been its inspiration, and cost Seton "five times the estimate, and yet it was well worth the price."[25] He immediately began stocking it with exotic species of ducks and geese, most of which fell prey to the pond's gigantic snapping turtles. Finally, only the Canada geese sailed majestically on Seton Lake.

On advice from Archbishop Robert Seton, the historian of the Seton family, the new house was christened Wyndygoul, after one of the estates of the earls of Winton. The original estate in Scotland had been given to the third earl's son Robert in 1671, but it had reverted to the earl when Robert died and was therefore confiscated by the Crown in 1715.

Although they continued to maintain a studio apartment over-looking Bryant Park in New York, Grace and Seton established their real home at Wyndygoul in the fall of 1902. Its official open-ing was delayed until New Year's Day 1903 when they gave a housewarming party, attended by such friends as the Hamlin Garlands, Richard Le Gallienne, Emory Pottle, Mary Fanton and Will Roberts, and the explorer Carl Lumholz. Garland helped Seton set up a tent in the snow-covered garden and watched while his host kindled a fire in the Indian fashion to dedicate a hearth to the god of hospitality. Garland wrote of the event:

> He was like a boy in his zest for every symbol of wilderness life and would have enjoyed eating his dinner in the tent, but all his guests, including myself, were disposed to hug the chimney indoors. . . . My wife and I left the party at midnight (the piano and the tom-tom were still sounding) and as we climbed the stairs at the north-east corner of the house, a keen wind was blowing and the air of our chamber was already near to frost. No doubt the bedding had been carefully apportioned among the guests, but that we needed more covering was plain. In the hall just outside our door lay a lovely white fur rug, and this, in spite of my wife's protests, I planned to appropriate. As soon as the house had quieted down I opened the door, caught this rug by the tail and snatched it in.
>
> It proved a grateful addition to our covering . . . at the first hint of dawn I arose and carefully relaid the rug in the icy hall. So far as I know, our hostess remained ignorant of our sufferings and my heinous social crime.[26]

Exactly twenty years earlier Seton had written to his friend Jack Willing that "there is no limit to the possibilities of him who *wills.*" Seton had willed and he had worked; now he was wealthy, he had a brilliant wife, socially prominent friends, an estate in the country, a troop of worshipping Indians, a reputation as one of America's best nature illustrators and public acclaim as one of the finest storytellers in the land. With his latest book still a best-seller, he was busy with the final revisions of his next one, *Two Little Savages,* which was to be serialized in *Ladies' Home Journal* beginning in January 1903 and was destined for publication in book form in the autumn of the same year. His first impulse had been to write an encyclopedia of woodcraft for the use of the rapidly multiplying Woodcraft Indian tribes, but he had been per-suaded that children would not read it. Instead, he disguised his woodcraft guide as fiction by writing the story of an unloved and persecuted lad who finds happiness and appreciation when he successfully organizes a group of boys into an Indian tribe. But in drawing on his boyhood experiences, Seton also drew from the deep well of injustices over which he had brooded throughout the years, and thereby unalterably established for himself, as well as for the hero of his book, the persona of the martyr. In fact, with this book, the reality of the persecution he had suffered became stronger than ever before.

Consequently, it must have been almost with a sense of the inevitability of martyrdom that Seton opened the March 1903 edition of *Atlantic Monthly* to find that he had been crucified by John Burroughs, the dean of natural history's philosophers, in an article entitled "Real and Sham Natural History." Burroughs accused Seton and the Reverend William J. Long of being fakes, and of seeking "to profit by the popular love for the sensational and the improbable." He continued:

One is keenly aware of the danger that is always lurking near the essay naturalist, the danger of making too much of what we see and describe, — putting in too much sentiment, too much literature — in short, of valuing these things more for the literary effects we can get out of them than for themselves. . . . In Mr. Thompson Seton's *Wild Animals I Have Known,* and in the recent work of his awkward imitator, the Reverend William J. Long, I am bound to say that the line between fact and fiction is repeatedly crossed, and that a deliberate attempt is made to induce the reader to cross, too, and to work such a spell upon him that he shall not know that he has crossed and is in the land of make-believe. Mr. Thompson Seton says in capital letters that his stories are true, and it is this emphatic assertion that makes the judicious grieve. True as romance, true in their artistic effects, true in their power to entertain the young reader, they certainly are; but true as natural history they as certainly are not. Are we to believe that Mr. Thompson Seton, in his few years of roaming in the West, has penetrated farther into the secrets of animal life than all the observers who have gone before him? There are no stories of animal intelligence and cunning on record, that I am aware of, that match his. . . . Such dogs, wolves, foxes, rabbits, mustangs, crows, as he has known, it is safe to say, no other person in the world has ever known. Fact and fiction are so deftly blended in his work that only a real woodsman can separate them.

In his story of the rabbit, Raggylug, he says: "Those who do not know the animals well may think I have humanized them, but those who have lived so near them as to know something of their ways and of their minds will not think so." This is the old trick of the romancer: he swears his tale is true, because he knows his reader wants this assurance; it makes the whole thing taste better. But those who know the animals are just the ones Mr. Thompson Seton cannot fool.

Burroughs then went on to analyze each of the stories in *Wild Animals I Have Known,* comparing Seton's animals with the animals he had known at Slabsides, his own retreat in the Hudson River valley. He concluded:

Since Mr. Thompson Seton took his reader into his confidence at all, why did he not warn him at the outset against asking any questions about the literal truth of his stories? Why did he not say that their groundwork was fact and their finish was fiction, and that if the reader find them entertaining, and that if they increase his love for, and his interest in, our wild neighbours, it were enough? . . . There should be nothing equivocal about sketches of this kind; even a child should know when the writer is giving him facts and when he is giving him fiction, as he does when Mr. Thompson Seton makes his animals talk; but in many of the narrations only a real woodsman can separate the true from the false.

(The second half of the article was devoted to excoriating Long, whose stories were little less than tall tales.)

The impact of the article was far-reaching because Burroughs was so widely respected. At sixty-six he was the grand old man of the scientific community which knew him affectionately as Uncle John; the reading public had acclaimed his six books of philosophical essays and regarded him as the new Thoreau. By his *Atlantic Monthly* article, he had managed to create the impression that anyone who read Seton's or Long's works was a sensation seeker while those reading his own books obviously were seeking pure truth.

The literary and scientific communities immediately took sides, some urging Seton to respond to the attack, some cautioning silence because of the respect in which Burroughs was held, and a few enjoying the spectacle of Seton's ego being punctured. The battle continued in the press, with some writers agreeing with Burroughs and others defending Seton, who had chosen to remain silent.

Then, three weeks after the article appeared, the financier Andrew Carnegie gave his annual literary dinner, and invited both Burroughs and Seton. Richard Watson Gilder, who engineered these affairs for Carnegie, was responsible for the seating arrangements at the dinner table, and, according to Carnegie's memoirs, Gilder accidentally placed Burroughs's and Seton's place cards side by side. When he realized his error, Gilder moved them apart, but Carnegie slipped into the dining room just before dinner was announced and put the cards back in their original position. "The result was just as [he] had expected. A reconciliation took place and they parted good friends."[27] Hamlin Garland, who was also at the dinner, recalls that the two men spoke together that night and that they both left in his company, but he does not recall seeing them seated together.

Seton's memoirs give a different story. He remembered approaching Burroughs immediately on entering the reception room of the Carnegie mansion, but being intercepted by Carnegie before he had a chance for a showdown with Burroughs. It was at this point that *he* persuaded Carnegie to move the place cards so that the two men could sit side by side. During dinner, according to Seton, he catechized the older man on his knowledge of wildlife until Burroughs "broke down and wept."[28] No one else present at the dinner seems to have seen Burroughs in tears.

What definitely did take place were intercessions by Seton's friends, who believed his stories were true in the sense that he ascribed truth to them. And it was these same friends who eventually arranged for Seton to visit Burroughs at Slabsides. Later, Burroughs came to Wyndygoul and allowed himself to be photographed in front of one of the Senewauk tribes' tents by the lake. Afterwards Seton showed the naturalist his library,

> some five thousand volumes then, my collection of two thousand photos of animals, taken by myself, my museum of one thousand mammal skins and two thousand bird skins collected and skinned by myself, one thousand drawings of birds and mammals by me; and, last of all, my journals, some thirty fat volumes, detailing my travels and observations during thirty years, [after which] he broke down and surrendered. 'I had no idea —' 'I never dreamed, etc. —' He, himself, never kept a journal, never made a drawing and never skinned a bird or a beast in his life.[29]

In July 1904 Burroughs published another *Atlantic Monthly* article, this time praising Seton's writing and his illustrations, but adroitly side-stepping the issue of truth which had so incensed him the previous year. Seton would later insist that, though hurt by Burroughs's attack, he had considered it so blatantly unfair and untrue that he had been amused by it.

However, the tenor of a little "allegory," which he wrote at the time but never published, indicates that his persecution complex was still functioning. The story tells of a land where people grow bigger or smaller according to the size of their accomplishments. The hero is an individual who had worked "very quietly for half his lifetime" on a number of projects which were all completed at roughly the same time. The villain, who wants to be big without working and therefore keeps getting smaller, schemes:

> . . if I can throw a handful of mud on this tall one that I hate, I shall at least have all eyes turned my way for a time.
> So he prepared a quantity of the nastiest filth he could find; and by climbing on a hill called Big-serial, he reached high enough to throw the muck, and the tall worker was plentifully splattered.

Everyone laughs at the spectacle of the big man covered in filth, and they wait to see how he will retaliate.

> But instead, he went on quietly with his work. The filth was easily brushed away, because it had no affinities there.

The villain then gets smaller and smaller and finally falls into the hole where he got the muck, and smothers in it. Seton concluded his story:

> Here endeth the tale of Little Mucky, the envious critic. Moral: Notoriety is a poisonous substitute for Fame.[30]

Unfortunately for Seton, before Burroughs capitulated, Theodore Roosevelt had become interested in Burroughs's charges, and had launched his own campaign against "Nature Fakers," or "yellow journalists of the woods" as he christened them. Roosevelt was by this time president of the United States, so his pronouncements on any topic tended to get more coverage by the press and carry more weight with the public than many of them deserved. In this case he was speaking not so much as president of the United States as spokesman for the Boone and Crockett Club. Roosevelt had founded the club in 1887, limiting its membership to one hundred men who had killed with a rifle in fair chase at least one adult male specimen of any three of the main big game animal species of America. Besides encouraging gun sports, the club promoted exploration, and worked for the preservation of big game, mostly by establishing zoos to prevent endangered animals from being extinct and consequently unavailable as game. The club journal was *Forest and Stream*.

Seton was totally ineligible, both because he was not in the correct economic bracket and because he had become a conservationist, but when the Camp Fire Club of America was founded in 1897, he was welcomed warmly by G. O. Shields, its founder and the publisher of the club's organ, *Recreation*. The Camp Fire Club, though at first not entirely against big game hunting, downplayed it, concentrating on nature study and conservation. They were the first large group to promote "hunting with a camera," a sport that Seton was already recommending to the readers of his *Ladies' Home Journal* column.

Seton's articles appeared most regularly in *Forest and Stream,* but they also appeared in *Recreation,* and Roosevelt had praised his story of Lobo when it was first published in *Scribner's Magazine* in 1894. This should have meant Roosevelt would support Seton when Burroughs attacked; instead, though he never actually named Seton in print as one of his Nature Fakers, everyone in the scientific and literary communities knew that Roosevelt included Seton in this category. Seton could neither confront Roosevelt, as he claimed he had confronted Burroughs, nor dismiss him as an envious critic, because he was desperate for Roosevelt's approval. Later that summer, an opportunity arose for Hamlin Garland to plead Seton's case. With Seton's tacit approval, Garland approached the president and told him bluntly that he should not include *Wild Animals I Have Known* in the books he was condemning:

> He reflected a moment in consideration of my friendship for Seton, then said slowly, "As *stories* based on wild animal life, I have no criticism to make of that book, but Seton in his preface goes too far in emphasizing the scientific value of his tales. If he had brought the book out on its merits as fiction — as a free transcription of animal life, no one would have accused him of 'pulling a long bow.' As stories they are admirable and in general they are based on accurate observation."

Garland then described Seton's studio full of specimens, scientific texts and field journals in an effort to emphasize the scientific basis of his friend's writing, but Roosevelt was not impressed.

> "I grant all that," Roosevelt replied; "but he should draw the line more clearly between his fiction and his zoology."
> On my return to Seton's home I told him substantially what the President had said, and while it was not as favourable as he had hoped, I think he felt relieved. To be included among "The Nature Fakers" by Roosevelt and Burroughs was no joke.[31]

As time passed, Seton reinterpreted the message Garland brought him that night, and was later convinced that Roosevelt had made a "vigorous protest" to Burroughs's attack, and had in fact said: "Burroughs and the people at large don't know how many facts you have back of your stories. You must publish your facts."[32]

Two Little Savages appeared in book form before Christmas 1903, and the lecture tour which Seton undertook to promote it led him back to Ontario. When he arrived in North Bay to lecture, he was met by his brother William, who had been living there for several years. William, although extremely proud of his successful brother, was puzzled that he no longer painted, and Seton told him: "In painting pictures you may labor on for months and when you realize on your work — if you do — the matter is settled, and the copyright goes with it, whereas the author may write a book and if successful the proceeds may come in for years afterwards." William concluded: "He said this more as excusing his defection than in giving it as a reason for the change."[33]

Actually, Seton had given his brother only half the story. It was true that he had given up art in order to make money and had found he could do this most efficiently by writing animal stories, but he never intended to commit himself to a lifetime of animal story writing. Grace, in fact, had made this quite plain in *Woman Tenderfoot* in 1900, when she wrote that her husband "desired to make his everlasting fortune, retire from the painting of pictures and the making of books, and grub in the field of science and live happily ever after"[34] — that is, return to the first goal of his life by becoming a naturalist and nothing else.

Yet Seton could not just abandon his storytelling career, for by now he had far too many commitments and responsibilities. Wyndygoul was the heaviest burden, but except for the house itself, which he had been unable to remodel with complete success, everything down to the smallest wildflower was exactly as he had ordered it. (He had even returned the estate's pasture lands to woodland by replanting them with seedling birch and pine sent from William Brewster's estate at Concord, Massachusetts.) To add to its value, it had become the base for his Woodcraft Indians, who were becoming more and more important to his career. It was an expensive establishment to run, however, as the house was drafty and difficult to heat, and it took a corps of employees to service it and its grounds.

To add to his responsibilities, he was about to become a father in January 1904. Although he had forecast two boys and one girl for himself and his English wife, the only child to be born to Grace and Seton was a girl. Christened Ann Seton Thompson Seton, she became known to the reading public in later years as Anya Seton, the novelist.

With all these responsibilities, there was no question that the books of animal stories must continue, at least for the present. The year 1904 brought *Monarch, the Big Bear of Tallac* and 1905 brought *Animal Heroes* and *Woodmyth and Fable* — but these were the products of earlier field trips and story drafts, not new work. Burroughs and Roosevelt had effectively put an end to Seton's defection. He would be preoccupied with only two things for the rest of his life: natural history and boys' work.

13

Black Wolf Meets B-P

It was Ernest Thompson Seton's conviction that "not one boy in a thousand is born bad. Boys have their badness thrust upon them. They are made bad by evil surroundings during the formative period between school and manhood; between twelve and twenty years of age."[1] All the experiences — real and imagined — that had made up his forty-one years of living had led Ernest Thompson Seton to the moment when he stood in front of a school assembly in Connecticut in 1901 and extended his invitation to a "picnic." Before him that day were the boys who had broken down his fences, attacked the animals within his park and written obscenities on his gates — boys who were obviously "bad" — yet he invited them to come back through those gates as his guests. The invitation was, in a sense, a deliberate gesture of defiance toward the Presbyterian upbringing which had taught him that children were foredoomed to hell because of their innate depravity; but it was also a challenge to himself to prove that his own instincts about children were correct.

At that time he had no children of his own, nor had he worked with children, yet from his own experience he was convinced that if a boy was given "something to do, something to think about, and something to enjoy in the woods,"[2] it was possible to channel his energies into positive accomplishments. As a small child his happiest hours had been spent in the family workshop, learning how to handle tools and creating things of use and beauty. He had found his "something to think about" in his investigation of his environment and in books, and in early youth he had found his "something to enjoy in the woods" of the Don Valley. These were the positive forces he recognized from his own childhood, the ones he was prepared to use to influence the lives of the youths who came to him on that weekend when "Seton's Indians" came into being.

When it came to finding a structure for his fledgling organization, he was hampered by his tendency to reject all the forces that he believed had warped his own life: formal religion, authoritarian controls and rigid discipline. "There are four possible forms of government," he wrote in *The Birch-Bark Roll of the Woodcraft Indians:* "First, the patriarchal, . . . it answers fairly for two or three, but fails with a considerable party. Second, the school system, which for several reasons, has not succeeded out of doors. Third, the Brigade, which many object to, chiefly because it fosters militarism; and last the Tribal or Indian form."[3]

Seton's choice of the Indian tribe as the unit of organization for his boys' group was inevitable. He had come to believe that "those live longest who live nearest to the ground, that is, who live the simple life of primitive times, divested, however, of the evils that ignorance in those times begot."[4] To Seton, the Indian living in harmony with his environment came the closest to this ideal, and the Indian form of organization was most clearly responsible for promoting that ideal. In *The Gospel of the Redman* he wrote:

> No man owns the wood of the forest, or the water of the rivers, or the soil of the earth. He did not make them, they are the harvest of the land that belongs to the whole people; and only so much of them is his as he can gather with his own hands and use in his own home. . . .
>
> The Tribe may give to one family the exclusive right to hunt or gather wood or forage or wild rice or fruit in one tract or range, but the family cannot sell this right, nor can they hire others to hunt or gather for them, lest the hunting be destroyed by overdrain.[5]

Seton believed that this "community," or "sociability," aspect of Indian life represented mankind's best hope for organizing itself to live in harmony with the environment, so the environment would continue to provide mankind with the necessities of life. Seton had not reached this conclusion simply by observing the Indian peoples' way of life since he had never actually lived among them long enough to have done so. And there is little to indicate that he had reached it through extensive reading on the various forms of political and economic structure. For example, in a conversation in 1903 he disappointed his brother William by saying that he had never read the works of Henry George on the Single Tax System because "he did not believe in scattering his energies but in sticking to one subject and doing that well."[6] He could not have escaped learning something about the subject from his brothers, however, for William, Enoch, Arthur and Alan were all rabid "Single Taxers," and William gave public lectures and wrote leaflets on the subject as well.

Most of his knowledge of socialism had been derived from discussions with James Mavor, the political economics professor at the University of Toronto whom he had met during the "Awaited in Vain" fiasco in 1893. Mavor was one of the signers of the Socialist League Manifesto in his early days in Glasgow, but he had reacted against the authoritarianism of Marxist socialism and was more closely aligned with the Fabian Socialists by the time that Seton knew him. After Mavor began to teach at the University of Toronto in 1892, he became interested in promoting labour colonies and co-operative societies on the Canadian prairies, and his investigation of the success of the Mennonite communal land-holdings prompted him to invite the anarchist Prince Peter Kropotkin to Canada. Kropotkin had been attempting to resolve the problems of Russia's Doukhobors, a deeply religious agrarian sect unwelcome in Russia because of their pacifism. When he found that Canada would not only grant them community land-holdings but also give them immunity from military service, he convinced Leo Tolstoy to provide passage money and, with James Mavor's aid, brought nearly eight thousand of them to Saskatchewan in 1899–1900.

There is little question that Mavor had considerable influence on Seton's thinking, especially since the two met so frequently in the ten years prior to the founding of Seton's Indian tribe. They were often together in 1893 during the "Awaited in Vain" affair, and met again in Paris in 1894. When Seton returned to Toronto for his mother's funeral in 1897, he was able to meet Kropotkin and hear his views on the democratic control of economic resources as it was practised in Doukhobor communities. Seton visited with Mavor again in 1898, and when he and Grace went to Toronto in February 1900 to speak on behalf of one of Mavor's charities, they stayed with the Mavors.

Probably Seton's most effective instructor in the art of communal living, however, was Charles A. Eastman, or Ohiyesa, a Sioux Indian from Minnesota. Eastman was a tiny child at the time of the Minnesota Massacre of 1862, and had been taken to Manitoba by his family when the army was called in to defend the settlers. Consequently, he was familiar with the country that Seton knew so well. (It had been his uncle, in fact, who had tried to claim Seton's moose in the fall of 1884.) Eastman had received a degree from the Boston University Medical School, but most of his work was carried out either among the Indian people or on their behalf. When he heard that Seton was interested in learning more about the Indian way of life, Eastman became his willing instructor.

Seton had also been moving steadily in the direction of conservation since he first realized the effect of the plough on the Manitoba prairies and had begun to see the land and the creatures closest to it endangered by the pioneering spirit. His own identification with the Indian and with wild creatures — especially the wolf — was leading him gradually into a lifelong crusade for recognition of the Indian system of government and shared use of resources, both of which could be adapted to the white man's way of life.

Although he was most familiar with the life of the Plains Indians, Seton drew from various tribal cultures in setting up his own tribe of boy Indians, justifying his selections with the motto: "The best things of the best Indians." Positions within his tribe's government of three elected war chiefs and twelve council members were based roughly on those of the Iroquois, as were their titles: Chief of the Council Fire, Keeper of the Tally, Keeper of the Wampum. But his system of honours was modelled on the Siouan quest for "glory," with feathers awarded for athletic prowess, and woodcraft skills judged against a standard of excellence rather than in competition with others. By making it a disgrace to lose one's "scalp" — a feather or tuft of hair worn in the lapel — for a dishonourable act, Seton also encouraged each individual's participation to the best of his ability. The games he invented for his braves, and the decoration of their costumes and tents, came from many tribes.

Seton's "Indians" were still in the laboratory stage in 1901, but they were formally introduced to the public in the May 1902 issue of *Ladies' Home Journal* in the column "Ernest Thompson Seton's Boys." Through this column, Seton presented his new organization's "Constitution, Laws, Games and Deeds," which were published later that year as *The Birch-Bark Roll of the Woodcraft Indians*. With Seton's column spreading the message, Woodcraft tribes began to spring up all over the United States, and within a year there were at least fifty of them with as many as fifty members in each. At this point Seton, or Black Wolf as he was now commonly known, introduced the concept of a confederation to be called "The League of Seton's Indians," later known as "The League of the Woodcraft Indians." Delegates to the league's annual grand council came from the councils of all the individual tribes. Probably the most important aspect of the whole organizational structure as far as Seton was concerned was the fact that adults only entered the scheme as advisors — medicine men — and never as authority figures, even in the grand council. He was convinced that control should be in the hands of the youths themselves, and he was equally convinced that though a grand council was necessary for the sharing of ideas, the real government of each tribe must rest with its membership, rather than be imposed from outside.

In October 1904, while Seton was on a lecture tour of England to promote *Two Little Savages* and *Monarch, the Big Bear of Tallac,* he decided to add a new lecture to his repertoire. "The Red Indian as I Know Him" was intended to test the English reaction to the Woodcraft Indian concept, but though some groups were established and Seton distributed copies of *The Birch-Bark Roll* wherever he saw an interest developing, the reaction was not encouraging. The average Englishman was not ready to allow his sons to emulate the red man.

In the summer of 1906, when Seton was again in England, he was shown a copy of a book on the training of military scouts, and promptly wrote to its author, Robert Stephenson Smyth Baden-Powell, to ask his help in popularizing his "boy camps" in

England. With this request he sent along a copy of *The Birch-Bark Roll*, by this time in its sixth edition.

Baden-Powell — or B-P as he was generally known — acknowledged receipt of the book on 1 August, and told Seton: "It may interest you to know that I had been drawing up a scheme, with a handbook to it for the education of boys as scouts — which curiously runs much on the lines of yours. So I need hardly say your work has a very special interest to me."[7]

The two met on 30 October 1906 at London's Savoy Hotel. After several conferences, it was decided that B-P would revise the scouting portion of *The Birch-Bark Roll* and be credited with this contribution in its next edition; however, he would not be helping to popularize Seton's "boy camps" because he had a "practically identical" plan for his own boy camps. When Baden-Powell brought out his *Scouting for Boys* in 1908, Seton "was astounded to find all [his] ideas taken, all [his] games appropriated, disguised with new names, the essentials of [his] plan utilized and not a word of acknowledgement . . . and not a word of explanation about why [he] should be left out of the movement [he] began."[8] Seton could find nothing in Baden-Powell's book that he had not already published in *Two Little Savages, The Birch-Bark Roll* or his woodcraft and scouting articles, and so far as he could see, the only changes Baden-Powell had made were to rename things and assume their authorship. All the new names were military in origin.

B-P's reply to Seton's protest was very courteous:

> Thank you very much for your kind letter. I much regret that I should have omitted mentioning the source of several of the games as being taken from your *Birch-Bark Roll,* but the truth is I had made a general statement to that effect in the introduction to the book which I afterwards cut out from at the beginning and have inserted it at the end where you will see it in Part 6. But in doing this I had not reflected that the remarks giving the authorship of the games would not be read by the people until after the games had appeared before them. I very much regret this oversight. It is very kind of you to take it in the good-natured way in which you have done.[9]

In spite of Seton's continuing protests, Baden-Powell did not give Seton credit in future editions. When Seton's British publisher complained, B-P replied that he had given Seton credit in ten places in the book, and furthermore he would undertake never to introduce *Scouting for Boys* into the United States so that it could not be considered competition in any case. However, in January 1910 Seton learned that a New York publisher had been offered the American publishing rights to the Englishman's book.

Seton's patriotism placed him at a disadvantage from the beginning in dealing with B-P because, in spite of his years of exile from England and more recently from Canada, he was still a British citizen, and though from time to time he would begin proceedings to become an American citizen, it would be another twenty-five years before he relinquished his British passport. Seton had contributed handsomely to Rudyard Kipling's Boer War Fund, and vigorously attacked American friends who upheld the rights of the Boers. Consequently, when he met Baden-Powell, what he saw before him was the "hero of Mafeking," not the man behind the legend.

In addition to being placed at a disadvantage by his admiration for Baden-Powell, Seton was hampered by his failure to judge the man's character correctly even after he had conferred with him on several occasions. Always eager to rub shoulders with the rich and famous, always anxious to increase his own status by associating with the "right" people, Seton had taken Baden-Powell at the value placed upon him by the press and the adoring British public during the Boer War. What Seton saw in Baden-Powell was exactly what he had wanted to be himself: the urbane upper-class Englishman, at home in the drawing rooms of the nobility. Baden-Powell would, in fact, later receive the knighthood that Seton had forecast for himself — though it would take him seven years longer than Seton's plan had stipulated.

Superficially, Baden-Powell was, of course, exactly what he appeared to be, but if Seton had realized that beneath that urbane exterior lay a man with "dedicated and almost frenzied ambition,"[10] he would never have put a copy of *The Birch-Bark Roll* in his hands, or been surprised at his actions when he did get hold of it. Baden-Powell was three years older than Seton, the son of an admiral's daughter and an Oxford geometry professor, neither of them wealthy. His father had been much older than his mother, and when he died she had been left to raise thirteen children and stepchildren on very limited funds. Being ferociously ambitious for her children, she invented a system for getting on in this world — a competition she called "grouping events." This term simply meant that each of her children's successes had to lead to two more successes or they did not "count." Spurred on by this incentive system, one of her sons became a Conservative MP and was knighted, another became a successful barrister and artist, another an aviation pioneer and president of the aeronautical society, another a judge and author in India, another a leading London barrister. Their mother, to provide all of them with a little more dignity, had hyphenated her husband's two names to give her sons the surname Baden-Powell.

For her third to youngest son, Robert, she wangled a scholarship to Charterhouse School and expected him to go on to Oxford like his brothers, but he was not accepted. He then sat for the open military exams for officer training, passed in the top six, and was sent to India with the 13th Hussars. From then on his only problem was how to stay in the competition with his brothers. This he did by publishing manuals on military topics and sports. He was not too concerned whether anyone bought them, but sent copies of them to influential people as "advertisements" for himself.[11] He also made sure he was seen at all social events of the British Raj so that his name frequently turned up in the English newspapers. Although he was not much of a scholar, he had made a reputation for himself at Charterhouse as a cartoonist and an actor in school plays, and he used both of these talents to good effect in the officers' mess, thus gaining more renown.

But B-P's real opportunity came when he was transferred to South Africa in 1899 and led his 5th Dragoon Guards into the settlement of Mafeking, remaining there under siege for 217 days. He emerged from Mafeking a hero, thereby surpassing anything his brothers had done or were ever likely to do for the rest of their lives. Facts uncovered in the last twenty years, however, indicate that he achieved his renown by less than heroic measures. By taking his troops into Mafeking in the first place and then remaining to be trapped by the Boers, he had been acting against explicit orders. Later, he could have withdrawn his force through one of the channels by which he sent out his regular dispatches — most of which were intended to enhance his own prestige — but he refused to budge. He even made arrangements through these channels to publish his newest book, *Aids to Scouting,* in order to take advantage of his hero status. He took credit for organizing the "boy scouts" of Mafeking, though the scouts had actually existed before the Guards arrived, and were then used as messengers by Baden-Powell's second-in-command, Lord Edward Cecil.

Robert Baden-Powell had, in fact, been trained to make the most of every opportunity, and when Seton sent him a copy of *The Birch-Bark Roll,* he did what he had been trained to do: he used it as the basis for his own scouting program in Britain and saved himself immeasurable time and energy. He did not possess half of Seton's creative ability, but he knew how to use what was put in front of him. What galled Seton most about his plagiarism was the fact that Baden-Powell had subverted his games and activities to militaristic ends. "My aim was to make a man," Seton wrote in his *History of the Boy Scouts;* "Baden-Powell's was to make a soldier."[12]

In August 1907 Baden-Powell held a trial camp at Brownsea Island in Dorset. The program was similar to that used by Woodcraft groups except that military terms were used for the organization, and the emphasis was on scouting in the military sense of the word. In December of the same year, Arthur Pearson of the London *Daily Express* gave Baden-Powell an office and began publishing the official paper of his new organization, *The Scout.* Thus were the Boy Scouts launched in Great Britain.

Meanwhile, in the United States, the establishment of new Woodcraft tribes had been slowly falling off, and Seton's publishers began pressuring him to drop the Indian model he had adopted for his organization. "There are too many Americans who think of Indians as dirty and loafing degenerates or as savages," wrote H. W. Lanier of Doubleday Page, "to make the idea popular when they think of educating their children."[13] Seton had always been aware of this problem and sought to overcome it by stressing that his organization was using only "the best things of the best Indians," but by 1910 he had to accept that "many people were repelled by the name 'Indian.' They imagined we were teaching the boys to imitate Indians."[14]

Seton's recruitment problem was not entirely the fault of the Indians' poor public image; he was also facing strong competition from the organizers of other boys' groups. The most successful of these was Dan Beard, whom he had first met at the Art Students

League classes in 1884. Like Seton, Beard was an illustrator and writer; he was also Seton's colleague in the Camp Fire Club. In 1904 Beard had become the editor of *Recreation* magazine and from that vantage point started an organization called "The Sons of Daniel Boone." Each of his recruits was signed up as a "tenderfoot," then, after passing certain tests, achieved the rank of "scout." When *Recreation* was sold in 1906, Beard took his organization to *Woman's Home Companion,* but two years later, when he resigned from this magazine, the publishers commissioned Baden-Powell to write a monthly column to replace Beard's. The name "The Sons of Daniel Boone" was allowed to lapse since B-P wished to address his young readers as "boy scouts." Beard, in the meantime, had gone to *Pictorial Review* and started a new boys' club which he called "The Boy Pioneers," though it seems to have been identical to his "Sons of Daniel Boone." Beard never published a manual but relied on his column to recruit new members.

Seton actually helped set up another of his competitors. Luther Gulick, as president of the Playground Association of America, persuaded Seton to adapt his program for use in the tenement areas of New York. This new program was christened "The Indian Scouts." There were three more groups calling themselves "scouts": "The Boy Scouts of the United States," organized by Col. Peter S. Bomus; "The National Scouts of America," by Brig.-Gen. William Verbeck, and "The American Boy Scouts," promoted by William Randolph Hearst in his New York *Journal.*

Consequently, when in January 1910 Seton learned that Baden-Powell was looking for an American publisher for *Scouting for Boys,* he was more worried than angry. With so many scouting groups already vying for the allegiance of American youth, none was strong enough to battle a concerted membership drive by Baden-Powell. Seton's own recruitment had fallen off drastically so that after eight years he had only 100,000 Woodcraft Indians enrolled in the United States; Baden-Powell in Britain had been able, in just two years, to sign up double that number. Seton reacted first by making one more attempt to divide up the territory between himself and Baden-Powell, and to gain recognition from B-P for the materials he had stolen from *The Birch-Bark Roll.* On 10 January he wrote an "open letter" to Baden-Powell which gave "A History of the Boy Scout Movement," that is, a history of the Woodcraft Indian movement and an outline of the specific things which Baden-Powell had borrowed from him without leave. Then he suggested that future editions of *Scouting for Boys* should include on the title page the words:

"with which is incorporated by arrangement *The Birch-Bark Roll* of the Indian Scouts by Ernest Thompson Seton." You could then incorporate as much as you like of the *Birch-Bark Roll* but keep it in my words and state at the place "from the Birch-Bark Roll." You should refrain from introducing the book into America. I for my part will shortly get out a new edition of *The Birch-Bark Roll* and will state on the title-page conversely "with which is combined *Scouting for Boys* by General Sir Robert Baden-Powell" and whatever I use from you in the body of the work I will make acknowledgement at the place. I will also withdraw my book from circulation in Great Britain and Ireland. . . . I learned from some of my friends on one of the large magazines here that *Scouting for Boys* has been offered to them for publication. If you accept my views as herein expressed you will withdraw this, leaving the American field entirely to me so far as that publication is concerned.[15]

When this appeal only brought another of Baden-Powell's courteous but inadequate replies, Seton realized that his alternatives had been reduced to one: to prevent Baden-Powell's inroads into the United States, Seton would have to amalgamate with other youth groups and use a more popular format. On 15 June 1910 representatives from thirty-seven youth agencies met at the YMCA in New York City, and within six days they had drawn up a constitution, and named an executive committee and an organization committee. After long deliberation, it was decided that the new movement should be called the Boy Scouts of America. Some warning bell seems to have sounded in Seton's head at this time, however, because instead of automatically making all his Indians into Boy Scouts, he continued to maintain his Woodcraft League as a separate organization, even though he was able to give them only scant attention during the next few years.

Seton was appointed chairman of the executive committee of the BSA, and began work by organizing a trial camp-out similar to Baden-Powell's experiment at Brownsea Island. The place chosen was Silver Bay on Lake George in upper New York state, where approximately 150 boys and leaders gathered on 16 August 1910. The boys were put through the routines of a standard Woodcraft Indian camp-out with Seton leading them; their adult leaders were given the standard British Boy Scout leadership course by W. B. Wakefield, who had come directly from B-P's office.

Up to this time, Seton's troubles had all come from Baden-Powell and the British Boy Scouts, but when he arrived back in New York City on 5 September, his difficulties with the Boy Scouts of America began. Most of the BSA executive had decided that for their organization they preferred the British Boy Scout model to that of the Woodcraft Indians, ostensibly because the Woodcraft League system was too decentralized and inefficient to allow the development of a nation-wide organization. In fact, they found the Woodcraft system less attractive because it allowed little adult intervention and set up the Indian as the standard of excellence. To switch to the British model, the BSA had to be reincorporated with a new constitution, and this time, the executive committee was composed of politicians, bankers, social workers, teachers and military men, instead of youth group organizers as in the first committee. Seton, who found himself left off the committee entirely, was given the title of Chief Scout, but it did not take him long to discover that he was now only a figurehead. Beard, Bomus and Verbeck had also been sidetracked as "National Scout Commissioners" without powers of any kind.

A lawyer named James E. West became the new executive secretary of the BSA. West was a close personal friend of Theodore Roosevelt who, though no longer president of the United States, still had enormous influence. He had just returned from a tour of Africa and Europe and, eager to be involved in the life of his country again, took an immediate interest in the new scouting group. West, who was already completely sold on Baden-Powell's concept of scouting, also believed as Roosevelt did that the BSA should be a prime training ground for the army. He was willing to retain Seton in the Scouts both as an advertisement for the "camping-out" aspects of the program, and because of his well-known name, but believed he should be kept at a distance from the actual machinery of the operation.

While the BSA was in this organizational upheaval, Baden-Powell had been on a cross-Canada promotion tour for the Scouts, and it was agreed that he would detour to New York to

ABOVE: Seton, Julia Moss Buttree and friends camping on first expedition to find land for a school in New Mexico, 1927 (Courtesy Seton Village).

LEFT: Julia Moss Buttree, c. 1921 (Courtesy Seton Village).

CLOCKWISE FROM TOP LEFT: Seton, Julia Moss Seton and the baby Beulah (Dee), 1938 (Courtesy Seton Village); Beulah (Dee) Seton, 1944 (Courtesy Seton Village); Beulah (Dee) and Julia Seton, 1944 (Courtesy Seton Village); Julia Seton in eagle-feather headdress with Seton, 1939 (Courtesy Seton Village); Seton and Julia Moss Seton, 1939 (Courtesy Seton Village).

Seton Castle seen from the west,
Santa Fe, New Mexico, c. 1938
(Courtesy Seton Village).

address the BSA executive at a dinner to be held in his honour. Seton, as Chief Scout, was required to act as his host. Baden-Powell, always equal to a potentially unpleasant situation, told his audience that he considered Seton and Beard to be the fathers of the scouting movement; he was just one of the uncles. Later, however, "Uncle" illustrated exactly where he believed he stood in the family when the three men were asked by the YMCA director to pose for a picture to mark the historic occasion. Wrote Seton: "The assumption was that we were equals. As we were about to pose, B-P said, 'I think I'll sit down,' and moved over to the ventilator [on the roof of the YMCA]. You [Dan Beard] and I had to stand, by which trick he made us his subordinates, although he was the latest to enter the field."[16]

Throughout the first three years of his new appointment, Seton was busy touring the country, visiting new Scout troops and lecturing community organizations on the value of scouting. When he came back to report to the executive council that many parents were concerned about the Scouts' emphasis on military drills and discipline, West and his council members were annoyed, but otherwise they could find no fault with his lecture tours since enrollment was steadily increasing. They overlooked his continuing emphasis on woodcraft activities even when he did a series of articles on woodcraft for *The American Boy* in 1912. In fact, when the BSA acquired *Boy's Life* as its official organ later that year, Seton was asked to produce a woodcraft series for it as well. In the meantime, the council had been busy on a massive revision of the Scout manual that Seton had prepared for the BSA in 1911. In the process of re-editing and inserting new material, Seton's name had appeared over policies and information with which he totally disagreed. To appease Seton's anger when he found out, the council appointed him associate editor of *Boy's Life,* along with Dan Beard.

Seton accepted the position but not the revised manual. Consequently, when the manual was ready for reprinting in 1914, the council decided to give the contract to Grosset and Dunlap instead of Doubleday Page, who had published the first manual and all editions of Seton's *Birch-Bark Roll.* Frank Doubleday, who was Seton's personal friend and therefore aware of the friction within the BSA, wrote to Seton on 19 August 1914 to suggest that his resignation from the BSA would straighten out many complications. "I think it would be unfortunate for everybody," he commented, "if it got around that there was a row; it would do neither you nor the Boy Scouts any good."[17]

This was not the first time one of Seton's friends had urged him to quit. On 12 December 1912 William Hornaday, the director of the New York Zoological Park, had written to congratulate him on his latest woodcraft book, then went on to scold Seton:

> . . . now for goodness sake, LET UP on Boy Scouting, Woodcraft and imitation Indians, and climb back to your legitimate field. I can't bear any longer to see such talents as yours frittered away on any of the three subjects I have named. . . . your side issues are now so engrossing your attention that your art has entirely disappeared and I feel that you will abandon your legitimate field forever.[18]

Although Seton was fully aware that the BSA was taking up too much of his time, and that the rewards for his work were steadily dwindling, he had up to this time stubbornly refused to resign. His "berserker streak" still lurked beneath the surface and made him determined that somehow he would force the executive to bow to his will. Doubleday's assurance that he had grounds to resign since his contributions to the manual had been altered without permission only made him change his tactics: he issued a warning that he *would* resign unless he was given a greater say in the policies of the organization. Convinced that he was indispensable to the BSA, Seton believed the executive could not afford to accept his resignation and they would have to give him the power he was demanding.

While West would have liked nothing better than to have Seton out of his hair, he could not accept his resignation because the public might interpret this as the BSA's ingratitude to its founding father. On the other hand, West had no intention of giving Seton more power, so he refused his resignation and sent an emissary to find out whether an arrangement could be made to "retire" him without a public scrap. In the meantime, West looked about for some way to discredit Seton so that he could be justifiably dumped without damage to the BSA's image.

While these negotiations were going on, war broke out in Europe and provided the solution to West's problem. Although the United States was not actively involved in the conflict, the tug-of-war between those citizens who felt their country should join the fight and those who felt she should not had made the question of patriotism and citizenship uppermost in everyone's mind. Seton, who was still a British citizen even though he had lived in the United States for eighteen years, offered his services to the British government in any capacity that would help the defence of the homeland. His gesture gave West the pretext that he needed: it was obviously unthinkable that an individual with loyalties to a foreign country should head a patriotic organization like the Boy Scouts of America. When West pointed this out, Seton immediately announced plans to take out his American papers — as soon as the war in Europe was over.

Either to avoid a showdown over this issue at the annual general meeting or by an oversight, Seton went to England on a lecture tour in February 1915 and was consequently unable to stand for his annual re-election as Chief Scout. No one else was nominated and the position was left vacant. When Seton returned later that spring, he submitted his official resignation as Chief Scout, but maintained his other positions in the hope of winning the next round of the battle with West.

He had not reckoned on the latest crusade of his old friend Theodore Roosevelt. Despite his defeat in the presidential election of 1912 and the complete rejection of his Progressive Party in the congressional elections of 1914, Roosevelt's pronouncements had a powerful effect on public opinion, and when he launched a campaign for military preparedness, there was an immediate groundswell of support. In speech after speech he thundered against the pacifists and the "peace-at-any-price men," and inevitably he looked toward the BSA in whose ranks he expected to find tomorrow's soldiers. It took very little suggestion to convince him that the safety of the nation was being sabotaged by the teachings of Ernest Thompson Seton.

On 30 November 1915, in a letter to James West in which he refused an invitation to speak on behalf of a scout fund-raising drive, Roosevelt cited his need to have "one or two things clearer in [his] mind" concerning the BSA's organization.

> It is my understanding that as a part of the wicked and degrading pacifist agitation of the last few years, certain leaders [of the Boy Scouts] . . . have used the Boy Scout organization as a medium for

the dissemination of pacifist literature, and have done everything they could to use the organization as a propaganda for interfering with the training of our boys to a standard of military efficiency. Now, I believe that the professional pacifists by their activities during the last half dozen years have done more damage to this country and to humanity than all the political and business crooks combined. The effort to prevent the boys of this country of the kind who naturally should be gathered into the Boy Scouts from being trained to arms so that they could serve the country in the time of need, and the effort to prevent their acquiring the spirit of self-respect which will make them eager and ready to fight for the right both as individuals and as members of the nation, these efforts from my point of view, represent treason to the country and treason to the cause of humanity.

A Boy Scout who is not trained actively and affirmatively that it is his duty to bear arms for the country in time of need is at least negatively trained to be a sissy, and there cannot be anything worse for this country than to have an organization of boys brought up to the mushy milk-and-water which is the stock in trade of the apostles of pacifism. . . . I am heartily in favour of an organization of boys which shall teach them, as these boys for example in England have been taught, that is, that shall teach them the duties of gentleness and chivalry toward the weak, of good citizenship in internal affairs, and as no less important, the duty of fitting themselves in mind and body so that they shall regard cowardice as an unpardonable sin and physical and moral flabbiness as disgraceful, and shall be eager and willing to bear their part in any war this country feels it necessary to engage in.[19]

When it was leaked to Seton that Roosevelt was about to label him publicly as a pacifist, Seton demanded that West accept the resignation he had submitted eight months earlier; at the same time, he relinquished all his other positions in the BSA. Seton had learned during the "Nature Faker" affair that being one of Roosevelt's targets was "no joke."

When West still delayed in accepting the resignation, Seton called a press conference and told reporters that in failing to act on his resignation, the BSA had treated him and the public unfairly, especially in continuing to use his name. The *New York Times* ran the story the following day:

Speaking of the Boy Scout Movement as he conceived it, Mr. Seton, summing up the situation, said: "Seton started it; Baden-Powell boomed it; West killed it."

To make his position clear, Mr. Seton said: "It should be clearly understood that I esteem the Executive Board of the Boy Scouts to be a splendid lot of men, giving freely of their time and money to the work. My only criticism is that they have allowed all direction and power to centre in the hands of James E. West, a lawyer, who is a man of great executive ability but without knowledge of the activities of boys; who has no point of contact with boys, and who, I might almost say, has never seen the blue sky in his life."[20]

Seton then told reporters that he had resigned because West had "robbed the movement of its spirituality and introduced purely material meanings to it."[21] West promptly accepted the resignation and responded with a statement the following day; it read in part:

As stated by Dr. William T. Hornaday of the New York Zoological Society in the appeal in the present campaign, "The Boy Scouts movement is a great national antidote for the devilish spirit of anarchy to the States and nation that is now cropping up like rank and poisonous weeds all along the path of our nation's progress." When it was discovered that Mr. Seton was in harmony with the views of anarchists and radical socialists on the question as to whether the Boy Scouts of America should stand for patriotism and good citizenship, no time was lost in developing the issue. Mr. Seton was given a reasonable, fair opportunity to make himself clear on this subject, but he hedged and stated that he could not make a definite promise that he would ever become a citizen of the United States.

Indeed, he went further and repeated his objection to the Boy Scout handbook, including a chapter on "Patriotism," and contended that the Boy Scouts of America should not undertake to have boys pledge allegiance to their country, but should leave them to support our country when they thought our country was right and to damn it when they thought it was wrong. He personally made clear that he damned our country for most of its past history. This is the real and only reason that Mr. Seton is not now Chief Scout of the Boy Scouts of America.[22]

Seton replied with a statement of his own.

> You notice that Mr. West does not reply to any of my statements, but contents himself with calling me an anarchist and socialist. It is quite the first time in my life that any one has taken such a view of me. Not long ago, West accused me of being a "monarchist" and said I was too "autocratic." If the Boy Scout Board will look up my letter they will find that in the same paragraph in which I criticize America for the Mexican Wars I was still more severe on England for the Chinese Opium War. In other words, I was denouncing all aggressive warfare. I am sorry to learn that the Chief Scout Executive approves such things.
>
> The case is very clear. First, I am not in sympathy with the present trend of the Boy Scout movement; second, I think I have a national message to deliver; and third, I can deliver that message best through the Woodcraft League. Henceforth I shall focus my activities on that work.[23]

When Roosevelt learned that Seton's resignation had been accepted, he telephoned West that he was "heart and soul behind the Boy Scout Movement."[24] *Boys' Life* marked Seton's departure with an anonymously written article entitled "Why Mr. Seton is Not Chief Scout," which explained that "the Scout Movement is in no wise affected by the dropping of Mr. Seton. . . . Mr. Seton was not a member of the Editorial Board which compiled the original handbook. . . . The comparatively small number of pages of material written by Mr. Seton are interesting, but nothing essential to the program of Scouting. They can be easily replaced in future editions by eminent American citizens."[25]

It was one of the eccentricities of Seton's character that having made up his mind to hate a man, it was almost impossible for him to ever think well of him again, and conversely, when he had decided on the essential goodness of a man, he could never think ill of him. Consequently, although Theodore Roosevelt had twice made him a target of one of his campaigns, Seton could not believe the great man had actually meant him harm, and at the time of Roosevelt's sudden death in January 1919, Seton was able to write in all sincerity:

It is very difficult to appraise fairly the gifts of a man in the highest possible place of power; but we whose business it is to learn, and gather up the learning of the world of the outdoors, do not hesitate to give to Roosevelt a position in the front rank of naturalist.

He and I have several times differed in matters of detail, but in all large issues of my interests we have been at one; . . .[26]

In later years Seton came to believe that his ouster from the BSA had not depended on his British citizenship or his supposed pacifism, but on a "conspiracy" that had been mounted to get rid of him. In a letter to Dan Beard he wrote:

I was charged, tried and condemned in my absence, without knowledge of offence or a chance to defend myself, expelled from the Scouts. Not a word is said [in W. D. Murray's *The History of the Boy Scouts of America*] about the fact that my secret offense was that I am in some matters a *socialist*. Nothing is said about the fact that the Wall Street Gang apparently dictated this conspiracy.[27]

Seton may have been right about the conspiracy, though the BSA executive certainly had grounds enough to remove him for his anti-war statements or even for his refusal to become an American citizen. But responsibility for Seton's defeat must really be laid at the feet of the one man who played no part in these final scenes of the drama at all — B-P. For it was Baden-Powell and what he stood for that conquered the Woodcraft ideal in the BSA.

14

The Living Animal

When John Burroughs had taken aim at *Wild Animals I Have Known* in 1903, Seton made up his mind that he would force Burroughs to take back his words, and eventually he had the satisfaction of seeing Burroughs make amends of a sort in the pages of *Atlantic Monthly*. But Burroughs had planted doubts in the minds of the magazine's readers that were not so easily dispelled, and Seton could hardly parade every one of these doubters through his study to see his "one thousand mammal skins and two thousand bird skins." Yet somehow he had to restore to his animal stories the authenticity that Burroughs's article had destroyed, because his income depended on the sale of his books.

Early in 1904 Seton was still trying to decide what Burroughs did believe animals were capable of, and trying to formulate his own views. Burroughs, he finally concluded, credited animals "with intelligence, gleams of reason, and altruism," but denied them "memory."[1] Seton, on the other hand, believed that an animal's intelligence came to it from three sources, all of them based on memory: its instincts or the inherited experience of its ancestors; the example of its contemporaries, and its own experience. (His story of "Tito, the Coyote That Learned How" illustrates all three.) His conclusions were based on his twenty-five years of field work, and while much of that time had been consumed in the collection, dissection and mounting of specimens, the bulk of his journal entries detailed his observations of mammal and bird behaviour. His animal stories had been the natural outcome of his belief that the study of behaviour was just as valuable, if not more valuable, than the collection and identification of specimens. "We and the beasts are kin," he wrote in *Wild Animals I Have Known,*[2] and therefore by understanding the animals' behaviour, man may understand himself better. Roosevelt, by complaining that Seton had gone "too far in emphasizing the scientific value of his tales," had struck at the heart of Seton's convictions.

Seton's interest in the study of behaviour had been evident in his two earliest attempts at purely scientific work: "The Mammals of Manitoba" in 1886 and *The Birds of Manitoba* in 1891.[3] Both of these works had needed much more specific data on distribution, abundance and habitat to make their behavioural information acceptable to the scientific community as science, rather than just nature lore. Following their publication, he had continued to gather information on Manitoba wildlife, and in 1898 had announced his intention to write a treatise on thirty species of North American horned ruminants; after the "Nature Faker" affair it came to him that by enlarging the scope of such a work, he had the means at hand to redeem his credibility.

He would prepare a monumental volume on northern animals, a work so comprehensive that no one would ever again question his qualifications as a naturalist. It would contain not only his own observations on the subject but all information that had been gathered to that time. The foundation for this work would be "The Mammals of Manitoba" which had been approved and published by the Historical and Scientific Society of Manitoba in May 1886 as their "Transaction No. 23." Although he lacked scientific training and sophisticated laboratory instruments, Seton, even in this first effort, had managed to identify and demonstrate varying degrees of familiarity with fifty-four out of a possible eighty species of mammal to be found in Manitoba. For the most part, however, it had not been much more than a list of animals; although he had been able to write more than five hundred words of information about the ground squirrel (*Spermophilus richardsoni richardsoni*), his comment on the star-nosed mole (*Condylura cristata*) had been limited to "Mr. Hine informs me that he has seen specimens of this mole taken within our province."[4] In spite of the limitations of this early work, Seton recognized its value as a starting point for his new book.

His first year was spent correlating his own data with the information collected and published by others on the animals living within the region of his first study — the province of Manitoba as it existed until 1905 (between the forty-ninth and the fifty-third parallels). After this preliminary review, he was able to establish the relevance of his study to a much larger area. The next step was to return to field work himself.

In spite of a heavy schedule of lectures for his Woodcraft Indian League, he was able to sandwich in a month in Manitoba in the late summer of 1904, and similar periods in 1905 and 1906. While in New York, he spent his time in the Museum of Natural History, and on visits to England on Woodcraft business and book promotion tours in 1904 and 1906 he haunted the British Museum. He carried on an enormous correspondence with game wardens, foresters, guides, sportsmen and anyone else who worked in the wilds in order to gather data on animal specimens which they had taken. "I am at work on marten notes with yours before me," he wrote to Roderick MacFarlane of the Hudson's Bay Company in Winnipeg. "Will you drop me a line (card) stating *how far apart your marten* traps were placed in the Mackenzie River experience you speak of when you got 60 skins, but were thwarted by the wolverines. Also how far apart the Saulteaux Indian traps were when he got 39 marten in 40 traps — i.e. *how long was the line in each case.*"[5]

Seton spent a month in the Lake Timiskaming area of Ontario studying the moose population and made an expedition to the Bitter Root mountains of Idaho to observe mountain goats at close range. In the late spring of 1906 he detoured from England to see the reindeer in northern Norway so that he could make comparisons with the horned animals of North America. His most ambitious field trip in search of data for this mammoth work, however, was his six-month safari to the Arctic Barren Lands in 1907 to see the caribou. His companion on this venture was Edward A. Preble of the United States Biological Survey in Washington, who had spent three seasons exploring the north, especially the Mackenzie River area and the District of Keewatin.

The destination they chose was Aylmer Lake, northeast of Great Slave Lake in Mackenzie District, where they had been told it would be possible to see enormous herds of caribou.

Preble joined Seton in Winnipeg on 5 May, and together they boarded the train for Edmonton. Thirteen days later they left Athabasca Landing in the canoe *Anne Seton,* with a convoy of thirteen scows loaded with supplies destined for northern communities. They were headed downriver toward the Arctic Ocean. At Fort McMurray, unwilling to wait for the steamer that was to carry them on the next leg of the trip, they bought a thirty-foot flat-bottomed boat, loaded their canoe and all the supplies they would need for six months on board, and continued north with only a Scottish-Indian guide to assist them.

At Smith Landing on the Slave River, Maj. A. M. Jarvis of the Royal North-West Mounted Police invited Seton to join him in a survey of the buffalo herds which were reported to exist west of the river. Seton saw a buffalo herd for the first time on 13 June; it was not the teeming thousands he had dreamed of when he first saw the Manitoba prairies twenty-five years earlier, but a mere dozen or so at a time, and he was once more impressed with the urgent need for conservation laws.

When they reached Fort Resolution on Great Slave Lake, Seton and Preble hired a York boat and seven Indian oarsmen to take them and their supplies to the northeast end of the lake. The trip was slow and made even slower by a lazy and rebellious crew; they certainly did not rank with Seton's "best Indians." He was appalled at their desire to kill everything that moved, and commented: "Each of them carries a Winchester and blazes away at every living thing that appears. They have volleyed all day at every creature big enough to afford a mouthful — Ducks, Gulls, Loons, Fish, Owls, Terns, etc. . . . It is nothing but kill, kill, kill every living thing they meet. . . ."[6]

They arrived at Pike's Portage on 28 July, and when the supplies had been unloaded, the crew was sent back to Fort Resolution in the York boat. From there Seton and Preble proceeded with only two men, travelling northeast on Artillery Lake, then northwest on Clinton-Colden Lake, and finally into the northern arm of Aylmer Lake, arriving at their most northerly point, Sand Hill Bay, on 20 August. The trip was crowned with "extraordinary luck" which began with the sighting of caribou while the men were still travelling on Artillery Lake; soon they encountered bands of four or five hundred at a time. They found musk-ox near Aylmer Lake and collected a nine-hundred-pound specimen. They also took an arctic fox in its summer coat and several lynxes.

The return trip took nearly two months of canoeing, and almost ended in tragedy when the canoe overturned in the Athabasca River Canyon. The men were able to save themselves and their damaged canoe, but the river carried away all their bedding, food, guns and specimens. Far worse for Seton, it carried off his "three precious journals" in their waterproof canvas bag — "600 pages of observation and discovery, geographical, botanical, and zoological, 500 drawings, valuable records made under all sorts of trying circumstances, discovery and compass survey of the beautiful Nyarling River, compass survey of the two great northern lakes, discovery of two great northern rivers, many lakes, a thousand things of interest to others and priceless to me — my summer's work — gone."[7]

By following the river bank, they were able to recover some of their belongings, and the journal bag itself was finally rescued by the two guides after they had run some fourteen miles downriver after it. Its precious contents were undamaged.

In Edmonton on 4 November Seton stopped only long enough to visit briefly with his friend Pauline Johnson and give a luncheon speech to the Canadian Club before he caught the train for home. The story of this canoe trip would eventually become *The Arctic Prairies,* published in 1911, but most of the information in the journals went immediately into his larger project.

Back at Wyndygoul, Seton set himself a gruelling work schedule, writing all morning and drawing all afternoon and evening, breaking only long enough for a brief walk before dinner. Within a short time the eye-strain headaches which had plagued him for nearly twenty years became acute. Seton had experimented with many different lenses, but on this occasion he was referred to an opthalmologist who recommended bifocals, which cured his headaches and saved the book. The manuscript was in the hands of his publisher by mid-August of 1908; for four years it had consumed most of his waking hours and the bulk of his energies.

Meanwhile, he had embarked on a new project, the outcome of discussions with Preble while travelling in the Arctic. Seton had been trying to devise a permanent "blind" which he could use for long-term observation of birds and small mammals. He had made blinds in the past in places which he knew to be frequented by animals, but they were generally temporary — usually natural hollows in the ground covered with brush, and once he had used a hollow in the garbage dump at Yellowstone Park. What he was attempting to design now was a structure that would provide a habitat for birds and small animals so that he could follow their activities over a period of months or even years, a habitat set up at a location convenient for *him* rather than for the creatures that would live in it. The product of his discussions with Preble was a design for a natural laboratory resembling a hollow tree with inside access for Seton.

As soon as he returned to Wyndygoul, Seton drew up his final plans for the laboratory, and in March 1908 he began building it on one of the islands in his lake. Thirty-five feet high, seven feet in diameter at the bottom and one and a half feet across at the top, it was sheathed with a layer of bark-covered chestnut planks that were perforated at intervals with holes of varying sizes; these led to nestboxes which had been nailed in place inside the "tree." A ladder allowed Seton to climb up to each nestbox and observe the activity within through peepholes and small doors.

The "tree" was completed by mid-July, but in early September it was still unoccupied, and while Seton worried, his friends speculated on his chances of success. Frank Chapman was sure it would remain empty; William Hornaday was convinced that starlings would become the sole tenants. Seton was determined that he would have an "osprey nest at the top, purple grackles between the sticks [dead branches that had been nailed to the top], bats in the garret, and purple martins, starlings, pigeons, et cetera, all the way down to the ground with woodchucks at proper intervals."[8]

In time the wild creatures did accept the "family flats" provided for them, though not quite as Seton had ordered them; he spent long hours inside the structure documenting their activities. Then, beginning in November 1908, he wrote a series of "progress bulletins" on life within his artificial tree for *Country Life in America*. There were ten bulletins in the series "Making a Hollow Tree and What Came into It," and then two follow-up articles in September 1911 and October 1912.

In 1909 he investigated the problems involved in raising mink and otter for their fur, but he garnered the most publicity for his experiments in raising skunks. These animals provided him with another series of articles, this time for *Field and Stream*. A number of photographs show him and his small daughter petting the skunks which, incidentally, had not been "denatured."

Meanwhile, to test reaction to his forthcoming work on northern mammals, Seton sold excerpts to popular magazines. He also published a booklet in November 1907 called *The Natural History of the Ten Commandments,* in which he expounded the theory he was formulating on moral evolution. The Decalogue, he suggested, was not simply an arbitrary set of moral injunctions for man, but a reflection of the moral order of all animals: the higher the animal is on the ladder of social development, the greater its morality. He noted, for example, that the Decalogue identifies monogamy as a highly moral trait, and that highly developed creatures such as wolves mate for life while animals low on the scale are promiscuous. Therefore, if man is the product of evolution, as Darwinians believed, it follows that he will only find true moral fulfillment in the strictest of monogamous relationships. Seton also saw models in animal behaviour for the sharing of tasks within marriage and for child-rearing. Reviewers were not sure whether to take the book seriously but played it safe by suggesting that it presented a "possible" argument for moral evolution.

As soon as his northern animals book went to the printers, Seton set to work revising his Woodcraft manual and completing his first "animal story" book in four years: *The Biography of a Silver Fox or Domino Reynard of Goldur Town.* The two-volume *Life Histories of Northern Animals* was released in September 1909 and dedicated to the Prince of Wales (later King George V), who had been in Quebec in July 1908 to dedicate a national monument on the Plains of Abraham. The books contained data on 59 animal species, 68 distribution maps, more than 100 full-colour plates made from Seton's watercolour animal portraits, and nearly 350 black-and-white drawings. Without exception, the members of the scientific community recognized the value of the work. Chapman wrote that "Seton has done for our mammals what Audubon did for our birds, but he has done it better."[9] William Brewster warned that "any attempt to criticize it would be likely to recoil like a boomerang upon him who made it."[10] J. A. Allen pronounced it "without a rival, and beyond comparison the best work of its kind that has ever been written. Indeed it is safe to say that nothing having the same scope and detail, either in text or illustrations, has ever before been attempted."[11] But it was Theodore Roosevelt himself who put the "Nature Faker" charge to rest at last when he wrote that *Life Histories* was "one of the most valuable contributions any naturalist has made to the life histories of American Mammals."[12]

Reviewers loved *Life Histories*. The *Nation* (2 December 1909) announced that it was "a serious, scholarly, exact, and at times almost painfully conscientious work of science, yet made clear and 'popular' for the benefit of the reading multitude and having also the most understandable and charming dissertations on the various habits of wild animals that have ever been laid before the public under the rules of science."[13] The *Literary Digest* (19 February 1910) commended the author for putting his "emphasis upon the mind of the living animal rather than upon the anatomy of the dead animal,"[14] and the *Spectator* (1 October 1910) said, "It must claim its place on the shelves of all libraries of standing, not only as a storehouse of pleasure and learning, but as a volume of reference which takes its rank at once as a classic."[15] And to crown this triumph, *Life Histories* was awarded the Camp Fire Gold Medal for 1909.

The best was yet to come, however, as far as Seton was concerned, for *Life Histories* had not only restored and enhanced his prestige as a naturalist but also returned his animal stories to favour with America's reading public. When *The Biography of a Silver Fox* was released no one dared to mention "sham natural history" or "nature faking." *Athenaeum* (29 May 1909) called the new book "a stirring, sympathetic narrative" with "the merit of being taken conscientiously from nature,"[16] and the *Literary Digest* (15 May 1909) reported that "in his hundred clever and suggestive illustrations Mr. Seton maintains his reputation as not only an artist but a naturalist."[17] These reviews would have delighted any writer, but especially one who had just spent four years writing a scientific treatise which, because of the cost of publishing it, would never make him any money. Seton's publishers immediately reprinted all his earlier animal story books, thereby making a small fortune in which the author shared.

Having at last proved the scientific value of his animal stories to everyone's satisfaction, Seton's output of this genre became only intermittent. *Wild Animals at Home* followed in 1913, *Wild Animal Ways* in 1916, *Bannertail, the Story of a Gray Squirrel* in 1922, *The Biography of an Arctic Fox* and *Great Historic Animals* in 1937 and *Santana, the Hero Dog of France* in 1945. Yet none of them ever achieved the popularity of his very first book, *Wild Animals I Have Known,* which had been so badly maligned by John Burroughs.

After her daughter was born in 1904, Grace Seton travelled with her husband less often and for shorter periods. They had a month together on the Ottawa River at the end of September 1904, Grace's first time in the woods in two years; this had been arranged, according to her, with "much violent uprooting from home duties."[18] And they travelled to England and Norway together in 1906. In the fall of that year, while Seton was in England, she had been busy putting the finishing touches on her second book of hunting and camping adventures, *Nimrod's Wife;* and in 1907, while he was canoeing in the Arctic, she had been promoting her book, organizing the Pen and Brush Club, and working for the Woman's Suffrage Association of which she was now vice-president.

Whenever Seton was in residence at Wyndygoul during the years from 1904 to 1908, he had put in sixteen-hour days on his *Life Histories,* and when at last it was complete, he had disappeared into the organizational maw of the Boy Scouts of America. As a consequence, the lives of the Setons progressed steadily in different directions and into separate careers. This situation should not have unduly disturbed Seton since he professed to believe in the emancipated woman, and had condemned his father — and St. Paul — for approving female subservence; yet he resented the independent woman in his own home. With the behaviour of the higher animals as his model, Seton had come to believe in a system of "God-given prerogatives" based on the law that capability confers responsibility: woman is capable of giving birth so she must take responsibility for the child; man is physically capable of fighting so he must defend the family; women cannot care for the children and hunt for food at the same time, so she must stay home while man hunts for food, but man by providing food earns a share of the right to train the child. Seton discussed this system of ideas in relation to pioneer life in North America in a chapter of his memoirs entitled "Primitive Home Life." He wrote that

> the home life of those frontier days was nearly ideal; and so sanely adjusted that it may have valuable lessons for those who are wrestling with modern problems of living. . . . Those who cooked and sewed did so in an atmosphere of fun and frolic. The men no more thought of serving food than the women did of cutting the firewood. When a woman was seen chopping or carrying in firewood it was understood to mean that she had failed as a man-charmer. When a man was seen washing the dishes it was understood to be like Hercules spinning at the distaff — that he had absolutely surrendered, and become the servile thrall of some female enchanter who was gifted far above the common of her sex.[19]

Although Seton was never reduced to playing Hercules to Grace's Omphale, he did see her independence as an erosion of his prerogatives, and this provided most of the grounds for friction in their marriage. The course of their lives, however, would probably have continued indefinitely on two separate but roughly parallel tracks if Grace had not become ill in the spring of 1913 while she was travelling in Spain with Ann. When they returned home, Grace's illness was diagnosed as typhoid fever. Seton, who was in the west lecturing, cancelled his tour and rushed home to learn that she was not expected to live. Throughout April she remained in a high fever, but in late May began a gradual recovery. During the summer, while she recuperated, Seton remained close at hand and, as a result, there was a renewal of the relationship they had enjoyed in earlier years.

It was during this period that Seton decided to sell Wyndy-goul and build a new home on property he had found on Lake Avenue closer to Greenwich; this time it would be exactly the house he had always wanted. In late July he began building a bridge over the stream which ran through the property, and by 1 August he was supervising the construction of the dam which would provide another lake, this one to be called Little Peequo Lake.

On 15 August he commissioned the English architect Frederick Rowntree to design a house of "pure Tudor architecture with square lead lights" similar to the home his friend Miller Christie owned outside London, only "a little bigger." The cellar walls were to be built of local stone, the first storey of rough stone very smoothly laid, or concrete, and the upper storey of plaster and timber. Seton stipulated that all the timbers used for the gables were to be hand-hewn, and "anything that pretends to be a beam *must be a beam.*"[20]

He had gradually evolved seven rules for obtaining "picturesqueness" in architecture, a concept which he defined as being fundamentally the same as "beauty" since the converse of both terms was "ugliness." The first of his rules was that the purpose of the building must dictate the plan, and that no structural element should be added for the sake of ornament. Secondly, he believed that solid permanent construction was essential: wooden buildings, "with frail wooden floors that cannot last twenty years and poor wooden roofs that cannot last ten years" deny "the dignity of strength."[21] Honesty was his third fundamental: cement floors should not be marked in squares to look like tiles, and fake timbers should not masquerade as real ones. Rule number four was variety: windows, for example, should be of a size and place to suit the needs of the room rather than the symmetry of the external design. Beautiful colours were his fifth requirement, and curved rather than straight lines his sixth. The seventh was simplicity. "There was a time," he wrote, "when builders in New York seemed possessed of the idea that complicating the surface was beautifying the building, and many pretentious structures went up, having every portion of the inside and out cluttered over with the most appallingly ugly machine-made ornaments. There are not a dozen buildings on Fifth Avenue below Fifty-ninth Street that could not be vastly improved with an ax, a jack-plane, or a hundred years of sand-blast."[22]

The Setons' new home, adhering exactly to its owner's rules for construction, was completed early in 1915 and named De Winton. On the far side of the new lake, the little house that had already been on the property was remodelled in the same style and christened Little Peequo. The remaining out-buildings — a combined workshop and woodshed, a garage with an adjoining apartment for the chauffeur, and a guest cottage — were all Tudor in design.

Unfortunately, by the time the new house was ready for occupancy, the Setons' lives had again taken separate courses. Grace, now fully recovered, had returned to writing and travelling to secure material for new books. She had also taken up the Allies' cause in the war and, according to Seton, "raised the money to buy, equip, and operate six Ford trucks for camp and transport service between Paris and the Front." The French government decorated her for this service.[23]

The cause, however, which occupied most of her time was that of women's rights, and she undertook extensive speaking tours to promote votes for women and to encourage women to take an interest in politics. Her forthright statements, found in many of the Connecticut Votes-for-Women League pamphlets and press releases, make plain her fundamental differences with her husband's philosophy. In February 1915 she wrote to the editor of the *New York Times:*

The day is past . . . when women shall be deemed unfit for politics because of biological differences from men. . . . Perhaps women have yet to learn the game of human selfishness a little better and the method of circuitous thinking! Perhaps they have to "hang around the places where votes are bought and watch the men who are willing to kill the people whose votes they cannot buy!" This is the advice of a mature dealer in politics to a young student. All that may be true. But to keep on insisting that women shall not have the vote on account of this or on account of that is wasting time.

Granting for a moment that women ought not to vote because they have not had the necessary business training, the question arises: How about the 8,000,000, at least, . . . who must compete with men in the struggle for that "home" where they are supposed to stay and which they would not have unless they provided it for themselves?

But to many this "alikeness" to man is not the argument. It is because woman is different, and her point of view often necessarily different, that no man can adequately represent her, and a Government where the two angles of the human race are represented is the only kind of a Government that can be called a democracy, the form under which we are supposed to be living. The younger generation will make better voters if mothers as well as fathers are able to improve and instruct the future citizens.[24]

Although most of Grace's grievances in her battles for women's suffrage were directed at men in general, she had one particular complaint against her husband. In the summer of 1914 she had learned that even if women were granted the franchise, she would not be allowed to vote. As Seton had never taken out American citizenship, Grace was considered an alien. Partly to mollify her, but mostly to placate the executive of the Boy Scouts of America, Seton announced plans early in 1915 to take out his papers; when he reneged on this promise a few months later, relations between the Setons deteriorated even more, and their marriage, which had once again drifted into a live-and-let-live state, erupted into venomous warfare.

Neither Grace nor Seton had been entirely faithful to their marriage vows, but within their social set this had been the rule rather than the exception so there had been no recriminations; now Seton's resentment at the BSA and the return of his latent persecution complex made him intolerant of Grace's infidelities, real or imagined. She retaliated in kind. Fortunately, their separate commitments restricted the time they spent together.

Then, in the summer of 1918, Seton met Julia Moss Buttree. She was one of a large audience at a Woodcraft meeting, probably in Connecticut, brought there by friends who felt she would find something of interest in Seton's Woodcraft philosophy even though her own work was along rather different lines. Many years later she wrote of that meeting:

When the speaker appeared, he was a tall, handsome, robust man with a vigorous, aggressive personality. His shock of heavy black hair was worn conspicuously long. His piercing black eyes darted this way and that as he gauged his audience before he began to speak. Even with his unusual appearance, my interest was not aroused, but when the first words came from his lips, an electric thrill went through me. The depth of tone, the roundness of enunciation, the clarity of diction, the sheer magic of speech gripped the whole assembly. . . . He told a simple tale which lasted for perhaps ten minutes. At the beginning I was engrossed in his technique, but soon I fell under the spell of the narrative, yet when the speaker ceased, I realized that I had not taken in the end of the story. I had been wholly lost in the cadence of his voice. . . .[25]

After the meeting, Julie — as she preferred to be called — was taken to meet the speaker, and Seton, looking down from his six-foot height to her four-foot-six inches, said, "Hello. We can have a lot of fun together!"[26] Seton was then fifty-eight years of age; she was twenty-nine.

She had been born in New York City in 1889, the eldest of Alexander Keilly Moses's seven children. Her father's family were Jews from England, her mother's family from Germany, but both families had been in the United States for several generations, and they practised a very liberal type of reformed Jewish faith. The Moses family was not wealthy, but Julie was able to remain in school until she graduated from Hunter Female College and Normal School with a degree in classics and a teaching certificate; later, she studied for a master's degree in drama.

The years of Julie Moses's youth in New York had coincided with the high point of immigration by eastern European Jews and the growth of discrimination against all of the city's Jews which that immigration had sparked. Therefore, as soon as she graduated from Hunter, Julie dropped the "e" from her surname in order to be less readily associated with the Jewish community. (Her blonde hair helped to make this strategy plausible.) So it was as Julie Moss that she took her first teaching position in an elementary school in Harlem.

Although she had enjoyed a very close relationship with her father, Julie and her mother were quite distant; Julie preferred instead the company of her mother's youngest sister, Blanche Rose, who lived with her husband in Port Chester, New York. On weekends, in a clubhouse built on the Roses' property, Julie Moss gathered a group of ten- to fifteen-year-old girls together and began teaching them dance and drama. She also collected a library for their use.

In 1914 Julie married Ted Buttree, an attractive Englishman who worked with little success as a typewriter salesman. A gentle, ineffectual man, almost incapable of making decisions, he was soon completely dependent on his wife's whirlwind energy and ambition. Immediately after their marriage, the Buttrees moved to Georgia where Ted had been offered a job. Soon after the move, Julie became very ill and was bedridden for almost a year. Probably as a result of this illness, she was unable to have children.

The following year they returned to Port Chester to live in the cottage that Blanche's husband had built for them on his property. They stayed there for the next five years while Buttree went from job to job and Julie worked with her girls' group. Soon after she met Seton in 1918, she reorganized her girls as a Woodcraft group and began working closely with the Woodcraft League's founder.

Ever since *Life Histories* had been published in 1909, Seton had been collecting more information on North American mammals with the intention of publishing another volume on the subject, but by 1919 it had become apparent that a complete revision would be necessary instead. To Frank Doubleday, who immediately agreed to publish the proposed revision, Seton explained that he intended to cover the lives of all the game animals of America north of the Mexican boundary:

> This is my attempt to set out on paper everything that I know or that is known about the home life of the wild animals, their joys, their sorrows, their domestic ways, their social games, their love makings, their marriage ceremonies, their ideas of property, their methods of communicating cross-country and direct with each other, their troubles, their diseases, their ideas of medicating themselves, their curious platonic friendships among themselves and with totally different animals such as fox and caribou, fox and skunk, badger and coyote, cougar and wolverine, and strange to say, fox and rabbit actually living together in good fellowship. This is the home life of the animals, the part of their lives that appeals to me, and yet to be sure that I am bomb-proof in all my assumptions, I am submitting every chapter of the critical revision to our friends of the Smithsonian Institute, the American Museum and the Biological Survey. That is, the book has a framework of absolutely sound science, the latest word on nomenclature, species and range.[27]

This new work would fill four volumes, to be published one each year from 1925 to 1928. They were to be as profusely illustrated as the *Life Histories,* but this time, at the end of each chapter Seton planned to include a cartoon showing animals in poses and occupations that were distinctly human. Doubleday was appalled at the idea of including such illustrations in a serious scientific work, but Seton was adamant that they belonged in his books, and his publisher finally gave in.

Although a large portion of his earnings had always come from his lecture tours, Seton decided to limit lecturing to Woodcraft promotion and devote all his time to his new and exhaustive treatise on North American animals. To help him with both Woodcraft and the book, he hired Julie Buttree as his secretary, at first only on a part-time basis. When it became necessary to have full-time help, he built a cottage — Fern Lodge — for her and her husband on the estate. Then, to make sure that she stayed, he financed the construction of a restaurant called The Black Bear adjacent to the estate, and installed Ted Buttree as manager.

In the meantime, with Grace busy with her own career, Ann already grown to womanhood and living on her own in Paris, and Seton totally immersed in his new project, De Winton had become too large for the family's requirements. In April 1922, while Grace was abroad, Seton moved into the cottage he called Little Peequo and leased out De Winton for a year. This move made it possible for him to live within his reduced income; Grace's travels were subsidized by her share of her father's estate and by the network of wealthy friends in faraway places who welcomed her as a house guest while she researched her travel books.

Grace heartily disapproved of the move into Little Peequo, as she considered it "a rotten little cottage."[28] As if in confirmation of her opinion, on the night of 3 November Little Peequo caught fire. Grace was once again on her travels, this time en route to China to research her *Chinese Lanterns,* but Ann, who had returned from Paris, was living with her father. The fire, caused by an overheated oil stove, gutted Ann's room and extensively damaged the house, but no one was hurt in the blaze. As De Winton had tenants, Seton, Ann and the housekeeper, Hannah, moved into the gardener's cottage temporarily. Grace took this opportunity to argue for a return to "the home that we love" as soon as the tenants' lease expired, rather than to Little Peequo when it was repaired, but Seton, completely committed to his treatise on game animals and unwilling to return to lecturing to support the larger house, promptly renewed the tenants' lease on De Winton for another year. He did make one concession: the tenants were required to give up the house for three days in June 1923 so that Ann could be given a proper society wedding to

Hamilton Cottier, a young Princeton graduate from Scarsdale, New York.

More than a thousand guests crowded into Christ Episcopal Church in Greenwich for the 30 June wedding. The bride's gown with its court train was made of heavy ivory satin embroidered with seed pearls, and its wide "bertha" had come from her mother's wedding gown. Her veil had belonged to her maternal grandmother. Five bridesmaids attended, most of them former classmates at the Spence School where Ann had been educated. The groom's attendants were all Princeton men.

After the ceremony, the guests were received at De Winton where they overflowed the house and the marquees set up in the gardens. Among the guests were industrialists like Cyrus McCormack, publishers like Edward Bok, literary people, scientists, suffragettes, and a large contingent from New York society bent on being seen at the season's most fashionable wedding. None of Seton's brothers and only a few of their children attended.

The weekend of the wedding was the last time that the Setons were actually in residence at De Winton. Ironically, in October 1923, *House and Garden* printed an article written by Seton describing the loving care that had gone into the construction of the house. It was entitled "The House that is Mine."

When Grace returned from China, she rented a cottage at a resort in upstate New York where she could write her new book, and except for joining Seton at De Winton for Ann's wedding, she remained in seclusion until she completed her book in October. Their contacts and correspondence during this time were almost entirely concerned with paying off the wedding expenses and — since this was the prohibition era — with the problem of supplying Grace's retreat with the odd bottle of gin or whisky. Seton and Grace were reunited in late October, and a short period of peace followed. This was less the result of some new understanding between them than of the natural amiability and benevolence toward the world that writers often feel when they have completed a long project, for Seton had also finished a book — Volume I of *Lives of Game Animals*. As a consequence of this renewed goodwill between them, it was agreed that as soon as Grace returned from a forthcoming trip to India, they would make another attempt to revive their marriage.

In making this promise to Grace, Seton was ignoring the fact that he had become involved elsewhere. Julie Buttree had originally been hired as a secretary, but as the work on *Lives of Game Animals* progressed, her help became indispensable to him and the two began working as a team. Gradually, she took over much of the administration of the Woodcraft League and became an associate editor of the *Totem Board,* the official Woodcraft magazine. In the spring of 1924 Woodcraft headquarters was moved to the estate, and Seton took time out from Volume II of *Lives* to set up a permanent outdoor kitchen and tenting area. In late May the first group of Woodcraft leaders arrived for training; Julie and Seton shared the teaching duties.

Their close association in work inevitably changed their personal relationship, and soon after Grace left for India in December 1923, Seton decided that he did not want a reconciliation with her after all. Although he had promised to move back into De Winton with her when she returned in the summer, by May he had renewed the tenants' lease once more. At the same time, he hired workmen to make a large addition to Little Peequo. In a letter to Grace dated 14 May, he explained:

I must sacrifice everything that I am doing or have got to the successful completion of the game book. It is a gigantic undertaking. . . . The galleys, 220 of them, have been gone over minutely with many a battle, Doubleday's help taking one view, the scientists another in many cases. I don't consider it an ordinary book in any sense. I have not the least doubt that it is the greatest natural history written within a hundred years. It is my monument. The consummation of my life work, and will stand for a hundred years to come as the standard on the subject, always provided that I finish it and keep it up to the level already attained. Of course, it does not represent me solely but every good naturalist that America has produced up to date dead or alive has contributed the best of his achievement to this very serious undertaking.

I think I have sufficiently set forth the magnitude of this work and impressed on you its importance to me. Now I know that I cannot continue the needed focussed intensity if I have to worry about raising money, etc., which would be implied by moving back into the big house, so I have decided against it definitely. I am sorry for your disappointment. I will take care that you have a comfortable place to live in, probably much as you did last year. Of course, your room is here awaiting you but I suspect that the need for concentrating on your own book will impose on you very nearly the same routine as that of last summer.

He then informed her that on recent trips to Washington for conferences with the Biological Survey, he had been "much hampered for lack of a secretary." On his last trip, therefore, he had taken Julie Buttree with him, leaving her in the chaperonage of Washington friends because he was aware that he "must of course be very discreet. So my secretary had the interesting experience of meeting all the men she had been writing letters to for months back, and getting some gauge of their personalities, as well as seeing Washington in the merry month of May."[29] From this time on, Julie accompanied Seton on all his business trips. Her husband remained in Greenwich supervising The Black Bear.

Seton was on hand in New York in early July to meet Grace when she returned from her travels in India and the Orient. At the train station, before putting her into the cab which would take her to the New York apartment of friends, he told her that he did not wish to live with her again. Although Grace found "the whole surprising change in [him] for the past year or two . . . like a bad dream,"[30] she refused to give up on the marriage. She had always been extremely independent, but she had grown "tired of this homeless condition" and wanted a "focus" in her life.[31] She resolved to win Seton back by being more accommodating. "I am willing to make sacrifices," she wrote to him, "but it means a real home and an affectionate husband. . . . Is there a little corner left in your heart that is not corroded with bitterness?"[32]

Seton does not appear to have asked for a divorce at this point, merely a separation, probably because, though Julie Buttree's marriage had become little more than a formality, she was still a married woman. Ted Buttree must have been aware of the relationship that existed between his wife and her employer, but his own dependence on her and his unquestioning devotion made complaints from him unlikely.

In November the Setons declared a brief truce before Seton left for a lecture tour of England. After this date, the fact that the marriage had finally broken down seems to have been accepted by both parties, so that although Little Peequo served as a home base for both of them, in the next four years they seldom touched base at the same time. No one made a move to change the status quo. Ted Buttree was resigned to the eventual loss of his wife, yet he did nothing to hasten the evil moment. Grace treated Julie with civility; she had always disapproved of her as a secretary for Seton — regarding her as a "port in a storm" and looking down on her because of her Jewishness — but she was careful not to give her husband grounds for complaint in her treatment of her rival. Julie did not consider herself Jewish, and for Seton her background was immaterial. His attitude to Jews had been conditioned by an encounter in the winter of 1883 when he first arrived in New York. He had little money and had tried to sell an old Russian sable hat to a Jewish furrier named Rosenstein. The furrier turned down the hat, but, realizing Seton was broke, had given him a dime, which was enough to buy a bread roll and a half pound of dates. Rosenstein's gesture established Seton's warm response to Jewish people for the rest of his life, and he believed he had found the same warmth and generosity in Julie Buttree. Being confident that she would be the ultimate winner in this quadrangle, Julie Buttree was content with the status quo. She need only remain completely indispensable to Seton and the situation would be resolved exactly as she desired. It is indicative of the nature of the relationship between them that she always called him "Chief"; Grace addressed him most frequently as "Dear Boy."

Seton, meanwhile, was completely preoccupied with the need to finish his magnum opus. At sixty-five years of age he had already lived one year past the demise he had predicted for himself when he was an art student in London. The bronchial trouble he had anticipated for 1924 had come on schedule, but it had not carried him to his grave, though he was convinced that this was only a slight postponement. He had, after all, fulfilled in some fashion all of his predictions except the number of children he would have and the knighthood, which had unfortunately gone to Baden-Powell.

Now he drove himself even harder to complete the next volume, and at the adjoining desk Julie Buttree worked with him far into the nights. Often they sent out for dinner — generally lobster or other seafood since these were Seton's favourites — taking time out to eat before the fire, while Ted Buttree sat at home alone.

Seton seems to have treated the man fairly as an employee, but scarcely even acknowledged his marriage to Julie.

As in the relationship with his father, the more Seton felt his actions restricted by his marriage to Grace, the more he blamed her behaviour for the anger that was developing within him. Eventually, he would convince himself that her actions and her personality were entirely responsible for the breakdown in the marriage.

In April 1927 Ernest Thompson Seton was awarded the John Burroughs Bronze Medal for *Lives of Game Animals*. After Burroughs's death in 1921, his fellow naturalists had formed a Burroughs Memorial Association; in 1926 they presented their first bronze medal for the best piece of nature literature published during the preceding year to William Beebe, the biologist, explorer and author. *Lives of Game Animals* was the selection committee's unanimous choice for 1927. The award was for the complete work based on the standard of excellence attained in the two volumes which had appeared to that date. Clyde Fisher, president of the association, in presenting the award, told his audience:

Ernest Thompson Seton belongs as much to the boys and girls of the world as he does to the naturalists and technical scientists. There are doubtless many fathers and mothers who feel that his greatest service has been to young people. John Burroughs himself was among those who appreciated highly the Woodcraft work which Mr. Seton began at Cos Cob, Connecticut, some twenty-five years ago. And perhaps he *will* be remembered longest by his delightful animal stories. Probably no others have been so widely translated into foreign languages. Who can measure the influence for good in such stories as *The Trail of the Sandhill Stag* and *The Biography of a Grizzly?* John Burroughs once wrote of Mr. Seton, "he easily throws all other animal story writers in the shade."

But the recognition which we wish to bestow today is for his magnum opus which has no peer either in text or in illustrations and like all his books, one of the most valuable features is the illustrations which are from Mr. Seton's drawings. One of our leading ornithologists has said that the first good drawings of birds after Audubon's time were those made by Mr. Seton about a quarter century ago. All of his drawings are artistically beautiful and yet accurate. In many cases, they are superior to photographs in that they frequently represent phases of action which have never been photographed and in all cases the drawings show what they were intended to show.

Ernest Thompson Seton, mammalogist, ornithologist, student of Indians, Woodcrafter, artist, literary naturalist and raconteur par excellence, with the authority vested in me by the board of directors of the John Burroughs Memorial Association, I present to you the certificate entitling you to the John Burroughs Bronze Medal, awarded for the best production of nature literature published during the past year.[33]

There was no one involved with this event who was not conscious of the irony of it, for it had been Burroughs's attack on the authenticity of Seton's animal stories that had driven Seton back to science, and it was his return to science that had made his animal stories once again salable.

15

Beulah Land

I've left the land of death and sin,
The road that many travel in;
And if you ask the reason why,
I'm going to seek a home on high.

Chorus:
Oh Beulah Land, Sweet Beulah Land,
As on the highest mount I stand,
I look away across the sea
Where mansions are prepared for me,
And view the shining glory shore,
My heaven, my home forevermore.

Though many would my progress stay
And beg me not to work or pray,
I dare not listen to their cry,
I seek a glorious home on high.

Oh Beulah Land, Sweet Beulah Land, . . .[1]

Although Seton had rejected organized religions nearly forty years earlier, and though he recalled almost all of his childhood experiences with bitterness, he had salvaged one happy memory from the services at the little Methodist church near the Lindsay farm: "Beulah Land," a hymn about the borderland between heaven and earth, the land of rest and peace. Perhaps it stayed in his mind because its rhythm had matched his purposeful stride, but it was the message in the lyrics that held him, because it spoke to him of a return to the simplicity of the west, a land closer to nature and God, a place to wait for the end.

Seton had never adapted to city life. After two years in London, he remembered it only as a city "of shivering cold, gloom and starvation";[2] Paris was "a wretched, much belauded village";[3] Toronto had been acceptable in his youth because he had seen it as merely an adjunct to the marsh, the island and the Don Valley, but when it spread over these beloved landmarks, he regarded it as just another big city.

Before he had ever seen it, Seton had dreaded "horrible, crowded, smoky, miserable New York";[4] in 1903 he told Hamlin Garland that it was only with his desk and drawing board before him that he could "ignore the rumble of the elevated train,"[5] and forty years after his first winter in the city, he wrote: "Every time I go [to New York] I am in a state of furious rebellion. I don't want to go to New York. I won't live there any more than I can help. Each time I go I hope it will be the last time I ever see it."[6]

His complaint with cities was really not so much that they were cold or smoky, or even that they were impersonal, but that they were actually malevolent. All the successes of his life had stemmed from his experiences in the wide open spaces; all his failures had taken place in the cities: the unsatisfactory *Birds of Manitoba* manuscript, the "Awaited in Vain" fiasco, the "Nature Faker" controversy, his defeat at the hands of the BSA executive, the failure of his marriage.

Even the triumph of the Burroughs Medal had been marred by terrible battles with Doubleday over the editing. Seton had taken the precaution of submitting every page of his manuscript to the Biological Survey, the Smithsonian Institution and the Museum of Natural History to be checked for misspellings of animal names, the correct type and composition for a scientific work, the symbols to be used and scientific references, and he felt confident that he had submitted a perfect manuscript. Doubleday's editors then made hundreds of changes which he discovered only when the galleys were sent to him for proofing. In the end he won the battle, but Doubleday billed him to make the changes which returned the manuscript to its original state, calling them "author's changes."[7]

At sixty-seven Seton had completed all the projects he had set for himself in the cities of the east and was prepared to retire. But not to inactivity. Instead, he was ready to climax his life's work with a return to nature, to a "peaceful" old age in the outdoors. In June 1927 he set off for New Mexico to find land on which to build a retirement home and establish a summer college of Indian arts and philosophy. Ever since he had been forced to resign from the BSA he had administered his Woodcraft League first from headquarters in New York, then from Greenwich; neither, however, had been satisfactory. He had not been able to give enough time to Woodcraft, and De Winton estate had not provided enough space for an adequate training centre. And while Seton did not believe in an authoritarian hierarchy for his Woodcraft tribes, his control of the organization had become so lax that in June 1922 the western tribes had set up an independent organization, and Seton had been forced to get an injunction to prevent them from using his training manuals and insignias. A new headquarters had become a necessity if he was to salvage the League.

After a long process of elimination, Seton selected New Mexico for his Beulah Land. He had never particularly enjoyed cold climates, even in his youth; now he wanted "no more cold weather" for his remaining years.[8] California seemed most likely to spare him from further discomfort of that kind, yet it was not a suitable area for the college he envisaged. He wanted high but not mountainous country — he regarded mountains "as highly impertinent" because they obstructed the view.[9]

New Mexico, especially around Santa Fe, seemed to offer the warmth he required for most of the year, and California was close enough that he could flee to it in the coldest months. There were large tracts of land available for his college, and at seven thousand feet it was high enough to give a clear view in every direction. It was also the home of the Indian peoples whose philosophy and life style came closest to Seton's "best things of the best Indians." He was convinced that the Indians of the southwest, more than any other native people, had developed a culture from their environment without destroying it. To him the fact that their kivas or houses of worship were partially underground was confirmation of their oneness with both God and earth. For many years Seton had refused to attend the white man's church where a long-faced preacher was prepared to intercede on his behalf with a difficult-tempered God, but he could appreciate the mysticism and direct-ness of the relationship between the Indians of the southwest and their God.

Having selected New Mexico as his destination, in the summer of 1927 he embarked by car in a modern version of the Manitoba land-hunts he had participated in forty-five years earlier. Of the friends and associates who accompanied him on this trip, Julie Buttree was the most important. She was there as his partner, a relationship accepted by all the other members of the entourage and even by their contacts in New Mexico. The pair had been planning this venture for nearly two years, yet when the time came to depart, Julie admitted to being "scared" because of the possible social repercussions.[10] Seton appears to have had no such qualms. Julie was the perfect mate for this venture: her interest in Indian cultures complemented his own; she was a whirlwind of energy and efficiency; she deferred to him in all things, and she wor-shipped him. He could hardly have asked for a better companion.

The June 1927 trip was the first of six trips — two per year — which they made to the area, checking out each piece of land the real estate agents discovered within a hundred-mile radius of Santa Fe. In 1929 they inspected a 2300-acre tract which had been part of the King of Spain's original grant to Governor Sebastion de Vargas in 1692. Seven miles south of Santa Fe, and nestled among piñon pines and juniper-covered hills, it had the most convenient location of any of the properties they had seen, as well as a reliable water supply. Purchase of the land was completed in February 1930, and by June, Seton and Julie had moved west for good. Ted Buttree accompanied them as general handyman.

The three years of land-hunting were not without disruptive incidents. Seton's income had dwindled in the years he had been preparing *Lives of Game Animals,* so that in order to buy the de Vargas tract he had to sell some of his other holdings. De Winton and its garage, barns, immediate out-buildings and ten acres of land were offered for sale in June of 1927 for $180,000, but the estate did not sell until early 1929 and then only by increasing the land offered with it to forty-six acres and lowering the price to

$175,000. In the meantime, in order to prevent Seton from selling everything and leaving his wife homeless, Grace's lawyers required him to sign a four-year agreement that he would not sell the house she was living in — Little Peequo, the "rotten little cottage" that she hated.

Seton's second brother, William, died in early May 1928. He was eighty-one; only brothers Joseph and Charles had predeceased him by a few years. Seton went to Toronto for the funeral and there received an unexpected request: Enoch and his wife asked him to visit Annie Wood, his old love, who was now confined to the Toronto Orthopedic Hospital.

Since the end of her love affair with Seton, Annie had been running a city mission out of the YMCA, conducting services for the city's derelicts and ministering to the spiritual needs of the men of the Toronto police force and their families. Every evening for the three years prior to her hospitalization, she had stood with a former rabbi on a street corner in a Jewish neighbourhood, preaching to convert the Jews to Christianity. Now she was dying of cancer, content to believe that she was being called "home" because her work was done. She only wanted to see her "beloved Ernest" one last time so that she "could die happy."[11]

Annie had never married, though she confessed to Seton that she had never been "without admirers, men who would have married me, but all knew my heart had been given away years ago, many knew to whom, and I never cared who knew, or that the man I loved had married another. . . . You know I have been waiting for you to arrive these forty years, a heart kept whole and yours, these long, long years."[12]

After their reunion, Seton visited her two or three more times, and, in spite of the fact that he was already committed to spending his remaining days with Julie Buttree, a rather pathetic love affair blossomed again between himself and the dying Annie, with a flow of passionate love letters flying between them whenever they were apart. The letters reveal a strange re-enactment of their first love affair: arguments over who was to blame for their parting, tender reconciliations and grieving over the lost years. "Think of it," Annie mourned, "all those years of heaven on earth, that's what it would have been."[13]

By late August Annie Wood's condition had deteriorated. She could no longer write. In early September she sent word through her brother (Sir James Wood) that she did not wish Seton to visit her again, but to remember her as she had been. She died on 8 October. Her funeral was one of the most impressive the city had seen. (Enoch commented that "one would have thought she was royalty.")[14] Her coffin was preceded from the church by the Silver and Pipe bands of the Toronto Police Department and followed by 150 uniformed officers and men of the police force; they escorted the coffin to the railway station where a special train of eight coaches took them to the town of Galt for the burial service in the Trinity Church cemetery. Seton did not return to Toronto for the funeral, but exchanged letters with Sir James. The effect of this interlude on him is unknown as the only reference in his journal simply notes that he had been to see his "old love."

During 1929 Julie Buttree began joining Seton on stage in his lecture tours. With her degree in drama and her growing interest in Indian song, dance and ceremony, she had developed an act which complemented his storytelling and lantern-slide presentation. She also added colour to the show by appearing in a variety of Indian costumes. Except for his early recruiting lectures for the Woodcraft League, Seton had never worn Indian costume on stage, preferring instead to appear in one of several three-piece tweed suits which he refused to discard until they had been reduced to complete shabbiness.

While Julie's participation enhanced his lectures, it did not help his relations with Grace. The wrangling over a property settlement began in earnest about this time and continued for the next five years, with neither willing to sue for divorce until a settlement had been agreed upon in case a court settlement should prove ruinous. When his lawyer suggested that an American court might look more kindly on Grace, who was an American subject, than on Seton, who was still a British citizen, in 1931 Seton once more began the process of becoming an American.

He was still torn in his loyalties, though not as he had been in the early years of the century when he had convinced himself that he was of value to the American government in his official position as naturalist to the government of Manitoba because he could act as a liaison with the Canadian government. He did act in this capacity in April 1908 after his Arctic journey, when he had approached Prime Minister Laurier, apparently at the request of Theodore Roosevelt, to determine the Canadian government's stand on forest protection and game reserves. He was not called upon for services of this kind again, and little by little his involvement with the BSA caused the value of American citizenship to outweigh British citizenship.

In February 1915 Seton had been ready to take out his papers as soon "as the European situation cleared,"[15] but after the BSA dumped him, he changed his mind again. In February 1924 he finally applied to the immigration department, but in August he cancelled his application. Later that year, aboard a steamer crossing the Atlantic, he wrote a short requiem entitled "Goodbye to England" in which he weighed up the good and the bad of his birthplace, "where houses are never warmed no matter how cold the winter" versus America "where wise methods keep the house at one temperature the year round."

Goodbye to the dear land where you're sent to jail if you stray one step from the ancient by-path through the woods. Goodbye to the land where no man works for wages but expects a tip in addition. Goodbye to the country where they invite you as guests to their houses and allow their servants to rob you so that it would have been much cheaper to have lived in a first class hotel. Goodbye to the land where they invite you to go shooting, then take from you everything that fell to your gun. Goodbye to the land where no man, unless of private fortune can serve his country as officer in army or navy, and where not so long ago it was a social disgrace to be advanced on the merit system.

I'm going home to the land where every public servant is paid a living wage, where the poorest if gifted with brains may reach the highest possible position of power. Goodbye dear land of trim lawns, emerald walks and finished farms. I'm going back where we have rubbish, billboards, tin cans and barbed wire fences everywhere. Goodbye old land, where age is respected and rank and achievement are saluted. I'm going back home where we worship dollars, where your janitor slaps you on the back, and niggers crowd your women into the gutter. Goodbye England, I'm going home.[16]

By 1931 he could no longer ignore the fact that his British citizenship had become a liability; once more he began the citizenship process, and on 6 November of that year he became an

American. He was now seventy-one years of age; he had first made his home in his adopted country almost forty-eight years earlier.

Ernest Thompson Seton and Julie Buttree selected the site for their first home together in June 1930. By the following summer they had constructed a small but comfortable adobe house for themselves and a half dozen other buildings for their staff: this was the nucleus of "Seton Village." A hundred and fifty yards away they built the "Indian Village" — cabins, tents and teepees — in a large circle around a central plaza. At the entrance to the village were two carved and painted totem poles; on the opposite side of the plaza were two dining halls — one for adults, the other for children — with a kitchen separating them. A "dance lodge," complete with stage, dressing rooms and auditorium, provided space for entertainment events, and the hogan — a round building with seating for one hundred on tiered benches — was used for council meetings. On the edge of the village stood the showers, toilets and a sweat lodge which was heated in the Indian manner with hot rocks plunged into water.

Across the arroyo was the kiva, or Pueblo ceremonial chamber, built under the supervision of Juan Gonzales, the San Ildefonso medicine man. There were no buildings designed strictly for classroom use since it was intended that, to take advantage of the setting, the school would be held mostly outdoors. But while everything possible had been done to allow the students to experience "the primitive life without its deterrent shortcomings,"[17] Seton made sure that living accommodation was not too primitive: he bought eight obsolete boxcars and a pullman car from the Santa Fe Railroad and renovated them to look like adobe houses.

In July 1932 the first six-week summer session of the Seton College of Indian Wisdom (later the Seton Institute of Indian Lore) was held with Julie Buttree as dean and administrator. She also served as chauffeur for the "Chief," since he had never learned to drive, and as his secretary. During the next ten years, there were also times when she filled in as camp cook. Both Seton and Julie taught courses in the school, but they also hired a number of qualified teachers, as well as local Indians known for their craftwork.

The curriculum they offered was divided into arts and crafts, outdoor and physical activities and leadership skills. Crafts included Navaho weaving, basketry, pottery making (Indian methods, coil and wheel), beadwork, porcupine quill work, leather carving, costume making and Indian design and its modern applications. The physical activities offered were Indian and modern dance, nature study, camping and horseback riding. Leadership skills included Indian philosophy and history and woodcraft. All students had access to Seton's library of close to eleven thousand volumes as well as his museum of Indian artifacts and mounted mammal and bird specimens.

By 1933 Seton had designed his final home. Seton Castle was situated on the rise of land that overlooked both villages. It was constructed in the adobe style so appropriate to the landscape; the carvings that decorated the doorways and windows were Seton's own work. When it was dedicated in 1934, it had five main rooms; these increased to thirty rooms by 1945 and to forty-five rooms by 1970. Of them all, the library is the purest "Seton" — a long, gracious "hall" with Navaho rugs on bare wooden floors, peeled poles across the ceiling, a huge fireplace of natural stone, and windows looking across an intimate courtyard toward the juniper-covered hills.

Julie Buttree was divorced from her husband on 26 September 1934. He remarried the following year, but the union lasted only a matter of months. In 1941 he married for a third time; this marriage lasted for the remainder of his life, but he continued to be totally emotionally involved with his first wife, staying on at Seton Village in order to be near her. She in turn always treated him with kindness, perhaps motivated by a certain degree of guilt.[18]

Seton's divorce from Grace became final on 22 January 1935. The agreement between them provided that all royalties from the books he had written prior to his divorce were to be assigned to Grace and that she would keep certain properties, including Little Peequo. It was further provided that neither Grace nor Seton would comment publicly again on the other's activities, and that, should either write memoirs, the other would have the right to edit portions pertaining to his or her life.

The day after the divorce was granted, Seton married Julie Buttree in a private ceremony conducted by Seton's friend County Court Judge Joseph McGill in El Paso, Texas. Seton was now seventy-five; his bride was forty-six. Immediately after the reception, the newlyweds set off on a three-week trip to California to promote Woodcraft and to lecture. By mid-February they were back in El Paso so that Seton could undergo another operation for hernia repair. There were some complications due to his age, but he had completely recovered in time for a lecture tour in May and the annual influx of students in July.

The couple embarked on the *Queen Mary* in October 1936 for the first of three annual European trips. This trip took them to England for a month of speaking engagements, then to Czechoslovakia in response to an invitation from the Woodcraft League which had been established in that country. They were presented with flowers and gifts everywhere they went, and even received a Yugoslavian delegation that had journeyed four hundred miles to meet them. In Germany, youth group organizers begged them to return the following year to lecture on Woodcraft, and tried to arrange a meeting with Hitler to seek approval for the proposed tour, but Hitler refused to see them. After each of their overseas trips, they drove directly to California or Mexico to spend the remainder of the winter in the sunshine.

Seton began writing his autobiography sometime during 1937, using his journals as the basis for the work. The impetus to begin came from William D. Murray who, while preparing the official history of the Boy Scouts of America, had written to Seton to ask for information about the early years. Seton offered to show Murray the voluminous correspondence between himself and Baden-Powell, letters which the British Boy Scout leader "had the impudence" to ask him not to publish until after he had "revised them." Murray was not interested in them.[19] About the same time, William Mill Butler of Maplewood, New Jersey, began an unofficial history of the BSA, and solicited information from all those who had been involved in the founding. This prompted Dan Beard to prepare his own version of the founding for inclusion in his memoirs, *Hardly a Man Is Now Alive.*

Convinced that none of them would tell the truth as *he* knew it about these long ago events, Seton decided to write his own memoirs. By 1938 he had negotiated a contract with Farrer and Rinehart for a three-volume memoir, but when the draft of the first volume was ready, the publisher rejected it, suggesting that Seton should collaborate with a younger writer on a revision. Seton refused and told them to forward the manuscript to Scribner's.

In the midst of this chaotic life of lecture tours, summer school, trips abroad, memoir writing, book promotion and winter holidays in California, the Setons adopted a baby. Ever since she had come west with Seton in 1930, Julie had been attempting to adopt a child. A young niece had spent two summers at Seton Village with the intention of coming to live there permanently and be legally adopted, but in the end she decided to return to her own parents. The year that Seton and Julie were married they had negotiated to adopt two Mexican children, but that plan came to nothing when the family's priest objected because the adoptive parents would not agree to raise the children as Catholics. Then, in February 1938, Julie learned of a young unmarried woman who would be having her baby in the summer and wished to put the child up for adoption. In exchange for a good home until her baby arrived and payment of all her medical bills, this young woman agreed to the Seton's adoption of her child.

When the little girl was born, her new father was seventy-eight. He named her Beulah, a name she would change to Deanna — because her dancing teacher nicknamed her Dee-anski — and would later shorten to Dee. She was baptized by the San Ildefonso medicine man in the Seton Village kiva; he gave her an Indian name which meant Blue Turquoise and Golden Rock, and his children also had a name to give her: Summer Flower. With all of these names, Dee grew up feeling that she had no identity of her own.

The new parents made no changes in their marathon schedule; instead, they developed a routine for the child which fitted their own life style. Four months after her arrival, they started off on a lecture tour with the baby and a nursemaid in the back seat of the car. Beulah was a precocious child, and by the time she was seven months old could keep time to music, so they took her on stage dressed in a diaper, a wide ribbon and a war-bonnet. She stole the show. At two years of age she was dancing on stage in miniature versions of her mother's costumes, and signing autographs with her name and the four-petalled blossom which was the insignia for Summer Flower. By the time she was two and a half she could sing "sixty-three songs — a total of one hundred and fourteen verses in all,"[20] and recite dozens of nursery rhymes, so her part in the family act was once more enlarged.

Seton's memoirs were in time accepted by Charles Scribner's Sons and placed in the hands of their famous editor, Maxwell

Perkins. The scope of the work had now been reduced to a single volume which would concentrate primarily on Seton's adventures in his boyhood and early manhood up to the founding of the Boy Scouts of America. On the insistence of his surviving brothers (Arthur, George and Walter), he removed the more rancorous portions about his father, and he submitted the short portion he had written about Grace to their daughter Ann for further editing. Maxwell Perkins suggested the removal of other sections in order to give the book more "unity and direction."[21] Then, on 8 January 1941, while the work was still being edited, Baden-Powell died, and, since it was considered neither good manners nor good business to speak ill of the dead, Seton was persuaded to delete the chapter which dealt with the controversy over the founding of the Scout movement. Thus, he was left with all his old resentments and feelings of outrage still intact.

The volume, which finally arrived on the bookstands in 1941, has nearly 400 pages of text: the first 340 cover his life until his marriage in 1894, the other 60 deal with a few of the high points of the remaining years. Many of the chapters are marred by a petulant tone and by Seton's insistence on the unwarranted persecution which he believed he had been subjected to so many times in his life; other sections, such as those on Burroughs and Roosevelt, do not correspond with historical fact.

Only two thousand copies were printed, and by the time these were sold, the United States was at war and all civilian publishing had been curtailed. The book was not reprinted after the war. In 1967 Julie Seton published *By a Thousand Fires: Nature Notes and Extracts From the Life and Unpublished Journals of Ernest Thompson Seton*. It included some of the deleted material about Joseph Logan Thompson, but she avoided the BSA controversy, for the book had been timed to coincide with the opening of a new Ernest Thompson Seton Memorial Library and Museum at the BSA's Philmont Scout Ranch near Cimmaron, New Mexico.

Seton was eighty-one when the United States entered World War II. He was still not ready to retire, though his health had suffered earlier that year as the result of an attack of whooping cough contracted from his young daughter. While he was more susceptible to colds and bronchial trouble after this illness, it was not his health but the war which restricted his life style for his remaining years.

Gas rationing forced the Setons to travel by train and bus for their lecture tours, but with service to civilians limited, it was almost impossible for them to maintain their usual schedule. In the winter of 1942–43, on their way to California for their usual winter vacation, they were stranded in the desert for hours when their overcrowded train broke down. They were refused entry into the dining car until all servicemen had been fed; Seton, unable to stand in line that long, returned to his seat without food. In Los Angeles they searched in vain for rental accommodations and finally had to settle for space in a friend's unfurnished house. They spent the remaining winters of the war years at Seton Castle, but the house had not been constructed for winter living; it was difficult to heat, fuel was scarce and there were no servants to help with the heavier work.

In the fall of 1942 Seton was commissioned by Vanguard Press to write a book on animals in war. Arrangements were made for him to visit a number of army training centres, and in December, Seton and Julie embarked by bus for Leadville, Colorado, where the army was using dogs for sled duty and mules for packing in areas inaccessible to horses or mechanized vehicles. On this trip they were on the road for seventy-two hours in tightly packed buses in which they were sometimes forced to stand; in Leadville they were allowed only four hours at the camp. On later trips they investigated methods for training attack and guard dogs, and even the use of bees to carry microdot messages. The book was finished early in 1943, but when Vanguard submitted it to Washington for approval, the army refused to allow it to be published because the training methods Seton had described were considered classified information.

In May 1943, after installing a thirty-gallon reserve tank in their car and accepting donations of gas coupons from friends, the Seton family drove to New York to lecture and deal with their royalty and publishing problems. Seton's royalty income was virtually nonexistent by this time as his publishers had been unable to reissue any of the books he had written since his divorce — *Great Historical Animals* and *The Biography of an Arctic Fox* in 1937, *Trail and Campfire Stories* in 1940, his autobiography in 1941, and *The Gospel of the Redman,* which he had written with Julie in 1936. In New York he took the manuscript of *Animals in War* to Max Perkins in the hope that he could induce the army to allow

Scribner's to publish it; he also offered Perkins the manuscript of a new book on tracking. As far as their publishing ventures were concerned, the trip was nonproductive, but Seton gave several lectures on animals in war, and this helped to pay their expenses.

The Seton Institute of Indian Lore did not reopen after the summer of 1941. Wartime travel restrictions had seriously reduced enrollment, and it was impossible to find replacements for the instructors who had gone into the services or war work. In January 1942 the Setons met with Eleanor Roosevelt to offer the school dormitories as a home for two hundred evacuees, but they were never used for this purpose. Because of the housing shortage, the staff houses were snapped up as rental units, and later, by sub-dividing the land around them, Seton was able to sell many of them. The camp facilities were allowed to deteriorate, as there were no workmen available to make repairs.

After his illness in 1941, Seton remained in moderately good health and vigour for four more years with only an occasional cold or pulled muscle to give him cause for complaint. In February 1945 Julie wrote to friends that he continued well, "although he is not able to do as much physical work as he used to do. He tires more easily and it distresses him very much. He still has all the enthusiasm of his earlier years, and it is hard to have to stop work before one is satisfied."[22] As if in defiance of his years, that summer, when he could not find workmen to do the job, he reroofed the library wing of the house himself with his seven-year-old daughter at his side handing him the nails.

The end of the war in Europe renewed his hope for the future. He worked steadily at his desk and at his easel to complete *Santana, The Hero Dog of France,* a story inspired by his research on war animals. In spite of the paper shortage, five hundred copies were published that year by the Phoenix Press of Los Angeles. He began making plans for a new ten-thousand-mile tour of the United States and Canada, a tour which would rekindle interest in his books and force his publishers to reprint them.

That winter the family drove to California for the first time in three years. Seton's energies had flagged in the closing months of the year, but in California Julie was pleased to see that "he picked up very greatly."[23] He gave a number of lectures, and his wife and daughter shared the program with Indian songs and dances.

After their return to Seton Castle in April 1946, his health slowly deteriorated. Angry that his body was letting him down, he pushed himself harder, and Julie reported sadly that "he is once more doing more than he ought to. But he would be entirely too unhappy if we tried to stop him from all the things that mean so much to him, so we must perforce leave him to tire himself out. It is hard to watch."[24]

As summer approached, he lost interest in food. He had never been a hearty eater, but he had always enjoyed his meals; now he began to pick at them. To tempt his appetite, Julie had seafood flown in. Rather than offend her, on the pretext that he was going to eat while he worked, Seton would take his plate to his desk and dispose of the food in his wastebasket. In July his ailment was diagnosed as cancer of the pancreas. He remained active throughout the summer, even lecturing at the University of New Mexico on 14 August, his eighty-sixth birthday. In September he was taken to hospital in Santa Fe, but after several weeks there, he asked to be taken home again to die.

When he returned to Seton Castle, well-meaning friends, believing that Beulah would be in the way at such a time, took the child to stay with Ted Buttree and his wife. After a week of anxiety and loneliness, she made her way home without permission, entered the house by the back door, and, by hiding behind furniture, moved from room to room until she found her mother. Julie comforted the child, then allowed her to be taken away again.

On 23 October Julie appeared at the Buttree home long enough to announce: "Daddy's not going to be sick anymore." For a brief moment, Beulah believed that her father had recovered and that she would be allowed to go home. Then Julie completed her message: "He's dead."

Epilogue

Ernest Thompson Seton's remains were cremated, and his ashes stored until 14 August 1960, the one hundredth anniversary of his birth. Then his two grandsons, Seton Cottier and Daniel Barber, scattered them from a plane over the land where Seton had chosen to end his days.

Seton's journals were sent to the American Museum of Natural History in New York City. In 1965 a duplicate set and the greater part of his library and natural history collections were donated to the Boy Scouts of America, to be housed in an Ernest Thompson Seton Memorial Library and Museum at the 127,000-acre Philmont Scout Ranch, Cimarron, New Mexico. The $150,000 building, a gift from L. O. Crosby of Picayune, Mississippi, was dedicated on 21 July 1967.

Grace Gallatin Seton continued her career as a writer and lecturer; her best-known books were *Yes, Lady Sahib, A Woman Tenderfoot in Egypt, Magic Waters, Chinese Lanterns, Poison Arrows* and *The Singing Traveller.* She died in Florida on 19 March 1959 at age eighty-three.

Ann Seton was divorced from Hamilton Cottier in 1929; her second husband was Hamilton Chase. She began writing short stories in 1932 under the pen-name Anya Seton. Her first historical novel, *My Theodosia,* based on the life of Aaron Burr's daughter, was a 1941 best seller, as were *Dragonwyck, Katherine, The Winthrop Woman* and *Devil Water*.

Julie Seton returned to the lecture circuit after the death of her Chief, but their daughter refused to accompany her. Julie became involved in theatre activities in Santa Fe, taking a prominent part in the city's annual melodrama. Her last appearance was on 5 October 1968; she suffered a disabling stroke the following day and was bedridden until her death six years later. She was the author of *By a Thousand Fires*, a book of reminiscences and extracts from her husband's notebooks, published in 1967. She also wrote *Rhythm of the Redman, Pulse of the Pueblo, Trail and Campfire Stories, Indian Creation Stories* and *The Quandary of Youth*.

Seton Village and Castle were registered as a national historic landmark by the National Parks Service on 11 July 1966. A cairn on the hillside below the house commemorates the occasion. The castle is now occupied by Dee Seton-Barber and her husband, Dale Barber, who maintain it as a shrine to her father's memory. Nearly forty years after his death, Seton's home is still visited by those whose lives were influenced by his animal stories and his Woodcraft teachings.

Notes

CHAPTER ONE

1. Julia M. Seton, *By a Thousand Fires: Nature Notes and Extracts From the Life and Unpublished Journals of Ernest Thompson Seton,* p. 12.
2. Ernest Thompson Seton to William Snowdon Thompson, New York, 30 October 1897, Seton Letterbook no. 1, p. 237, Seton Memorial Museum and Library, Cimarron, New Mexico.
3. Ernest Thompson Seton, *Trail of an Artist-Naturalist: The Autobiography of Ernest Thompson Seton,* p. 6.
4. William Snowdon Thompson, "Early Memories and Experiences in Two Hemispheres: An Autobiographical Sketch," p. 116.
5. J. M. Seton, *Thousand Fires,* p. 76.
6. Justina Leavitt Wilson, ed., *The Book Review Digest* (Minneapolis: H. W. Wilson, 1909), p. 396.

CHAPTER TWO

1. William Snowdon Thompson, "Early Memories," chap. 1, p. 1.
2. Julia M. Seton, *By a Thousand Fires,* pp. 19–20.
3. "Presentation of an Address to Mr. J. L. Thompson, June 1866," mss. in possession of J. Carl Thompson, Waterloo, Ontario.
4. J. M. Seton, *Thousand Fires,* p. 13.
5. W. S. Thompson, "Early Memories," chap. 26, p. 3.
6. Ernest Thompson Seton, *Trail of an Artist-Naturalist,* p. 6.

7. J. M. Seton, *Thousand Fires,* pp. 12–13.
8. W. S. Thompson, "Early Memories," chap. 11, p. 2.
9. Ibid., chap. 2, p. 2.
10. Ibid., chap. 3, p. 1.
11. Ibid., chap. 8, p. 6.
12. E. T. Seton, *Trail of an Artist-Naturalist,* p. 6.
13. W. S. Thompson, "Early Memories," chap. 3, p. 6
14. Ibid., chap. 8, p. 3.
15. Ibid., chap. 18, p. 1.
16. E. T. Seton, *Trail of an Artist-Naturalist,* p. 11.
17. Ibid.

CHAPTER THREE

1. Ernest Thompson Seton, *Trail of an Artist-Naturalist,* p. 11.
2. William Snowdon Thompson, "Early Memories," chap. 24, p. 1.
3. Ibid., chap. 24, p. 2.
4. E. T. Seton, *Trail of an Artist-Naturalist,* p. 27.
5. W. S. Thompson, "Early Memories," chap. 24, p. 5.
6. Ibid., chap. 24, p. 6.
7. E. T. Seton, *Trail of an Artist-Naturalist,* pp. 25–26.
8. Ibid., p. 26.
9. Ibid., p. 16.

CHAPTER FOUR

1. Ernest Thompson Seton, *Trail of an Artist-Naturalist,* p. 54.
2. Ibid., p. 55.
3. Ibid.
4. Ibid., p. 56.
5. Julia M. Seton, *By a Thousand Fires,* p. 44.
6. Ibid.
7. E. T. Seton, *Trail of an Artist-Naturalist,* p. 374.
8. Ibid.
9. J. M. Seton, *Thousand Fires,* p. 21.
10. Ibid., p. 43.
11. E. T. Seton, *Trail of an Artist-Naturalist,* p. 9.
12. J. M. Seton, *Thousand Fires,* p. 9.
13. Ibid., p. 20.
14. E. T. Seton, *Trail of an Artist-Naturalist,* p. 13.
15. Ibid., p. 180.
16. Ernest Thompson Seton, *Two Little Savages,* p. 5.
17. E. T. Seton, *Trail of an Artist-Naturalist,* p. 68.

18. Grace G. Seton to Ernest Thompson Seton, 20 December 1929, Seton Papers, Seton Village, New Mexico.
19. William Snowdon Thompson, "Early Memories," chap. 3, p. 6.
20. E. T. Seton, *Trail of an Artist-Naturalist*, p. 55.
21. J. M. Seton, *Thousand Fires*, p. 55.
22. Ibid., p. 15.
23. Ibid.
24. Ibid., p. 14.
25. E. T. Seton, *Trail of an Artist-Naturalist*, p. 70.
26. Ibid., p. 71.
27. Ibid., p. 75.

CHAPTER FIVE

1. Ernest Thompson Seton, *Trail of an Artist-Naturalist*, p. 77.
2. Ibid., p. 90.
3. Ibid., p. 86.
4. Ibid., pp. 84–85.
5. Ibid., p. 103.
6. Ibid., p. 106.
7. Ibid., p. 109.
8. Ibid., p. 113.
9. Ibid.
10. Ibid., p. 114.
11. Ibid., p. 142.
12. Ibid.
13. Ibid., p. 125.

CHAPTER SIX

1. Ernest Thompson Seton, *Trail of an Artist-Naturalist*, p. 392.
2. Sir James Balfour Paul, ed., *The Scots Peerage*, p. 593.
3. Geoffrey White, ed., *The Complete Peerage*, p. 821.
4. Paul, *Scots Peerage*, p. 603.
5. E. T. Seton, *Trail of an Artist-Naturalist*, p. 4.
6. Ibid., p. 393.

CHAPTER SEVEN

1. Ernest Thompson Seton, *Trail of an Artist-Naturalist*, pp. 128–29; and Ernest Thompson Seton to Jack Willing, Carberry, Manitoba, 19 August 1883, Manitoba Provincial Archives, Winnipeg, Manitoba.
2. *Saturday Globe* (Toronto), 2 March 1895.

3. Unpublished draft of deleted portion of Ernest Thompson Seton's autobiography, Seton Papers, Seton Village, New Mexico.
4. William Snowdon Thompson, "Early Memories," chap. 38, p. 9.
5. E. T. Seton, *Trail of an Artist-Naturalist,* p. 130.
6. Ibid.
7. Ibid., p. 131.

CHAPTER EIGHT

1. Ernest Thompson Seton to "Rufus" (Henry Milford Steele), Paris, 13 December 1890, Seton Papers, Seton Village, New Mexico.
2. Ernest Thompson Seton to William Snowdon Thompson, New York, 30 October 1897, Seton Papers.
3. Ernest Thompson Seton, *Trail of an Artist-Naturalist,* p. 135.
4. Ibid., p. 145.
5. Ibid., p. 137.
6. Ibid., p. 145.
7. Ibid., p. 146.
8. Seton Papers.
9. E. T. Seton, *Trail of an Artist-Naturalist,* p. 152.
10. Ibid., p. 153.
11. William Snowdon Thompson, "Early Memories," chap. 26, p. 3.
12. E. T. Seton, *Trail of an Artist-Naturalist,* p. 154.
13. Ibid., 283; and E. T. Seton to W. S. Thompson, 31 October 1897, Seton Papers.

CHAPTER NINE

1. Ernest Thompson Seton, *Trail of an Artist-Naturalist,* p. 175.
2. Ibid., p. 162.
3. According to other sources, the Winnipeg Wolf had been captured as a cub and kept chained outside a Winnipeg hotel owned by a man named Hogan. It was befriended by Hogan's son, but after the boy's death, it roamed the nearby woods until it was shot a few years later. According to Hartwell Bowsfield ("The Winnipeg Wolf," *Manitoba Pageant,* January 1960), the animal was born in the summer of 1880 and was about three years old when it was killed.
4. E. T. Seton, *Trail of an Artist-Naturalist,* p. 181.
5. Ibid., p. 198.
6. *Manitoba Tribune,* 1 February 1883.
7. Arthur Septimus Thompson, unpublished memoir.
8. Ernest Thompson Seton to Jack Willing, Carberry, Manitoba, 19 August 1883, Seton Papers, Seton Village, New Mexico.

9. E. T. Seton, *Trail of an Artist-Naturalist,* p. 247.
10. Seton to Willing, 19 August 1883, Seton Papers.
11. Seton to Willing, 10 September 1884, Seton Papers.
12. E. T. Seton, *Trail of an Artist-Naturalist,* p. 299.
13. Ibid., 264.
14. Ibid., 274.
15. Ernest Thompson Seton, *Trail of the Sandhill Stag,* dedicatory page.
16. A. S. Thompson, memoir.

CHAPTER TEN

1. Ernest Thompson Seton, *Trail of an Artist-Naturalist,* p. 279.
2. William Snowdon Thompson, "Early Memories," chap. 38, p. 13.
3. Annie Wood to Ernest Thompson Seton, 29 May 1928, Seton Papers, Seton Village, New Mexico.
4. Wood to Seton, 2 June 1928, Seton Papers.
5. E. T. Seton, *Trail of an Artist-Naturalist,* p. 284.
6. Ibid., p. 285.
7. Ernest Thompson Seton to "Rufus" (Henry Milford Steele), Paris, n.d. (c. September 1890), Seton Papers.
8. Seton to "Rufus," December 1890, Seton Papers.
9. Ibid.
10. E. T. Seton, *Trail of an Artist-Naturalist,* p. 286.
11. Seton to "Rufus," 1 May 1891, Seton Papers.
12. E. T. Seton, Trail of an Artist-Naturalist, p. 286.
13. Seton to "Rufus," n.d. (c. October 1890), Seton Papers.
14. Richard W. Murphy, *The World of Cézanne* (New York: Time-Life Books, 1968), p. 162.
15. E. T. Seton, *Trail of an Artist-Naturalist,* p.285.
16. Robert Ridgway to Ernest Thompson Seton, Washington, 30 June 1890, Seton Papers.
17. Reprinted in Manitoba Naturalists Society, *Ernest Thompson Seton in Manitoba, 1882–1892.*
18. E. T. Seton, *Trail of an Artist-Naturalist,* p. 300.
19. E. T. Seton to W. S. Thompson, New York, 31 October 1897, Seton Memorial Museum and Library, Cimarron, New Mexico.
20. *Saturday Night,* 10 December 1892.
21. Rachel Grover and Francis W. Mavor Moore, *James Mavor and His World,* p. 4.
22. E. T. Seton, *Trail of an Artist-Naturalist,* p. 290.
23. William Brymner to Ernest Thompson Seton, Montreal, 6 April 1893, Seton Papers.
24. *The Week,* 7 April 1893.

25. *Saturday Night,* 1 April 1893.
26. Robert Harris to Ernest Thompson Seton, Montreal, 4 April 1893, Seton Papers.

CHAPTER ELEVEN

1. *Companions on the Trail: A Literary Chronicle,* p. 14.
2. Ernest Thompson Seton, *Trail of an Artist-Naturalist,* p. 310.
3. Ibid., p. 304.
4. Ibid., p. 339.
5. Seton Papers, Seton Village, New Mexico.
6. E. T. Seton, *Trail of an Artist-Naturalist,* p. 343.

CHAPTER TWELVE

1. Ernest Thompson Seton, *Trail of an Artist-Naturalist,* p. 344.
2. Ibid., p. 291.
3. Ernest Thompson Seton to William Snowdon Thompson, New York, 30 October 1897, Seton Letterbook no. 1, p. 237, Seton Memorial Museum and Library, Cimarron, New Mexico.
4. Ibid.
5. William Snowdon Thompson, "Early Memories," p. 116.
6. Grace Gallatin Seton, *Nimrod's Wife,* pp. 74–75.
7. E. T. Seton, *Trail of an Artist-Naturalist,* p. 349.
8. Ernest Thompson Seton to the editor of the *New York Herald,* 22 November 1912, Seton Papers, Seton Village, New Mexico.
9. Julia M. Seton, *By a Thousand Fires,* p. 120.
10. Grace Gallatin Seton-Thompson, *A Woman Tenderfoot in the Rockies,* p. 233.
11. Ibid., p. 218.
12. Gertrude Thompson to W. Deacon, *Saturday Night* Book Department, 2 November 1926, Seton Papers.
13. *Toronto Globe,* 11 February 1893.
14. Grace Seton-Thompson, *Woman Tenderfoot,* p. 212.
15. Jules Archer, *From Whales to Dinosaurs,* p. 31.
16. *Toronto Globe,* 21 March 1901.
17. Ernest Thompson Seton to James Mavor, New York, 23 April 1902, Thomas Fisher Rare Book Library, University of Toronto, Ontario.
18. Hamlin Garland, *Companions on the Trail,* p. 99.
19. E. T. Seton, *Trail of an Artist-Naturalist,* p. 354.
20. W. S. Thompson, "Early Memories," chap. 39, p. 16.
21. Garland, *Companions on the Trail,* p. 99.
22. Ernest Seton Thompson, "The Story of Wyndygoul," *Country Life in America* (August 1909) p. 400.

23. Ibid., p. 448.
24. Seton gives various dates for this event, but since the fence was not erected until the fall of 1900, and he was absent in Colorado from August to October 1901, and absent again in March, April and May of 1902, yet had firmly established his Woodcraft Indians by the time he wrote his May 1902 column for *Ladies' Home Journal*, late spring 1901 seems to be a likely date for the event to have occurred.
25. E. T. Seton, "The Story of Wyndygoul," *Country Life in America* (September 1909) p. 505.
26. Garland, *Companions on the Trail*, pp. 112–13.
27. Andrew Carnegie, *Autobiography of Andrew Carnegie*, p. 281.
28. E. T. Seton, *Trail of an Artist-Naturalist*, p. 371.
29. Ibid.
30. J. M. Seton, *Thousand Fires*, pp. 222–23.
31. Garland, *Companions on the Trail*, pp. 205–6.
32. E. T. Seton, *Trail of an Artist-Naturalist*, p. 373.
33. W. S. Thompson, "Early Memories," chap. 39, p. 4.
34. Grace Seton-Thompson, *Woman Tenderfoot*, p. 3.

CHAPTER THIRTEEN

1. Ernest Thompson Seton, "Organized Boyhood: The Boy Scout Movement, Its Purposes and Its Laws," *Success Magazine* 13 (December 1910) 804.
2. Ernest Thompson Seton, *The Birch-Bark Roll*, p. 4.
3. Ibid., pp. 2–3.
4. Ibid., p. 1.
5. Ernest Thompson Seton and Julia M. Seton, *The Gospel of the Redman: A Way of Life*, p. 26.
6. William Snowdon Thompson, "Early Memories," chap. 39, p. 16.
7. Robert Baden-Powell to Ernest Thompson Seton, London, 1 August 1906, Seton Papers, Seton Village, New Mexico.
8. Open letter from Ernest Thompson Seton to Robert Baden-Powell, January 1910, Seton Papers.
9. Robert Baden-Powell to Ernest Thompson Seton, London, 14 March 1908, Seton Papers.
10. Brian Gardner, *Mafeking*, p. 18.
11. William Hillcourt with Olave Baden-Powell, *Two Lives of a Hero* (London: Heinemann, 1964), p. 59.
12. Ernest Thompson Seton, "A History of the Boy Scouts," undated manuscript, p. 42, Seton Papers.
13. H. W. Lanier to Ernest Thompson Seton, New York, 11 August 1908, Seton Papers.

14. E. T. Seton, "Organized Boyhood," p. 805.
15. Open letter from E. T. Seton to Baden-Powell, January 1910.
16. Ernest Thompson Seton to Dan Beard, Santa Fe, 22 December 1938, Seton Papers.
17. Frank N. Doubleday to Ernest Thompson Seton, New York, 19 August 1914, Seton Papers.
18. William Hornaday to Ernest Thompson Seton, New York, 12 December 1912, Seton Papers.
19. Eltin Morison, ed., *The Letters of Theodore Roosevelt* (Cambridge, Mass.: Harvard University Press, 1951) 8:992–93.
20. *New York Times,* 6 December 1915, p. 1.
21. Ibid.
22. *New York Times,* 7 December 1915, p. 1.
23. Ibid.
24. Morison, *Theodore Roosevelt,* 8:993.
25. "Why Mr. Seton is Not Chief Scout," *Boys' Life* 6 (January 1916) 28; reprinted in John Wadland, *Ernest Thompson Seton: Man in Nature,* p. 442.
26. Julia M. Seton, *Thousand Fires,* p. 135.
27. Ernest Thompson Seton to Dan Beard, Santa Fe, 22 December 1938, Seton Papers.

CHAPTER FOURTEEN

1. Ernest Thompson Seton to William Brewster, Cos Cob, Conn., 3 March 1904, Seton Papers, Seton Village, New Mexico.
2. Ernest Thompson Seton, *Wild Animals I Have Known,* p. 12.
3. *The Mammals of Manitoba* was also published as *A List of the Mammals of Manitoba* (Toronto: n.p., 1886).
4. Ernest Thompson Seton, *The Mammals of Manitoba,* p. 13.
5. Ernest Thompson Seton to Roderick MacFarlane, Bremen, Germany, 8 January 1906, MG29 A11, vol. 2, pp. 197–99, Public Archives of Canada, Ottawa, Ontario.
6. Ernest Thompson Seton, *The Arctic Prairies,* pp. 172–74.
7. Ibid., pp. 292–93.
8. Ernest Thompson Seton to C. Hart Merriam, Cos Cob, 23 July 1908, Seton Papers.
9. Address by Clyde Fisher at presentation of the Burroughs Medal, New York, 2 April 1927, Seton Papers.
10. John Wadland, *Ernest Thompson Seton: Man in Nature,* pp. 294–95.
11. Justina Leavitt Wilson, ed., *The Book Review Digest* (Minneapolis: H. W. Wilson, 1909), p. 396.
12. Wadland, *Man in Nature,* pp. 294–95.

13. Wilson, ed., *Book Review Digest,* p. 396.
14. Ibid.
15. Ibid.
16. Ibid.
17. Ibid.
18. Grace Gallatin Seton, *Nimrod's Wife,* p. 272.
19. Ernest Thompson Seton, *Trail of an Artist-Naturalist,* p. 48.
20. Ernest Thompson Seton to Frederick Rowntree, Cos Cob, 15 August 1913, Seton Papers.
21. Ernest Thompson Seton, "Achieving the Picturesque in Building," *Country Life in America* 35 (October 1918) 44.
22. Ibid., p. 47.
23. E. T. Seton, *Trail of an Artist-Naturalist,* p. 349.
24. *New York Times,* 21 February 1915, Letter to the Editor, p. 5.
25. Julia M. Seton, *Trail and Campfire Stories* (San Gabriel, Calif.: Willing Publishing, 1940), p. 1.
26. Author's interview with Dee Seton Barber, September 1983, Santa Fe, New Mexico.
27. Ernest Thompson Seton to Frank N. Doubleday, Greenwich, Conn., 28 November 1923, Seton Papers.
28. Grace G. Seton to Ernest Thompson Seton, Hong Kong, 24 January 1923, Seton Papers.
29. Ernest Thompson Seton to Grace G. Seton, Greenwich, 14 May 1924, Seton Papers.
30. G. G. Seton to E. T. Seton, Ceylon, 16 April 1924, Seton Papers.
31. G. G. Seton to E. T. Seton, New York, 9 July 1924, Seton Papers.
32. New York, 18 July 1924, Seton Papers.
33. Seton Papers.

CHAPTER FIFTEEN

1. "Beulah Land," credited to John P. Benson and Edgar Page Stites.
2. Ernest Thompson Seton, *Trail of an Artist-Naturalist,* p. 151.
3. Ernest Thompson Seton to "Rufus" (Henry Milford Steele), Paris, 17 December 1890, Seton Papers, Seton Village, New Mexico.
4. Ernest Thompson Seton to Jack Willing, Carberry, Manitoba, 19 August 1883, Seton Papers.
5. Hamlin Garland, *Companions on the Trail,* p. 182.
6. Ernest Thompson Seton to Grace G. Seton, Greenwich, 14 May 1924, Seton Papers.
7. Ernest Thompson Seton to Ivan von Auw Jr., Santa Fe, 25 February 1937, Seton Papers.

8. Ernest Thompson Seton to Grace G. Seton, Los Angeles, December 1929, Seton Papers.

9. Myra Emmons, "With Ernest Thompson Seton in the Woods," *Ladies' Home Journal* (September 1901) p. 4

10. Author's interview with Dee Seton Barber, September 1983, Santa Fe, New Mexico.

11. Annie Wood to Ernest Thompson Seton, Toronto, 15 June 1928, Annie Wood Letters, Seton Papers.

12. Ibid., 18 June 1928.

13. Ibid., 15 June 1928.

14. Mrs. Enoch Thompson to Ernest Thompson Seton, Toronto, 12 October 1928, Annie Wood Letters, Seton Papers.

15. Ernest Thompson Seton to Grace G. Seton, 31 January 1915. Quoted in John Henry Wadland, *Ernest Thompson Seton: Man in Nature*, p. 441.

16. Ernest Thompson Seton, "Goodbye to England" (December 1924), manuscript, Seton Papers.

17. Brochure, c. 1936, for the Seton Institute of Indian Lore, Seton Papers.

18. Author's interview with Dee Seton Barber, September 1983, Santa Fe, New Mexico.

19. Ernest Thompson Seton to William D. Murray, Santa Fe, 22 March 1935, Seton Papers.

20. From the Diary of Julia Moss Seton, Seton Papers.

21. Maxwell Perkins to Ernest Thompson Seton, New York, 13 February 1940, Seton Papers.

22. Julia Moss Seton to Edward H. Blackmore, Santa Fe, 6 February 1945, Glenbow Museum, Calgary, Alta.

23. Ibid.

24. J. M. Seton to E. H. Blackmore, 13 April 1946, Glenbow Museum, Calgary, Alta.

Selected Bibliography

(Only the principal works of Ernest Thompson Seton are listed here, i.e. the collections in which his stories originally appeared; not included are the numerous anthologies and collections which have been drawn from these original works in the last seventy-five years. Also omitted are the titles of the hundreds of articles Seton wrote for periodicals. Articles relevant to this biography are cited in the chapter notes.)

Adam, G. Mercer. *Toronto, Old and New*. Toronto: The Mail Printing Company, 1891.

Anderson, Edward F. *Peyote: The Divine Cactus*. Tucson, Arizona: University of Arizona Press, 1980.

Archer, Jules. *From Whales to Dinosaurs: The Story of Roy Chapman Andrews*. New York: St. Martin's Press, 1968.

Art Gallery of Toronto. *The Ontario Society of Artists: One Hundred Years: 1872–1972*. Toronto: The Gallery, 1972.

Artibise, Alan F. J., ed. *Winnipeg, an Illustrated History*. Toronto: James Lorimer and Company, 1977.

Beard, Daniel Carter. *Hardly a Man Is Now Alive: The Autobiography of Dan Beard*. New York: Doubleday, Doran & Co., 1939.

Burroughs, John. "Real and Sham Natural History." *Atlantic Monthly* 91 (March 1903).

Carnegie, Andrew. *The Autobiography of Andrew Carnegie*. Boston: Houghton, Mifflin, 1920.

Carr, Violet M., ed. *Ops: Land of Plenty*. Ops, Ontario: Ops Township Council, 1968.

Clark, C. S. *Of Toronto the Good: A Social Study*. Montreal: The Toronto Publishing Company, 1898.

Duval, Paul. *High Realism in Canada*. Toronto: Clarke, Irwin, 1974.

Eastman, Charles A. *Indian Boyhood*. New York: McClure, Phillips, 1902.

Edmiston, Susan, and Cirino, Linda D. *Literary New York: A History and Guide*. Boston: Houghton Mifflin Company, 1976.

Emmons, Myra. "Ernest Thompson Seton — Artist, Naturalist, Writer." *Recreation* (May 1897), pp. 315–30.

Gardner, Brian. *Mafeking: A Victorian Legend*. London: Cassell, 1966.

Garland, Hamlin. *Companions on the Trail: A Literary Chronicle*. New York: Macmillan, 1931.

———. *Roadside Meetings*. New York: Macmillan, 1930.

Glazebrook, George P. de T. *The Story of Toronto*. Toronto: University of Toronto Press, 1971.

Grover, Rachel, and Mavor Moore, Francis W. *James Mavor and His World*. Toronto: University of Toronto Press, 1975.

Halsey, Francis Whiting. *American Authors and Their Homes: Personal Descriptions and Interviews*. New York: James Pott and Company, 1901.

Holloway, Jean. *Hamlin Garland: A Biography*. Austin, Texas: University of Texas Press, 1960.

Hurdy, John Major. *American Indian Religions*. Los Angeles: Sherbourne Press, 1971.

Landgren, Marchal E. *Years of Art: The Story of the Art Students League of New York*. New York: Robert M. McBride and Company, 1940.

Lingle, Walter L., and Kuykendall, John W. *Presbyterians: Their History and Beliefs*. Atlanta: John Knox Press, 1978.

McCullough, David. *Mornings on Horseback*. New York: Simon and Schuster, 1981.

MacTavish, Newton. *The Fine Arts in Canada*. Toronto: The Macmillan Company of Canada, 1925.

Manitoba Naturalists Society. *Ernest Thompson Seton in Manitoba 1882–1892*. Winnipeg: Manitoba Naturalists Society, 1980.

Masters, Donald C. *The Rise of Toronto, 1850–1890*. Toronto: University of Toronto Press, 1947.

Maurice, Arthur Bartlett. *The New York of the Novelists*. New York: Dodd, Mead and Company, 1916.

Mess, Henry A. *Industrial Tyneside: A Social Survey*. London: Ernest Benn, 1928.

Middleton, Jesse Edgar. *The Municipality of Toronto: A History.* Vol. 1. Toronto: Dominion Publishing, 1923.

————. *Toronto's 100 Years.* Toronto: The Centennial Committee, 1934.

Miner, Muriel Miller. *G. A. Reid: Canadian Artist.* Toronto: Ryerson, 1946.

Murray, William D. *The History of the Boy Scouts of America.* New York: Boy Scouts of America, 1937.

Page, William, ed. *The Victoria History of the Counties of England: A History of Durham, Volume II.* London: Archibald Constable and Company, 1907.

Parry, Albert. *Garrets and Pretenders: A History of Bohemianism in America.* New York: Dover, 1960.

Paul, Sir James Balfour, ed. *The Scots Peerage.* Vol. 8. Edinburgh: David Douglas, 1911.

Pearson, W. H. *Recollections and Records of Toronto of Old.* Toronto: William Briggs, 1914.

Reynolds, E. E. *The Scout Movement.* London: Oxford University Press, 1950.

Ross, Edward. *Diary of the Siege of Mafeking: October 1899 to May 1900.* Edited by Brian P. Willan. Cape Town: Van Riebeeck Society, 1980.

Seton, Ernest Thompson. *Animal Heroes.* New York: Scribner's, 1905.

————. *The Arctic Prairies: A Canoe Journey of 2,000 Miles in Search of the Caribou, . . .* Toronto: William Briggs, 1911.

————. *Bannertail: The Story of a Gray Squirrel.* New York: Scribner's, 1922.

————. *The Biography of an Arctic Fox.* New York: Appleton-Century, 1937.

————. *The Biography of a Grizzly.* New York: Century, 1900.

————. *The Biography of a Silver Fox.* New York: Century, 1909.

————. *The Birch-bark Roll of the Woodcraft Indians.* New York: Doubleday, Page, 1906.

————. *The Book of Woodcraft and Indian Lore.* New York: Doubleday, Page, 1912.

————. *Great Historic Animals: Mainly About Wolves.* London: Methuen, 1937.

————. *Life Histories of Northern Animals.* 2 vols. New York: Scribner's, 1909.

————. *Lives of Game Animals.* 4 vols. New York: Doubleday, 1925–28.

————. *Lives of the Hunted.* New York: Scribner's, 1900.

————. *Mammals of Manitoba.* The Historical and Scientific Society of Manitoba, Transaction No. 23. Winnipeg: The Manitoba Printing Company, 1886.

————. *Monarch, the Big Bear of Tallac*. London: Archibald Constable and Co., 1905.

————. *The Natural History of the Ten Commandments*. New York: Scribner's, 1907.

————. *The Preacher of Cedar Mountain*. New York: Doubleday, 1917.

————. *Rolf in the Woods*. New York: Doubleday, 1911.

————. *Santana, the Hero Dog of France*. Los Angeles: Phoenix Press, 1945.

————. *Studies in the Art Anatomy of Animals*. 1896. Reprint. Philadelphia: Running Press, 1977.

————. *Trail of an Artist-Naturalist: The Autobiography of Ernest Thompson Seton*. New York: Scribner's, 1940.

————. *The Trail of the Sandhill Stag*. New York: Scribner's, 1899.

————. *Two Little Savages*. New York: Dover, 1962.

————. *Wild Animals at Home*. New York: Grosset and Dunlap, 1913.

————. *Wild Animals I Have Known*. New York: Scribner's, 1898.

————. *Wild Animal Ways*. Garden City: Doubleday, 1916.

————. *Woodmyth and Fable*. Toronto: William Briggs, 1905; New York: Century, 1905.

Seton, Ernest Thompson, and Seton, Julia M. *The Gospel of the Redman: A Way of Life*. Santa Fe: Seton Village Press, 1966. Also published as *The Gospel of the Redman: An Indian Bible* (Garden City, N.Y.: Doubleday and Co., 1936).

Seton, Julia M. *By a Thousand Fires: Nature Notes and Extracts from The Life and Unpublished Journals of Ernest Thompson Seton*. New York: Doubleday and Co., 1967.

Seton, Grace Gallatin. *Nimrod's Wife*. New York: Doubleday, Page, 1907.

Seton-Thompson, Grace Gallatin. *A Woman Tenderfoot in the Rockies*. London: David Nutt, 1900.

Thompson, Arthur Septimus. Unpublished memoir, c. 1940. Mss. property of David Arthur Thompson, Guelph, Ontario.

Thompson, William Snowdon. "Early Memories and Experiences in Two Hemispheres: An Autobiographical Sketch." August 1923. Mss. property of John Carl Thompson, Waterloo, Ontario.

Wadland, John Henry. *Ernest Thompson Seton: Man in Nature and the Progressive Era: 1880–1915*. New York: Arno Press, 1978.

Weaver, Emily P. "Pioneer Canadian Women." *Canadian Magazine* 49 (May-October 1917) 32–36.

White, Geoffrey, ed. *The Complete Peerage: or A History of the House of Lords and All Its Members from Earliest Times*. Vol. 12, pt. 2. London: The St. Catherine Press, 1959.

Index